Bad Moon Rising

Bad Moon Rising

A SOCIOLOGY ON EMERGING SOCIAL PROBLEMS

DAVID LIEBERT

Open Knowledge Books, LLC
https://www.OKbooks.online
Corporation Registered in Florida

First edition: 2020

The publisher is not responsible for websites (or their content) that are not owned by the publisher. All images used in this work are believed to be in the public domain, have provided appropriate attribution, and are being used for educational purposes.

Direct inquires on public speaking events or other related questions to the author at Liebert.David@SPCollege.edu

Names: Liebert, David, author.
Title: *Bad Moon Rising: A Sociology on Emerging Social Problems*
Description: First edition | Florida | Open Knowledge Books, LLC | Includes bibliographical references and index.
Identifiers: ISBN-13: 9781703368031
Subjects: Social Problems—Sociology—Existential Sociology

ISBN-13: 9781703368031

Open Knowledge Books, LLC
http://www.OKbooks.online

Let there be free words!

I see a bad moon a-rising
I see trouble on the way
I see earthquakes and lightnin'
I see bad times today

Don't go 'round tonight
It's bound to take your life
There's a bad moon on the rise

I hear hurricanes a-blowing
I know the end is coming soon
I fear rivers over flowing
I hear the voice of rage and ruin

Don't go 'round tonight
It's bound to take your life
There's a bad moon on the rise

I hope you got your things together
I hope you are quite prepared to die
Look's like we're in for nasty weather
One eye is taken for an eye

Oh don't go 'round tonight
It's bound to take your life
There's a bad moon on the rise
There's a bad moon on the rise

- *Bad Moon Rising,*
by Creedence Clearwater Revival (1969)

CONTENTS

Bad Moon Rising

Preface

This book is different from other works on the topic of social problems. Most books are straight-up textbooks. Certainly, there is nothing wrong or inappropriate about a textbook. They are excellent sources for encyclopedic figures and facts on just about any topic. Unlike this book, textbooks tend to adopt, to either a greater or lesser degree, an agnostic perspective on the subject. The state of race relations, for example, is explored first from a conflict perspective explaining how socioeconomic inequality for ethnic minorities is sustained through exploitation followed by a symbolic interactionist look on how a small, marginalized population of African-American men establishes and conveys a sense of masculinity amongst themselves. Rarely are there bold positions taken in a textbook. Controversy in textbooks bites at the reader with similar ferocity as a grandmother wearing full dentures. This book, however, is embedded with ample opportunity to ignite controversy.

Additionally, textbooks on social problems tend to be authored by properly educated sociologists holding a Ph.D. in the field. Whereas, an academic mongrel writes this book. I majored in sociology as an undergraduate and then completed a master's degree in the discipline as well. My doctorate, however, is in counseling psychology, which was an applied degree intent on preparing me to listen carefully to the woes and troubles of patients. At the time of this publication, I have over

21-years of experience teaching undergraduate-level courses in both psychology and sociology at a Florida state college, which is the new lingo used today to refer to the community college.

Most who are unfamiliar with these two disciplines assume sociology and psychology are closely related fields of study. The simple answer: not so much. Psychology and sociology are distinctly different. True, they are both within the broader field of social sciences and share some similar methodologies, and a few topics are overlapping here and there. We may sometimes refer to some of the Fathers of Sociology as Uncles in psychology and vice versa.

In my travels, I haven't bumped into many others, like me, who have their graduate training spanning between sociology and counseling psychology. To this end, my graduate training makes this book somewhat different from others; it permits me to infuse more of the person into the dialog which lies ahead in this book. Sociology is a discipline examining the dynamic connection existing between the individual and societal. It's at that place where these two elements in the equation connect and spark that the sociologist often attends to most. My psychology background permits me to see a little deeper into the human side of things.

The path more often taken views social problems as emanating within the social institution or at least coming to rest within the institution. For example, poverty is seen as a problem of an economic system, which permits an elite class dominant reign and control over the weak, so exploitation is inevitable. Moreover, the ever-increasing incidence of depression rates in society is viewed, in part, as the result of a society that casts a blanket of stigma over any mental health label keeping the motivation for those inflicted low in seeking help, and when they do reach out for help, they are met by an institutional healthcare system that denies access to costly care by pushing onto the emotionally wounded cheaper pharmaceutical potions. Whereas in this book, there is greater emphasis on identifying—or at least acknowledging—the catalyst contributing to this spark of connection between the individual and societal. Both the many ways people affect and influence this dynamic connection brings light in the pages that follow. The discussion, at times, reflects a sort of existential sociology.

The discussion that lies ahead should not be confused for hijacking the issues from the lens of *clinical psychology*; rather, the actual analysis is more towards the *clinical sociology* of the phenomenon. The clinical psychologist's chief concern lies with identifying what social or environmental factors have contributed to her patient's anxiety (unless she is completely absorbed by the neurobiological theories assuming a genetic or faulty neurochemical etiology is completely at fault), differentiating the presenting symptoms to form a precise diagnosis of a specific anxiety disorder against all the other possible anxiety disorders (i.e., phobia, panic attack, post-traumatic stress disorder, and generalized anxiety disorder), and finally coming up with a treatment plan that once executed will ameliorate her patient's psychopathology.

Rather, by embracing a clinical sociology lens, our analysis takes us beyond the institutional side of the topic and directs focus onto the individual. For example, the social institution of marriage and family is experiencing a decrease in marriage rates; fewer people are married today than were married 50-years ago. Likewise, there is also evidence suggesting married couples cultivate greater levels of intimacy than couples sharing other types of paired relationships or that single people do with the social networks available to them. Lack of emotional intimacy is related to higher rates of anxiety, loneliness, and depression. A clinical sociologist is interested in all the ways other social institutions (i.e., education, political, healthcare, and so forth) might absorb, project or—perhaps—attempt to care for these feelings of anxiety, loneliness, and depression. For example, keeping these points in mind, perhaps there was a societal response missed by the lawmakers, sociologists, advocates, and organized opponents during the height of the gay-marriage debate that speaks to the timing for the debate. Gay or straight, we want legal opportunities available to us for forging deeper levels of intimacy in our relationships with significant others.

This book differs from others on the subject to the extent this book focuses on *emerging social problems*. Too often textbooks on social problems feel like the last department budget meeting I had to attend, where our copy costs had gone down 17% from last year, but we saw a 78% increase in money being used to purchase whiteboard markers for the classroom. To a similar extent, chapters on social problems report on the current ratio between every dollar earned by a man and woman for doing the same job, the decrease of violent crimes, and the increase in rates of drug addiction. An increase or decrease in the overall percent of violent crimes is important, and it is just an awful thing to be a victim of a crime, but it is highly unlikely the statistic could ever swing so much from one edition of the book to the next edition that societal collapse is possible. By emerging social problems, I'm attempting to identify those social problems that have the capacity to both radically and adversely impact the current stability of our society, to change us in ways like movie makeup artists quickly morph a bitten victim right in front of our eyes into a flesh dripping, shuffling, mumbling zombie. To clarify, I am not identifying possible events that are outside of our control which can eradicate us down to dust, nor am I suggesting the worst of our social problems, if left unresolved, would result in apocalyptic outcomes arousing images of that old movie the *Road Warrior*. I am attempting, however, to identify a class of social problems that would fundamentally change us in ways opposed to being free, happy, and well. Central to this book is the premise that all people have human/inalienable rights of life, liberty, and the pursuit of happiness.

Another difference with this book that is often missing in other books on social problems is the political dimension. Indeed, political leanings and advocating towards a preferred social policy we find in many parts of the text and subtext alike in just about every book ever written on the topic of social problems. The political and the sociological go somewhat hand-in-hand together. To say a discussion on social problems can occur apolitically would be like an archeologist suggesting digging up artifacts can occur without becoming sweaty and dirty.

Political policy always shares some degree of either celebration or culpability to any social problem and is oftentimes the social institution which the population looks to as a remedy for what is troubling us at the moment. This book is apolitical in the sense that it is not advocating for social policy and doesn't align with any political party's platform. The trap that lies in doing so: our contemporary politics divides thinking dichotomously. We have two political parties (because suggesting any third party has a chance is ridiculous); it's always argued a vote for them will take us down the road to utter ruin, but a vote for us will finally fix this problem once and for all.

Additionally, the political text and subtext unfolding inside of many social problems books have not been traditionally inclusive of diverse political thoughts. There tends to be a left political leaning within the sociological curriculum, and when discussing the right, it's not done so by presenting such ideas in a favorable light. I recognize what is suggested here to be a bold, maybe even an extremist statement, as I seem to be suggesting there's a presence of political bias within the ranks of sociology. At the very least, I should be backing up such a claim with a properly APA formatted citation. Well, here it is, full disclosure: I lean towards the right. I have spent enough years as a student in undergraduate and graduate sociology classes to be taken seriously when I say, "finding a politically conservative sociologist on a college campus today is as likely as finding a Jedi Knight in the business section of a Barnes and Nobles bookstore looking over David Ramsey's latest book on risk-free financial planning." Again, let me repeat myself, which is something right as well as left professors never get tired of doing; this book is apolitical. This book addresses the subject of social problems, not conservative sociology. There is no political remedy to any social problem suggested in the pages ahead or is any left-leaning politician demonized for causing or fueling on a social problem. In turn, I ask the reader not to prematurely draw any conclusions about my *moral* leanings on any topic discussed herein. Do not assume what my actual position is on issues like gay marriage, climate change, economic disparity, and so forth. Once honest debate leaves the arena of dichotomous politics, positions on such topics may range both far and wide.

Moreover, and even more importantly, perspectives based on morality, political ideology, and sociological points of view are rarely fully congruent with each other. Where you can expect my political leanings to influence the chapters that lie ahead in this book will be in those areas where individual rights and responsibilities confound with the needs and interests of the group. Additionally, in those areas where social science appears to have rested their case and advocate some universal truth, you may find that I, nevertheless, present an opposing point of view. For instance, I remember so clearly all our desks forged into an oddly shaped circle (as graduate students in sociology just loving sitting in circles and calling their professors by their first names) on the second floor of Cooper Hall at the University of South Florida. Assigned to read Al Gore's *Earth in the Balance* (1992), I made a comment that he seemed to be prophesizing much like Nostradamus on the world ending in just a couple of decades (Still Here!) as a sort of economic shakedown. Although we have changed the term from Global Warming to Climate Change, the same politics are in place still today suggesting the world is only a decade or at most two from complete collapse, and ruin and only one political party can save us with their New Green Deal. The conservative in me does not accept this as absolute truth, and the sociologist in me is going to look at different possible perspectives to explain what might also be occurring and present these ideas without any moral superiority. Political bias in sociology texts often presents in the form of the author's *position* on the matter, drawing a line in the sand, explaining why this side on the position is correct and the other side is wrong. I have refrained from taking positions. Instead, my focus is on drawing out the *interests* on the matter, even at times excavating existentially into the individual psyche to tease out that which truly worries, inspires, and motivates our individual, as well as, collective behaviors.

Upon further thought and consideration, perhaps there is one position taken with this book: the answers to the social problems we face today as a society are possible, but the first step in fixing these types of problems is to engage in rowdy, robust, and respectful debate. We must once again listen to the ideas of folks we, at first look, completely disagree with them. Civil debate requires that we listen to the ideas of others as if our ideas may be wrong.

1   Introduction

Bad Moon Rising is a book on the sociology of social problems, which is different from other books on social problems. This is not a review of the countless social entanglements and challenges appearing to be embedded into our society's many social institutions and are suggested to represent the primary source for personal gloom and despair. Such was the position held by Sigmund Freud who argues, "…civilization is largely responsible for our misery, and that we should be much happier if we gave it up and returned to primitive conditions" (1961, p. 33). Instead, this book challenges the reader to consider a social problem, not as a phenomenon that has infiltrated into the social system, infecting it as a bacterial agent might do to its human host, but to see a social problem more as a systemic phenomenon. A social problem at times results from the act of an individual connecting to his or her society. Dynamic friction takes place between the societal and the individual, and it is at this is this point of connection between the two which identifies the etiology for social problems.

By placing the individual as a central element in the discussion, this book does what most other texts on the subject of social problems too often ignore. The individual is not passive in the process; instead, the individual is an active agent in the etiology of social problems. This idea is not new. The humanistic movement in psychology popularized in the decades ranging from the 1950s through the 1970s embraced the central importance of the individual, arguing there existed a connection between the ills of the social world and the plight of the individual. These humanists (i.e., Abraham Maslow and Carl Rogers) viewed the nature of the individual as pure and ideal before social corruption. The individual aspires only to achieve his or her unique potential, being no different from that of an acorn aspiring to become a tree. Abraham Maslow (1968) referred to this as "self-actualizing" and Carl Rogers, in a similar fashion, referred to this as the "fully functioning person" (1986). However, it was the barriers established by a tainted social world in which people inhabited that prohibited the likelihood of such achievement from ever manifesting. For humanistic psychologists, like both Maslow and Rogers, the elucidation was obvious: make the world a better more ideal place. For instance, professors should not arrive at the classroom on the first day with syllabi outlining the term's learning objectives ready to hand out to their class. Instead, the professor only needs a blank sheet of paper and pen to write down the needs his or her students have already brought with them to the class that might prove helpful in their journey towards self-actualization.

Although humanists also identify the individual as being central in the discussion, this book does not reflect similar ideas on the nature of the relationship between the individual and societal. There is no assumption that human beings are ever *ideal* in either their current or future states, regardless if humans should find themselves existing either in utopian communities or in "primitive conditions." Although a central theme expressed many times throughout this book is that social problems can be fixed and ameliorated, never is it suggested a perfect society is achievable; there is always "tyranny in the womb of every utopia" (de Jouvenel, 1957, p. 10). *Chapter 10*, the final chapter of this book, does end with a few suggestions for improving some of our contemporary social problems, but these suggestions are not prescriptive for achieving utopian outcomes. Instead, these suggestions are squarely pragmatic where debate is encouraged by the reader over acceptance.

This book does argue that human beings are born with innate needs that do attempt to align up and connect with societal interests, but these needs are not self-actualizing in nature. The central focus for *Chapter 5: The Existential Dynamic*, shows these needs to be existential. These needs are reflective of the fact that we are born with inalienable rights, as argued by John Locke, to include life, liberty, and the pursuit of happiness. These rights are not dependent on laws or government for experiencing their direct benefits. Another authority cannot forfeit these rights as they do not first come from the government. Inalienable rights slice across all governments and cultures, as they are universal. Realizing the personal value and benefit of these inalienable rights through existential self-reflection by being made aware of the human plight is essential. Achieving existential self-awareness occurs through psychological confrontation with the four givens of human existence: death, freedom, isolation, and meaning (Yalom, 1980). Chapter 5, moves beyond a discussion on psychological existentialism, where the focus remains set on the individual but pushes the analysis into the realm of sociological existentialism by acknowledging those social forces which influence us and inhibit our ability to reflect on the givens of human existence and—in turn—realize our inalienable rights.

Before any discussion and analysis of existential factors contributing to contemporary social problems can take place, a sociological foundation first needs to be established. This book begins with a look at the societal side of the social dynamic. *Chapter 2: Social Problems: Yes, No, or Maybe* explores the various attributes necessary to operationalize a *problem* as being a *social problem*. Some problems are merely troubles which are confined to just one or a very few people but do not breach the gate and connect dynamically to social institutions, even if others happen to connect to the other person's plight through empathy emotionally. Moreover, some problems fall into the category of existential threats, where it would be best for social scientists to avoid taking the lead to address these types of problems. Instead, the government needs to claim the reign of control since existential threats pose the real possibility of annihilating society, as was the case with World War II, for example.

Chapter 3: The Sociology of Social Problems provides a theoretical and methodological context upon which to view and analyze social problems. Social problems by their nature span as well as drift through various disciplines; thus, they behave sociologically, suggesting a dynamic connection between the individual and the societal. In this chapter, the social dynamic connecting the individual with the societal is established, explaining the ebb and flow linking the two. Explaining theories such as conflict, functionalism, and symbolic interactionism occur in this chapter, which provides the reader with the various lens of orientation to understand the many possible explanations for the social dynamic.

Again, one of the goals for this book is to challenge the reader to consider a social problem, not as a phenomenon that has infiltrated into the social system, but as a systemic phenomenon emerging from the point of connection between the individual and the societal. To this end, social problems are considered as *emerging social problems* and center—more or less—around an existential framework. *Chapter 6: Free Will and Thinking*[E] explore the possible societal, and individual effects technology is now imposing on our most succinct inalienable rights: freedom of thought and the right to freely debate our ideas within the public square. Human neurological functioning naturally processes information though uses of schemas, algorithms, and heuristics in predictable ways in which search engines are now beginning to influence. Moreover, technology is now begun to alter and influence our most valued freedoms for debate and free speech by relocating the public square to virtual platforms that do not support free speech for all. *Chapter 7: The Melting Middle-Class* addresses the social problem of economic inequality—not through an analysis looking at the assorted range of inequality occurring between the group who has the least contrasted against the group who has the most—through the effects of a redistribution of the center rung of the socioeconomic ladder by pushing these folks onto either a higher or lower rung. Happiness is an inalienable right achieved, in part, by securing purpose and meaning in life. Achieving actual meaning in life is compromised when lifestyle including the ability to have and afford to raise children and earn an affordable higher education leading to a certificate of value is no longer in reach for many in our society today. *Chapter 8: Social Isolation* explores emerging social problems stemming from technology's anti-socializing effects. Human intimacy through ample societal opportunities to connect is essential. As more schools encourage online classes over face-to-face classroom experiences and social networking platforms inhibit real opportunity for actual physical, synchronistic contact with each other, society is witnessing an epidemic of mental illness the likes of depression and anxiety along with suicide rates which are now aggressively on the rise. This chapter also examines the effects of decreasing marriage rates in favor of alternative lifestyles like cohabitation is having on intimacy and happiness. In *Chapter 9: Social Meaning*, we again return to the issue of happiness, and the existential need to experience purpose and meaning in life. The proliferation of marijuana's legalization in states across the country in recent years proposes some social problems that may not be widely considered alarming or even benign, but are verrucous.

Once again, this book is not intended to be a call for action. It is not a manifesto proposing the reader to follow any scripted behavior. Instead, it does offer the reader the opportunity to cultivate a sociological skillset for analyzing social problems, that extends beyond the need to create a professional space to distance one's feelings from a given social problem. C. Wright Mills refers to this as the *sociological imagination*, which also includes the ability "to grasp history and biography and the relations between the two within society. That is its task and promise. To recognize this task and promise is the mark of the classic social analyst" (1959, p. 6).

This book pushes beyond Mills' *sociological imagination* and encourages the development of four skills in *Chapter 4: Emerging Social Problems* to sociologically analyze a social problem. First, social problems vary in their degree of ethical alignment between respective positions of morals and values, where *values*, refers to those things people genuinely care about, and *morals* refer to those ways motivation binds our behavior to shared human emotions and experiences. As the degree of congruency between these two ethical attributes increases, social problems take on less severity. In turn, the more these two attributes become incongruous with each other, the more socially risky the problem becomes. Second, as attention is misdirected away from the societal interests to various positions about a social problem, possible risk and harm to society increase, especially as the degree of involution increases whereby the social problem is entangled with multiple layers of complexity in the many different positions taken. Instead, sociological attention is best when redirected away from a particular position and focuses on social interests instead. Third, when the free, open, and reciprocal exchange of communication is present, the severity of risk decreases but will otherwise remain high when debate falls upon deaf ears indignant to acknowledging any other possible alternative position. Fourth, as aegis authority increases, so too does the inherent risk associated with social problems. In other words, when a few sources of social authority maintain authority and control over the social problem, the level of social risk rises. Finally, *Chapter 10: Conclusion: Making it Better for the Middle-Class* provides an opportunity to apply these four skills to interpret and debate on a speculative plan to address and correct an emerging social problem concerning our nation's decreasing citizenry within the middle-class. The goal is to provide a model that serves as the basis to engage the necessary and free debate on those matters that concern us most.

Bad Moon Rising: A Sociology on Emerging Social Problems is foremost intended to bring our nation's most pressing problems out into the public square, referring to that space where the norms of pleasant civility are pushed aside for the moment and—disrobing ourselves of titles, status, and rank—we debate freely and exchange ideas. This is the proper space to sound the alarm as we sniff out these emerging societal concerns, especially when our politicians are telling us there is no concern, "nothing to see here; move along!" To this point, there is much that needs to be said.

2   **Social Problems: Yes, No, or Maybe**

Bad Moon Rising is a book about the *sociology* of *social problems*, referring not only to those social phenomena that concern and trouble us as a society, but those tribulations that on one end of the continuum may significantly alter our way of life by eradicating deeply held and shared value systems. It is, after all, our societal values, not the color of our currency which is—in fact—the essence that binds us as a shared, cultural collective. Social problems tug and snip away at social values. At the opposite end of the continuum, social problems compromise our inalienable rights as individuals. Our society, referring specifically to the geographic boundaries making up the United States of America has since its inception functioned as an institution with the belief everyone is bestowed with inalienable rights, referring to rights that do not flow from the state; instead, these rights originate from one's creator. The philosophers may have argued on the range in which such rights exist, but it is always safe to rest with those suggested by John Locke: life, liberty, and the pursuit of happiness. Social problems can erode these rights.

I completed my first social problems class in undergraduate school back in 1991. I still have the assigned textbook from this class defining a social problem as "…a condition affecting a significant number of people in ways considered undesirable, about which it is felt something can be done through collective social action" (Horton, 1991, p. 2). Two years later, I taught my first social problems class as a Teaching Assistant. Our textbook defined a social problem as "… a condition that is harmful to society" (Coleman, 1993, p. 2). A recent textbook I have used for this class defines a social problem as "… a social condition or pattern of behavior that has negative consequences for individuals, our social world, or our physical world" (Leon-Guerrero, 2019, p. 4). There is nothing unusual with definitions for a social problem evolving. The first definitions used early in the Twentieth Century were heavily based on a medical model. Bad people afflicted with alcoholism or homosexuality, for instance, were considered to be at the root of societal ills. By the 1920s and 1930s, the focus had shifted to the poor, inadequate social conditions with particular attention to a society's inability to accommodate and adapt to the changing social needs brought about by increased immigration, rapid urbanization, and the role industrialization were now regularly having on vocation. Most definitions nonetheless tend to stagnate. The social problem is anchored somewhere out in the social world where the ill effects creep into the human condition; otherwise, the social malignancy first has taken root in the individual and then proceeds to seep out into the social environment.

This book embraces a different approach, conceptualizing social problems as a dynamic phenomenon where the etiology originates at the point of connection between the individual and societal institutions and flows from this point of origin breaching the gap in varying degrees of permeability. In other words, some *problems* are *social problems* because a dynamic connection exists to one degree or another between the society and the individual, whereas other *problems* are not *social problems* because no permeability exists between these states.

The word *dynamic* has been used to refer to an active connection between these two reciprocal entities: the individual and societal. Social problems are connected communally and fueled by their interests to varying degrees of permeability. For instance, an individual who holds radical beliefs and engages in the act of domestic terrorism likely faces a swift and immediate response by various social institutions. Here we see how individual beliefs may affect social institutions where this active connection reflects broad permeability. However, consider a middle-aged curmudgeon who despises children splashing about in the neighborhood's swimming pool. Even if he gripes and barks at the children from time-to-time, social institutions remain unaffected, as there is no effective permeability between the individual beliefs and societal institutions. At worst, parents instruct their children to skip over that neighbor's house on Halloween.

Moreover, the same is said for a social problem originating within societal institutions. Consider, for example, that a fraudulent election may have devastating consequences for people who are now represented by an imposter. Therefore, some problems lie outside of any possible dynamic connection, where the issue is merely a problem for the individual or the environment, but objectively not a social problem. An illness may have devastating consequences for the individual but possess no impact whatsoever on the larger social landscape. Yet, when a scientist identifies a cure for a deadly virus that was once isolated to the environment, assigning costs to a vaccine and restricting access to the vaccine for specific populations opens the aperture of permeability. Now friction of sorts erupts at this point of connection between the personal and social, which we now identify as a social problem. Also, environmental occurrences may lie far outside of human control. For example, an asteroid is hurtling straight at Earth, which is a quarter the size of the moon. True, the consequences for people are devastating, but no reasonable argument prevails that there is something that can be done to ameliorate or even resolve the event. Although it is "Game Over," it is not a social problem, as there is no permeability between the environmental problem and either societal institutions or individuals.

A social problem is not merely limited to the experience of a *social trouble*, referring to an adverse event experienced by another. A social problem extends beyond the personal experiences of people by adversely affecting societal institutions. Moreover, a social problem is not limited to a *social concern*, referring to negative feelings and a general state of anxiety directed toward a social phenomenon where the primary evidence for the concern isolates within feelings and personal anxieties. Instead, social problems refer to a social phenomenon operationalizing through the lens of empirical evidence directing such evidence through the scientific method. Additionally, social problems refer to a social phenomenon that tends to limit its parameters of operationalization around both the theories and methodologies of *sociology*, which—most importantly—recognizes social problems as being dynamic. A social problem refers to a social phenomenon which either places at risk or compromises the sustainability of societal functioning or the inalienable rights of those impacted directly or indirectly by the problem. Finally, when reasonable argument prevails, it is believed there is something that can be done to ameliorate or even resolve the social problem.

Not Everything is a Social Problem

Sociologists who focus their efforts on studying the social dynamics between mental illness and societal institutions have pointed out the ongoing expansion—if not proliferation—of psychiatric diagnoses in recent decades. *The Diagnostic and Statistical Manual of Mental Disorders (DSM)*—frequently referred to as the psychiatric bible—routinely appears to be including new diagnoses of psychopathology with each new edition of the manual, which appears to be doing nothing more than pathologicalizing everyday normal behavior into mental illnesses (Kutchins & Kirk, 2003). Being a woman and having a menstrual cycle means one is most likely now suffering from *premenstrual dysphoric disorder*, a child's temper tantrum is diagnosed as *disruptive mood dysregulation disorder*, and grief over a loved one's death is without reservation conforming to a diagnosis of depression. For every uncomfortable behavior, there now seems to be a psychiatric condition explaining it.

Unfortunately, a review of textbooks on the subject of social problems suggests just about any social and personal adversity falls under the scope of a social problem. For example, one recent textbook includes illiteracy as a social problem. While being illiterate undoubtedly will adversely affect one's likelihood to grasp onto that rung of the socioeconomic ladder yielding self-sufficiency, our society's current rate of illiteracy is not posing any reasonable risk of ill effect to the ongoing sustainability of our social institutions. Illiteracy is not a social problem.

Social Concerns and Troubles vs. Social problems. Several weeks ago, I found myself rather caught up on all the tasks I planned on tackling when the day first began. Quiz grades from the morning's class were posted, tomorrow's lecture was prepared, and the last of my adjunct faculty evaluations were finally completed and now on their way to the Dean for final review. So, I made the rare decision to leave the office a little early. My wife had been pestering me for the last few days to spend some late afternoon hours together at our neighborhood's pool.

Now fifty-years-old, I seem to be fighting myself from exposing my internal curmudgeon, which ever so slowly has been gestating in my psyche in more recent years. The pool was filled with children splashing about. I grumbled just loud enough for my wife to hear. "Let's head down to the other side where there aren't so many children," she said. Bad decision, as some twelve-year-old sunbathing on the pool deck, had set her iTunes to Katy Perry. "Who the #*&! wants to have to listen to that!" My wife splashed me.

Two weeks later while sitting on folding chairs at the community homeowners' meeting, my wife leaned over and whispered, "Do you want to raise the concern or should I: our neighborhood is going to hell-in-a-handbasket; we need to put a stop to children having fun in the pool, and Led Zeppelin must be the only music permitted in any of the common areas." Although tempted, a community HOA meeting is not the forum for venting *social troubles*. As sociologist C. Wright Mills explains, such troubles "occur within the character of the individual and within the range of his immediate relations with others; they have to do with the self and with those limited areas of social life… A trouble is a private matter: values cherished by an individual are felt by him to be threatened" (1959, p. 8). It is not the responsibility of the neighborhood HOA to assist me in wrestling with my inner-curmudgeon. Too many children in the neighborhood pool is a challenge that is best left with me to explore together with my psychoanalyst.

Surprisingly, a neighbor whom I would have never recognized but happens to live two doors down from me on my street raised her hand during the HOA meeting and immediately spoke up. "I am concerned about the ducks; I see them every morning swimming in the pool. I am worried that duck-poop in the pool will make our children sick." In no more than a few quick seconds, a dozen comments ricocheted about the room, none of which the ducks nesting in the flower beds by the pool would have appreciated hearing. As it turns out, ducks—not just Katy Perry—is the real conundrum facing the safety and wellbeing of my neighborhood.

Now, the real epicenter of intellectual exchange at any college or university occurs in the faculty lounge right at the point the coffeepot makes contact with a mug. "Will duck-poop in the swimming pool make someone sick?" I asked the biology professor the next morning. "No, I wouldn't think so as long as the pool is properly chlorinated. Actually, I would be more concerned if I weren't wearing any sunscreen while floating around in water saturated with duck-poop. Nearly twenty people die every day in this country from melanoma. I don't believe the CDC keeps statistics on duck-poop related injuries or deaths."

I am still not dropping my Katy Perry concern, but are sun-related cancers, noise pollution, population growth (meaning too-many or too-few children) and duck-poop a concern? When is a *social concern* just that: a concern, rather than a problem which has the potential to adversely affect our neighborhood, state, nation, or world? At this point, let us agree some express *social concerns* which for some fills, not only their head, but the rest of the room with worthless noise. Nevertheless, there are those social problems that are of actual concern, where such problems have the potential to affect our inalienable rights adversely, which includes life, liberty, and pursuit of happiness.

Figure 2.1, Social ecological model on social problems, troubles, concerns, and existential threats

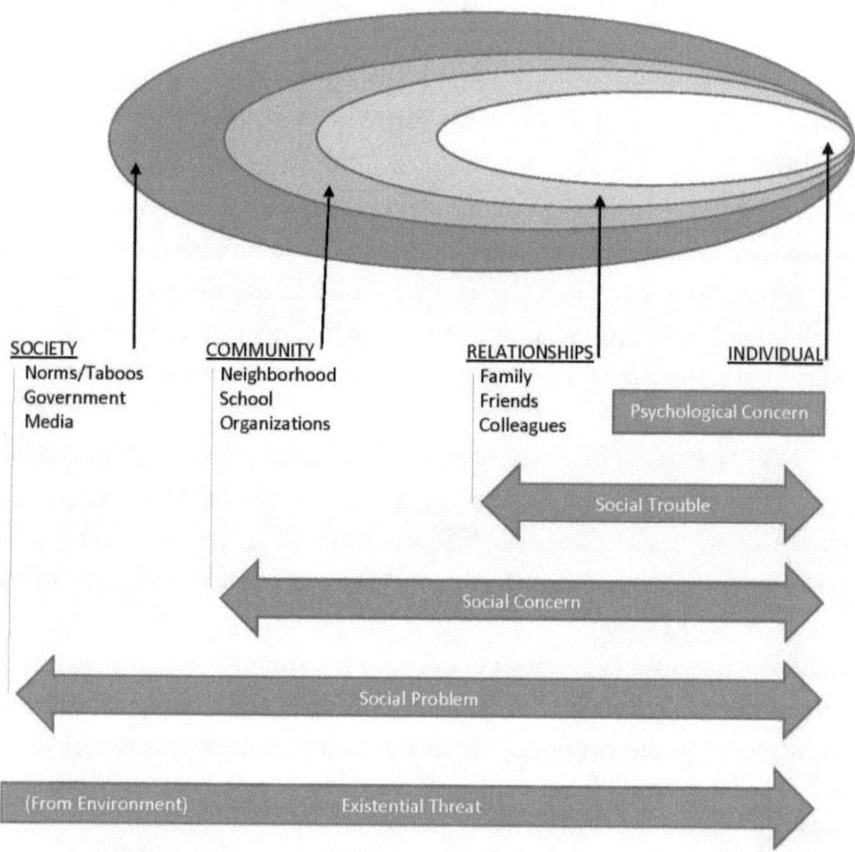

Let us think of a *social concern* as a meaningless form of internal chatter that is inevitably shared externally to others as a sort of social-gossip where there is no significant threat beyond one's own emotional reaction. It made me feel sad, for instance, to learn all of the ducks who had made their nests—meaning their homes—around the community's pool were caged and relocated. Nevertheless, my feeling *sad* does not confirm the decision to relocate the ducks was wrong, unjust, or only a sad event. Some of my other neighbors who helped to facilitate the event shared different feelings about the ducks' relocation. Still, often we witness when discussing and debating social concerns as if an actual threat is real, authentic, and validated. Lukianoff and Haidt (2018) for example, explore this point in their recent book, arguing we are seeing amongst America's youth today a growing sense of being fragile and vulnerable to real threats posed in the world. In turn, parents need to keep their children closer and at home more because the world has increasingly become a particularly dangerous place to live. Interview parents today and the typical response confirms the belief: *the world is more dangerous for children today than it was for me when I was their age.* Is this the case? Harvard cognitive psychologist, Steven Pinker (2018) provides robust data showing evidence to the contrary: we are living in the safest period in human history. The likelihood of being murdered, for instance, is at the lowest point for all of human history. This is the case looking at the data globally (Pinker, 2011) as well as nationally (See Figures 2.2 & 2.3; James, 2018).

Simply because we *feel* the world is a dangerous place, schools are not safe to attend, immigrants from Central and South America should be able to enter into the United States freely, abortion is wrong, or ducks should live any damn place they wish to live does not mean it is so. *Feelings* often serve to guide our thoughts and behaviors, but this does not mean these resulting thoughts and behaviors are correct or even justified because feelings first confirmed them. Try this: put on a pair of sunglasses with blue lenses and hold up a lemon. What color is the lemon? If you answered green, then perhaps you should pack up all of your belongings and move out to a remote lake with some ducks I once knew. The lemon is yellow! Our feelings—may at times—confuse the truth just as blue sunglasses may confuse our capacity for accurate color perception.

*Figure 2.2, National homicide rate between years 1960 and 2016**

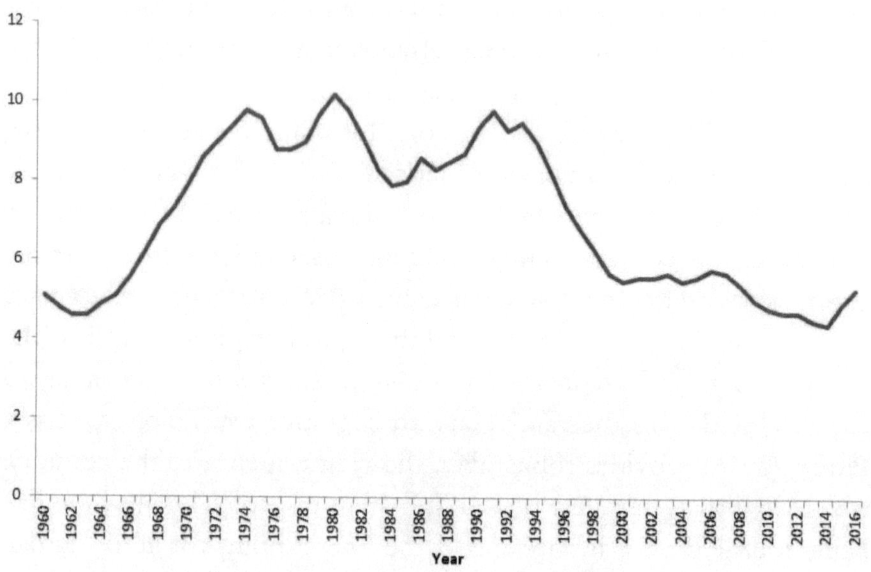

* Rate per 100,000 people

*Figure 2.3, National violent crime rate between years 1960 and 2016**

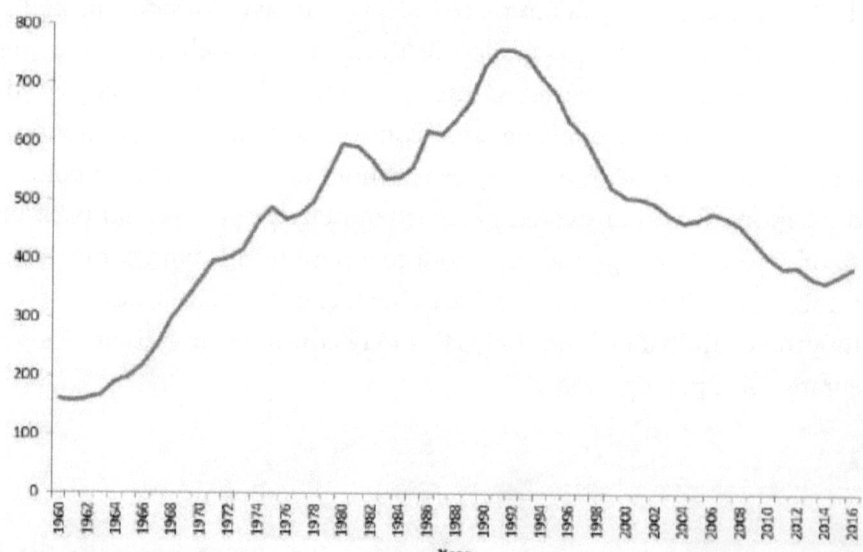

Environmental Woes vs. Social problems. CBS News journalist Edward R. Murrow sat down for an interview with Dr. Jonas Salk in the spring of 1955. Salk was a virologist who had recently discovered a vaccine that would prevent the disease polio (correctly called *poliomyelitis*), which results in devastating muscular paralysis. "Who owns the patent on this vaccine?" Murrow asks the doctor. With no hesitation, Salk responded, "Well, the people, I would say. There is no patent. Could you patent the Sun?" (*See it Now*, 1955), and in the year before Salk's death in 1994, the United States was declared to be polio-free (Centers for Disease Control and Prevention, 1994). Human nature aspires to adapt and overcome environmental challenges. Advances made by science and technology not only seek to improve the quality of life, (which is the case for the new ice cream machine I recently purchased) but to conquer that which we were once merely victims. Parents in the first half of the Twentieth Century feared and fretted over the possibility their children might contract the polio virus. Until the time of Salk's vaccine, the virus was invincible; the only possible outcome for the exposed was to assume the role of the victim.

Picture 2.1, Jonas Salk

Nevertheless, until there is a cure or inoculation, a virus is not a social problem. Once the means to ameliorate the virus is in the grasp of societal institutions that determine who is permitted to receive it or not receive it and at what cost, approaching the discussion through the lens of a social problem is mute. Moreover, when addressing problems stemming from environmental events, emphasis needs to be on the criteria of when reasonable argument prevails, there is something that can be done to improve or even resolve the social problem as a means for effectively differentiating *problems* from *social problems*. Often is the case, as we can see from this example when science solves an environmental problem, it may also create social problems in its wake. As Kazuo Ishiguro (2005) suggests in his dystopian novel:

> I saw a new world coming rapidly. More scientific, efficient, yes. More cures for the old sicknesses. Very good. But a harsh, cruel, world. And I saw a little girl, her eyes tightly closed, holding to her breast the old kind world, one that she knew in her heart could not remain, and she was holding it and pleading, never to let her go.

Science and technology have overcome many problems rooted in the environment where prior generations saw no mercy whatsoever. As devastating as a hurricane's wrath may be to a community lying directly in its path, the hurricane is not a social problem; instead, it is an environmental catastrophe resulting in *social concerns* and *troubles* for those affected by the elements of the storm. On the other hand, failure to get access to relief and aid to the suffering may undoubtedly constitute a social problem. Hurricane Katrina was a massive Category Five storm that ravished the city of New Orleans to near apocalyptic proportions in 2005. The city's response to adequately prepare for the storm's wrath in the hours before Katina's landfall was woefully poor. Desperately needed humanitarian relief and supplies were delayed in the immediate aftermath of this storm, resulting in finger-pointing between local, state, and federal government agencies, with the federal government suggesting the state had greater responsibility to take the lead in pre-storm preparations and post-storm relief, and the state arguing the charge should have been led by FEMA. When essential supplies and relief are available and the inability to deliver it in a reasonable amount of time is due to a breakdown in communication and confused government policy, those who directly suffer are experiencing a social problem. Today, Hurricane Katrina has set the benchmark against which all other Category Five hurricanes are measured in both pre-storm preparation and post-storm relief response.

The term *catastrophe* was used to describe the devastating affects a significant storm has on a community. Nevertheless, a hurricane, even one as powerful as Katrina, will not put an end to our civilization. When society's complete and total existence is at risk, then it may be said society is facing an *existential threat*, as the result of such a problem holds a reasonable likelihood of society's annihilation. For instance, Global Warming (now more commonly referred to as Climate Change) has been hoisted by some into this category of *existential threat*. The Earth's air and ocean temperatures, according to many scientists have been steadily rising as a result of emissions of greenhouse gas, identifying human-activity as the primary cause. Therefore, as a result of human-abuse to the environment, the planet is now on the brink of annihilation, not in centuries or even in decades, but in the same year I was hoping to start drawing on Social Security[1] (Hains, 2019). Assuming we have exceeded that point of "no return" where any human intervention can reasonably alter the course of Climate Change, this problem is an *existential threat*, not a social problem.

This is not to suggest that the only outcome from an existential threat is societal annihilation. The trajectory an existential threat pursues can be either altered or extinguished; otherwise, annihilation is a likely outcome. For example, Adolf Hitler posed such a threat to our nation as his forces moved west across Europe during World War II.

---

[1] Freshman Congresswoman, Alexandria Ocasio-Cortez (D-NY) while speaking at a public event for Dr. Martin Luther King Day (2019) addressed her concerns over this topic of climate change by explaining, "Millennials and people, you know, Gen Z and all these folks that will come after us are looking up and we're like: The world is going to end in 12 years if we don't address climate change and your biggest issue is how are we gonna pay for it? This is the war — this is our World War II."

Defeating Nazism was not a social problem; it was an existential problem where the only solution was political.

Social Change is Not a Social Problem

Several years ago, one of my adjunct faculty members walked into my office. He had retired from a successful career spanning across both academics and industry, now enjoying some part-time teaching. He was an outstanding instructor in the classroom, making me feel humble in my classroom skills whenever I sat in to observe him. He loved teaching, and students also loved him as well; his classes were some of the first in the department to fill up, closing on the first day of open registration. Today, however, he looked distraught. "I have to talk to you about next semester. I'm not in a position to teach for you any longer."

I thought the worse: a terminal diagnosis. I softly pressed for details. "No, it's nothing like that. I am just no longer able to do the job expected of me." I argued back; "You're one of our best instructors. What you're saying makes no sense to me." I thought of what it must be like for a teenager to "come out" to his or her parents as I saw the anxiety welling up in the professor. "It's okay; you can tell me." To which he finally said the words, "I'm computer illiterate." I knew technology was not his strong suit. He never used email, preferring to use his home phone number with instructions to leave a message on his recorder, and he still used old transparencies in lectures rather than PowerPoint. Our college had just made changes requiring uploading all syllabi into the Learning Management System (LMS) where the grade book was kept as well. The LMS was also the required means by which email exchanges had to occur. For my professor, it was all too overwhelming, and in spite of many pleas on my part to receive training on the use of our LMS, the professor refused. One certainty of our social world: change is absolute.

Social change, in and of itself, is not a social problem. Harvard sociologist Talcott Parsons (1902-1979) suggests any change in one social institution will result in subsequent changes in other social institutions, almost like aftershocks following an earthquake, as the society attempts to reestablish a state of *homeostasis*, or normal functioning (1977). Consider, for example, the licensed practice of clinical psychology. The state is responsible for licensing psychologists. Moreover, it is the state licensure boards that govern the practice of the profession by establishing laws and regulations which, in turn, establish protections for both patients and those practicing psychology. In the last few years, there has been significant use of telemedicine tools providing secure, confidential video linking psychologists with patients. How relevant is state licensure becoming? Let us say in the city of San Francisco the average cost to see a psychologist is $225 per hour, but the same cost to see a psychologist via a secured video link in Birmingham, Alabama is $150; the state of California is now stepping in and warning the Birmingham psychologist he or she is practicing without a valid California license and will be reported to their home licensure board. The problem which this issue is currently bogged down into is that states are not able to regulate in other jurisdictions, as doing so refers to interstate commerce which is overseen by the federal government, not the state. At this time, there is no such thing as a federal license to practice clinical psychology. Using Parsons' model, a sociologist, therefore, might forecast that federal standards will soon develop for licensure, as insurance companies favor lower reimbursement and can lobby with more force than any single state can do. In turn, graduate programs in psychology will need to shift curriculum and normalize it towards these newly established federal standards versus their prior focus on state guidelines.

Additionally, psychologists who frequently have to consider setting up their practices in large metropolitan areas to cast a wide net to find patients may now consider setting up residence in regions of the country with the most favorable socioeconomic living standards. It is easy to forecast that this current problem will balance out as homeostasis is achieved again for clinical psychologists. The process in doing so, however, is not a social problem; instead, it is the normal process of a society recalibrating itself.

Towards Defining a Social Problem

Any proper study of social problems, as previously discussed, avoids navigating into a discussion on *social concerns*. Our feelings need to be kept in check. That is not to suggest feelings ought to continually be kept in check. Like most others, I have strong feelings on topics the likes of abortion, access to healthcare, voting rights, and so forth, but I strive to avoid bringing such emotions out openly when engaging in a classroom lecture, sitting on a discussion panel with a name placard identifying my professional title, or writing a document such as the one you are reading at this moment. Instead, I present such topics as a social scientist avoiding at all costs the emotional lens in favor of the objective, empirical lens of social science. Outside of the classroom, I vote, march, yell at the television when some politician is cutting the fool, and I might even feel tempted to scream at some twelve-year-old vanquished of all musical appreciation when imposing Katy Perry on my ears. From an academic perspective, feelings do not justify or confirm any position taken on a given social problem; instead, feelings inhibit and corrupt the pursuit of meaningful dialogue on the subject.

One undisputed fact about any social problem: both the concern and any possible solution to ameliorate a social problem is confounding, meaning there is no clear, conspicuous, and straightforward solution to remedy it. Social problems are about as complex as the synaptic tapestry weaving the neural networks of the human brain together. How we feel about a social problem is irrelevant, only leading the dialogue further away from purposeful and productive ends.

Moreover, social problems are also not philosophical; rather, social problems grind into actual human experience. Recently, I was watching a political debate. One of the candidates made a statement, something to the effect, that at the core of every social problem in our nation is the undisputed fact our society has an extensive income gap between those who have the most versus those who have the least, and we must first address this problem if we ever hope to experience true peace and prosperity. It sounds something like a politician might say when pounding the stump of likely voters, especially in lower socioeconomic neighborhoods. To suggest wide diversity in income ranges is at the crux of all social problems is simply a philosophical idea. What if for the sake of this idea, the government were to give every citizen a check for $50,000, meaning everyone is a bit richer, but the income gap remains the same, would we see any change in specific identified social problems? Thus, an accurate definition of a social problem must operationalize the phenomenon of concern within an empirical context. In other words, social problems are verifiable by observation or actual first-hand experience.

Consider, for instance, the post-Vietnam heroin epidemic that never was (Hall, 2016). Many US soldiers were known to be using and abusing heroin while serving in Vietnam. Their use was not casual, instead their heroin intake was sufficient enough to experience withdrawal from the drug immediately upon its disuse, and the number of active addicts might be as high as 34%, raising severe concerns back home in the US of a looming epidemic in heroin-addicted Americans about to erupt onto the streets which, in turn, would result in surging crime and violence.

In response to these predictions, President Richard Nixon appointed the first US Drug Czar and established a new executive agency, The Special Action Office for Drug Abuse Prevention. The US government committed a substantial amount of money and resources to fight this anticipated epidemic of drug addiction that many believed would soon hit the streets all across America. A surprising fact: the epidemic never happened. Only an estimated 1% of returning soldiers brought their heroin-addictions home with them (Hall, 2016). Most gave it up, managing the uncomfortable withdrawal symptoms on their own without the aid of any government resources. Substance abuse experts are not in full agreement with one another; nonetheless, a common explanation to account for this epidemic that never was is that these soldiers became addicted in a unique and stressful environment; when the environment changed to one not nearly as stressful, the addiction did not transfer along. As a result, we can say the fear of escalating heroin addiction amongst Vietnam Veterans was not a social problem. Although, there may have been reasonable empirical evidence to substantiate a concern for a social problem (i.e., referring to the estimated 34% use of the drug among soldiers at the time), the fact only a minimal number of veterans were observed to have carried on with their prior heroin abuse rules out the presence of a social problem.

Social Problems as Empirical Science

The astute reader has already taken notice the above conversation has slipped into the dialogue a little more than just observations and first-hand experiences. There were a few numbers presented as well. Observations and first-hand experience tend to be evasive and possibly subjective as well. "How did we do?" I hear some students call out to me as I walk into a classroom clutching a batch of graded exams from earlier in the week. How helpful is it to randomly call out 38 grades, no names, just numbers? It makes a lot more sense to say to the class average was 80%; the highest grade was 97%, and no one earned an F on the exam. Sociologists, including those who specifically study social problems, are social scientists. Sociologists—like any scientist—employ the use of the *scientific method* referring to a rigid, careful process for vetting questions used to explore observations and experiences. The process leads to the formation of a *hypothesis*, referring to a sort of proposed assumption deduced from the available evidence which then leads to scientific testing of these hypotheses. The inevitable objective is to deduce down, concluding, that at their best lead to sustainable prediction. Sociologists employ the use of several different methodological designs to navigate their application of the scientific method.

Descriptive designs describe a phenomenon as it occurs. This design is rather weak because drawing any causal reference cannot occur at its conclusion. These designs employ the use of *descriptive statistics*. In other words, this type of design is describing a phenomenon by using concepts such as percentages, averages, and ranges, meaning all a researcher can do is paint a picture of a phenomenon. No causal statements occur. For example, a researcher can determine that of all those students pursuing a degree in early education in the College of Education at their university, 80% are women, but the data does not support the conclusion that this lack of male representation is due to any gender discrimination. Although descriptive designs draw relatively weak findings, often, this design is used when studying a new social phenomenon, and sociologists routinely encounter new social phenomenon in a dynamic, ever-changing world. Descriptive designs represent a great place to start a scientific inquiry.

Qualitative designs are similar to descriptive designs in many respects. For instance, the purpose of a qualitative design is to describe a social phenomenon. Where qualitative designs differ from descriptive designs is how the researcher describes a phenomenon. With qualitative designs, the researcher uses *words*, not *numbers*. Qualitative designs are about *thick description*. There are several different ways that researchers conduct qualitative research. For instance, sociologist psychologist Lillian Ruben (1976) conducted an original study of middle-class working families using a qualitative design. In this instance, Ruben scheduled interviews with many different working-class families. At the time of the interview, these families knew she was a university professor, and their stories would be part of a research study. Ruben tape-recorded these interviews. After that, she transcribed these interviews and began the methodical process of finding common themes and common stories from all of the individual stories. In the final analysis, the researcher is looking for a single story that is reflective of all the stories.

Sometimes, however, researchers feel that if they let their subjects know that they are being researched, they will alter their behavior, and the real story is not being told. Sometimes then, when doing qualitative research, the researcher may secretly join the group to obtain an insider's account of the group's activities. For example, David Rosenhan (1973) had eight researchers admit themselves to various psychiatric hospitals back in the early 1970s. In his study, Rosenhan wanted to know if the *sane* could be objectively told apart from the *insane*. In this instance, these eight researchers never let anyone from the hospital staff know their actual purpose for being hospitalized. These researchers made careful observations and took notes when able. This form of research methodology does raise some ethical considerations.

Figure 2.4, Directional association relationships on scatter plots

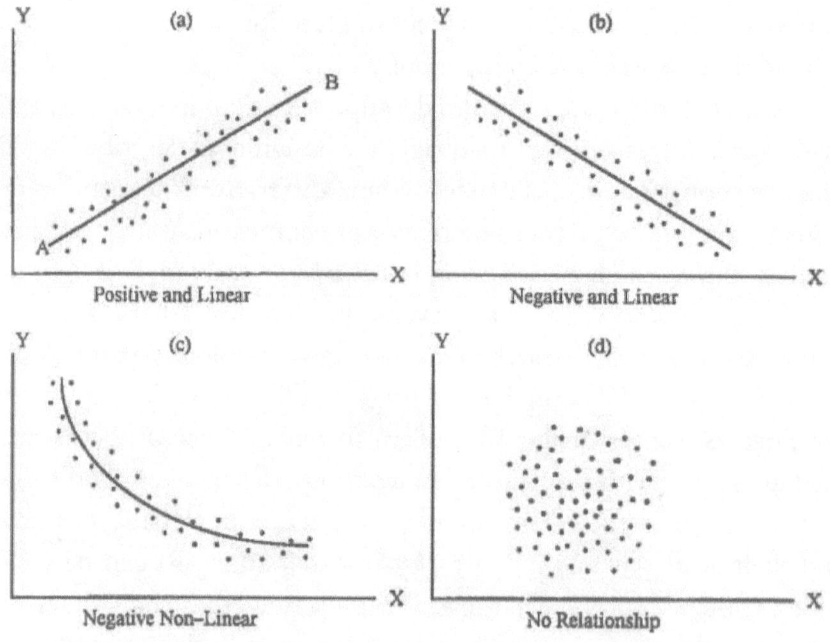

Correlational designs are methodologically stronger than the previous designs so far discussed, as this type of methodology measures association existing between two variables. Yet, this design is not strong enough to yield causal statements about the relationship between the two variables. Correlational analysis always begins by gathering data—measuring the two variables. Before these variables can be measured, they first must be *operationalized*. That is, the variables need to be clearly defined. For instance, if you plan to measure a variable entitled *social support*, define what you mean by the term. Clearly, define all of the variable's attributes. An unambiguous definition is essential because frequently, what sociologists measure is ambiguous. Just what is *social support* anyhow? Is it loaning someone $5.00, or is watering their plants or providing a shoulder to cry on during times of emotional distress? Because not all sociologists perceive the concept the same way, it is essential to clearly define its meaning within the context of the study at hand.

Once the variables have been operationalized and measured, it is necessary to place the data on a graph with an X and Y axis called a *scatter plot*. It is imperative to look at the data visually. Sometimes data can do odd things which otherwise may go unnoticed if not assessed by the human eye. Thus, obtaining the correlation coefficient occurs, reflecting a value measuring the degree of association existing between the two variables. The correlation coefficient will always be a number between −1.0 and +1.0. Both −1.0 and +1.0 correlation coefficients represent a perfect correlation. The positive or negative value refers to the direction of the relationship. For a +1.0 correlation coefficient, Variable A increases at the same rate as Variable B, and for a −1.0 correlation coefficient, Variable A is decreasing at a consistent rate as Variable B increases. If the correlation coefficient is 0, there is no relationship between the two variables.

When the coefficient is strong, it is tempting to say that absences cause grades to go down. However, with this type of design, all we can say is there is an association between these two variables. We cannot make a causal statement for two reasons. First, we may have found a *spurious relationship* (sometimes referred to as a *third variable problem*), as there may be some third hidden variable explaining the relationship. Second, the *problem of direction* is also in question. Is it Variable A that causes the change in Variable B, or is it Variable B that causes a change in Variable A? Because we do not know the direction of the relationship, we cannot make causal statements.

An *experimental design* is the most robust design. The strength of an experimental design lies in its ability for manipulation of variables. Unlike the other designs discussed thus far, with experimental designs, the researcher must make modifications in the environment to assess the outcome of the experiment. For this reason, when working with variables, the researcher must now clarify specifically the variable used. There are two types of variables: *independent variables* and *dependent variables*. An independent variable refers to the treatment variable; it is the variable that is being used to modify the environment. In which case, the dependent variable changes in value as a result of the independent variable's influence. For example, suppose a pharmaceutical company develops a new antidepressant medication. The company wishes to set up an experiment to substantiate the antidepressant's efficacy. In this experiment, the antidepressant medication is the independent variable (treatment), and the level of depressive symptoms is the dependent variable (medication alters the level of depression). Although there are different ways research employ experimental designs, typically the *pretest/posttest* method is preferred. This approach begins by randomly assigning subjects into either an experimental group or a control group, which is then followed by measuring a baseline value of the dependent variable for both groups. This follows the control group's exposure to the independent variable. Finally, both groups again have the dependent variable measured. The difference observed between the pretest and posttest is assumed to be the result of the independent variable.

These research designs only address how data is methodologically analyzed; it does not address the process for gathering the data. There are several ways to gather the data used in research. The type of design the researcher uses influences the type of data gathering technique.

One commonly used technique is to have a subject respond to a set of questions. The respondent's responses are recorded and compiled with responses from others. The subject may also complete a *questionnaire*. In so doing, the subject is responding in writing to a series of questions. However, the subject is completing a *survey* when recording responses. Observation is yet another way of obtaining research data. When respondents' behaviors are being observed and recorded, a *field study* is taking place. In some field study research, the respondents are unaware that they are being studied. Sometimes, to ensure validity, the respondents cannot know that they are being studied. When subjects know that they are being observed, their behavior may alter, referring to the *Hawthorne effect*.

Final Remark

At this point, we have differentiated what phenomenon may fall into the category of being a social problem from those phenomena where a label of a social problem does not appropriately apply. Excluding the use of personal feelings is an appropriate means for analyzing social problems, while always seeking emotional objectivity. Empiricism is how social problems should be analyzed, as the purpose of such analysis is to move towards the problem's resolution. It now becomes necessary to house the topic of social problems into a particular discipline or school of thought. To this end, social problems have traditionally been the subject of sociologists. Not that other disciplines (i.e., economics, psychology, anthropology, political science, as well as others) do not have meaningful contributions to make in the study of social problems. Sociologists routinely employ the use of these other disciplines in their study of social problems. A proper study of social problems resides in the discipline of sociology because this discipline's emphasis is to analyze the dynamic connection between the individual and the societal, and this is where social problems live.

3   The Sociology of Social Problems

A study of social problems aligns with the subfield of *sociology* within the social sciences, which directs its attention to the scientific study of social activity. Sociologists are concerned with empirically understanding social relationships and the many social institutions making up our society. Sociology as an academic discipline began to emerge sometime around the mid-Nineteenth Century as both a product of the Enlightenment as well as a direct reaction to it. The Enlightenment refers to an age of philosophy that dominated the ideas of the Western World, particularly around the Eighteenth Century which greatly influenced government, law, art, science, religion, and education. Concerning government and politics, it was John Locke who argued we all have inalienable rights, including life, liberty, and the pursuit of happiness. These rights, moreover, exist even in the absence of a government established to protect them. In other words, the essential elements of the world now become the individual, not the state. Additionally, the natural world was argued to behave according to its laws, sometimes referred to as *natural philosophy*. By employing empiricism, these natural laws could be deduced and known which help to usher in many scientific advances including new insights on the use of electricity, development of modern chemistry, and advances in medicine to name only a few.

The clash between political ideas of representative governments and new advances in the sciences help to prime the way for old social systems to collapse as was the case with the French Revolution and a little earlier, the American Revolution. It was about at this time Auguste Comte (1798-1857), a French philosopher, and now considered to be the *Father of Sociology*, began suggesting a new idea which he referred to as *positivism*; this idea continued to embrace the value of empirical science as a means for knowing the truth. Where Comte's ideas parted company most significantly from that of the Enlightenment was on the individual's status to the universe. For Comte it was not the individual serving as the essential, fundamental element of the universe; instead, it was the society. Comte explains, "Every social system… aims definitively at directing all special forces towards a general result, for the exercise of a general and combined activity is the essence of the society" (cited in Lenzer, 2009, p. 2). Although the natural laws governing society were not yet deduced, Comte argued by using empirical science they could be known. Moreover, such a scientist—he suggested—be called a *sociologist*. Although the philosophy of positivism fizzled, the discipline of sociology remains.

This is not to suggest the contemporary study of social problems is strictly viewed through the sociological lens. Sociologists draw liberally from other disciplines—often behaving at times like mongrels—scavenging routinely from economics, psychology, biology, government, communications, anthropology, history along with many others. It is those social problems by their nature span as well as drift through various disciplines; thus, they behave sociologically, suggesting a dynamic connection between the individual and the societal. As noted earlier, the degree to which the individual and the societal dynamically connect through this mutual ebb and flow it not set to a constant, as the degree of permeability varies greatly. Nevertheless, what supports an understanding of the nature of this connection is sociological theory. Such theory supports and provides context to explain facts about our social world. Essential sociological theories include functionalism, conflict theory, and symbolic interactionism. This theoretical triad refers to the *three pillars of sociological thought*. A brief overview of each theory follows. Although not one of the three pillars, our review begins with a look at the ideas of social Darwinism, as the discussion offers relevance moving forward.

Social Darwinism. Not one of the *three pillars*, but it was sociologist Herbert Spencer who coined the phrase, "survival of the fittest," not Charles Darwin, who favored the idea of *natural selection* where it was the biologically fit who were able to propagate leaving the weak to perish. Spencer has become to be known today as the sociologist who retrofitted Darwin's theory of natural selection by injecting into it a sort of social twist by applying it to the social world, now referred to as *social Darwinism*. Spencer viewed the social landscape as endlessly evolving, moving towards a better state, which marks a significant point of departure from Darwin who saw the process of natural selection as a means to increase the likelihood of passing genes along to the next generation. Darwin does not argue that the next generation is improved from the former, just that there are more genes passed along to predecessors. Spencer, however, is suggesting where one finds him or herself on the socioeconomic hierarchy is the result of their individual abilities and efforts which are, to one extent or another, limited by their biology.

Moreover, with deliberate intention to influence the social condition by directing attention to those on the lower rungs of the socioeconomic hierarchy,[2] society can be improved. As Spencer explains,

---

[2] Every society has a stratification system for socially ranking people. Some people are deemed to have a higher ranking than do others. Although stratification systems are universal, they vary widely in specific applications from one culture to the next. In the United States designations such as upper-class, middle-class, working-class and lower class are frequently used to clarify rank. The elements used to determine raking are not limited to economics. Social status, vocation, and educational attainment also come into play.

Moreover, some societies do not permit movement between rankings, as is the case for example, with a caste system. The United States does permit movement.

"The poverty of the incapable, the idle stresses that come upon the imprudent, the starvation of the idle, and those shoulderings aside of the weak by the strong, which leave so many in shallows and in miseries, are the decrees of a large, farseeing benevolence" (cited in Bliss, 1897, p. 568). It is at this point, the discussion on social Darwinism meets a fork in the road, as its application takes us in two different directions.

First, Spencer favored an approach where the lower classes bearing the brunt of social adversity were given aid and resources to lift them out of their ill state. Although Spencer believed their plight was due to inherited characteristics, nevertheless, he also believed changing genetic states for the better was possible. Spencer adhered to a *Lamarckism* belief on evolution, meaning that an organism can pass on characteristics acquired during its lifetime to the next generation. This notion of a "soft" inheritance was first proposed by the French biologist Jean-Baptiste Lamarck (1744–1829), suggesting individual efforts during the one's lifetime could serve as a primary means for driving species to adapt to current social challenges as they evolved towards a state of higher functioning (Wright, 1994). Spencer, in life, was not the cold and heartless sociologist who believed society was best served by allowing the poor and weak to wither on those lower rungs of the socioeconomic hierarchy. Rather, Spencer supported social advocacy favoring charity to help the society's fragile, by aiding such people to rise out of their situations. Consider the philosophy of giving a man a fish for today versus teaching him how to fish for a lifetime.

The other approach to applying social Darwinism is solidly rooted in *eugenics*, believing the only way to ensure society's continued progress is to directly intervene through deliberately purging the corrupted gene pool of those who would—otherwise—find themselves and subsequent generations falling again and again to the lowest rung on the socioeconomic hierarchy. For example, many psychiatrists took lead-

---

We can come from humble beginnings, as was the case for Steve Jobs for example, and later in life find ourselves at the top of the heap.

ing roles, even serving in membership roles in the Committee on Eugenics in the 1900s, lobbying states to pass forced sterilization laws to inoculate future generations from the ravishes of mental illness. By 1924 an estimated three thousand persons in this country who were residing in mental institutions had, as a result, been involuntarily sterilized (Harrington, 2019).

Today, it is unlikely to find any biologist or genetic psychologist advocating for a Lamarckism approach to studying evolution. Moreover, the idea of genetic characteristics that can directly influence the likelihood of placement on the socioeconomic ladder is a bit farfetched. Additionally, the mere suggestion for eugenic strategies to purify the gene pool leading to a better world results in crickets being the only noise left in the room as everyone has bolted for the exits. Nonetheless, Spencer's social Darwinism is still routinely brought back to light in a dialogue on social problems to raise an essential point: there is a dynamic connection between the individual and the societal. Where one finds himself or herself on the socioeconomic ladder is not purely the result of individual ability and effort. For example, sociologists Pitirim Sorokin probably worked very hard on writing his doctoral dissertation, but his defense was delayed at the University of St. Petersburg due to the Russian Revolution. One can never forecast when their lives will face a challenge due to economic swings, environmental disasters, or even political revolutions.

Functional Theory. Although we consider Auguste Comte as the *Father of Sociology*, rarely is he provided much attention these days, perhaps a paragraph or two in the introduction to sociology textbooks. Attention shifts quickly to our *Three Fathers* of sociology: Karl Marx, Max Webber, and Emil Durkheim. The latter of these fathers, French philosopher Emile Durkheim (1858-1917) is most often associated with the functional theory, frequently referring to his seminal 1879 work *Suicide* (1951) as the theoretical starting point for this theory. A massive undertaking, the book also serves as one of the first instances where statistical, rather than merely philosophical analysis is used to explore a question and secure findings. In *Suicide*, he suggests a functional connection linking individual incidences of suicide to those larger social currents occurring at the time. For example, *egoistic suicide* occurs when one feels isolated and estranged from society. Whereas, *altruistic suicide* results from being too enmeshed and close to a society where the group is generating the act, as can be explained with historical Sati practices where the widow sacrifices herself by heaping herself upon her dead husband's funeral pyre. *Anomic suicide* results in times of rapidly changing societal instability which might be the cause of an economic crash or even winning the Power Ball. Finally, *fatalistic suicide* occurs in a society that restricts personal freedoms.

> It is the suicide deriving from excessive regulation, that of persons with futures pitilessly blocked and passions violently choked by excessive discipline. It is the suicide of very young husbands, of the married woman who is childless... To bring out the ineluctable and inflexible nature of a rule against which there is no appeal, and in contrast with the expression 'anomie' which has been used, we might call it *fatalistic suicide*. (Durkheim, 1951, p. 243)

Functional theory applies a lens to the social landscape by which the ebb and flow of social movement are explained first by its consequences by identifying how these actions contribute to the ongoing stability of society. Starting with Durkheim, the analogy of the human body has been used to help understand this theory. Just as the human body has various systems (e.g., circulatory, neurological, or digestive), where these body systems function differently from each other but, nevertheless, all these systems function collectively in keeping one alive. So, too, is the case with the societal, wherein this instance it is the social institutions (e.g., education, government, healthcare, criminal justice etc.) which comprise the societal and act towards their own consequences, but in doing so still function collectively in keeping the societal system alive. The abrupt demise of one social institution from the fold would possibly have nihilistic results.[3] Moreover, these consequences may be purposefully intended, referred to as *manifest functions* or be of secondary intent, referred to as *latent functions*. A manifest function of the public school system, for example, is to teach children how to read and write, but a latent function of it is to provide a source of free daycare.

Functional theory when applied to study of social problems pays particularly close attention to the adjustments necessary in the face of a social change or environmental event where those social institutions immediately impacted by the change or event, along with those social institutions that are indirectly affected by a sort of rippling effect, must make calculated corrections so as to ensure continued overall societal stability. In other words, it is much the same when observing children playing on a teeter-totter. One rather large child is sitting on the very end, as is the other much smaller child but on the opposite side. The small child is stuck up in the air. To correct the situation, the larger child needs to move closer to the fulcrum in order to balance out the situation.

Consider, for example, a historically religious university as a *societal microcosm*[4] composed of such institutions as academics, security, administration, and housing. Sadly, there were two separate events recently taking place where students were seriously injured in alcohol-

---

[3] Kiefer Sutherland plays the role of President Tom Kirkman in the television series *Designated Survivor* which applies a fictional twist to the fact a member of the President's Cabinet is left back at events such as the State of the Union address. Should a devastating event, like the US Capital being blown up as depicted in this television show, presidential succession is ensured, as anarchy otherwise ensues along with social tumult, ending in complete societal collapse. Netflix & Chill!

[4] A social microcosm refers to a sociological analysis based on the assumption that a community, social institution, group of organized people, or even an individual person is regarded as encapsulating a miniature image of the larger society, embodying all of its characteristics, qualities, and features. A *macrocosm*—on the other hand—refers an antonym for a microcosm where sociological analysis now addresses wider social structures, interdependent social institutions, and global social life. Theories like conflict and functionalism tend to align to a macrocosm point of view; whereas, theories like symbolic interactionism and ethnomethodologies align with a microcosm points of view.

related car accidents while returning to their dorm rooms in early hours over the weekend. The university's administration has declared this to be a serious problem that must be corrected. Currently, the university has a strict no-alcohol policy but now wishes to loosen the language of the current policy to be more tolerable to the presence of alcohol on campus only on weekends, believing if students stay on the campus to drink, their risk significantly diminishes of being involved in a drinking-related car accident. This change in policy will have a direct effect on campus-security who had been previously responsible for enforcing the policy, now fundamentally changing their job description. Those who work in housing, however, are now responsible for ensuring that no drinking is taking place inside the dorms during the week, where this responsibility had not typically been a part of their job description. The faculty is having a fit, as it is their position the university is going to collapse as a result of adopting such a policy because students will not be spending their Friday and Saturday evenings studying in the library. Six months later, the administration is horrified to learn their charitable donations have dropped by 50%, as many prior donors oppose the new policy and stopped making donations to the university.

This perspective faces a dilemma:

> The strength of functional analysis presumably lies in its ability to do skilled dissection and analysis of the ways in which social actions interplay in a network of interdependence within a given system, and thus presumably clarify in some as yet unnamed way "why" the practices are present… But now we find that it is precisely this ahistoricity which makes out analyses often of such dubious value. And even worse, it is future history rather than past history that we seem to need to control. And how do we do that? (Tumin, 1965, p. 382)

Moreover, this dilemma is more so the case for the functional theorist then the others we will be looking at in this chapter. The ability to identify and extract out the confounding elements which are at play with a social problem is not the same as being able to offer a remedy for fixing it. What is often referred to as social engineering has shown at times to have adverse consequences. Consider the passage of Social

Security benefits for the elderly, initially called *Old Age Assistance*, which beginning in 1934 provided a funding stream for the elderly. Before this, poor elderly persons were cared for by adult children. Perhaps penniless, nonetheless, their needs we being addressed. However, with the passage of Social Security, the elderly now had money at their disposal, a fixed monthly budget, but the amount was often insufficient to meet all their expenses, and increasingly we saw more reluctance from their adult children to step in to assist. It was at this time we saw the rise of a new class of poverty, the elderly. It was at this time we see the start of retirement homes where old folks were now sent to live out their final days (Liebert, 1998).

Conflict Theory. Still considered one of the three primary pillars of thought in sociological theory, *conflict theory* came into its theoretical right as a means of challenging ideas of structural functionalism following World War II. The very core of this theory centers on the use of power, whereas structural functionalists' attention squarely centers around a society's use of social norms and values as the primary means for interpreting the ebb and flow of social movements. When the interests of any particular group within a society are at odds with the norms and values necessary to obtain their objective, power is the means used to circumvent and achieve goals. *Coercion over consensus* is the process that falls into place from this perspective (Marshall, 1994). Moreover, this can only be possible, from a conflict perspective, when first, there exists an imbalance of social power between various groups. Such *social power*, for instance, may take the form of having higher socioeconomic status, political influence, or racial and ethnic authority, whereby this becomes the currency that gets the job done.

The development of conflict theory originates from the writings of Karl Marx (1818-1883). German by birth, Marx completed his studies at the University of Berlin where he became actively involved with a radical and bohemian intellectual group known as the Young Hegelians, as their intellectual pursuits centered around the philosopher Georg Hegel (Sperber, 2013). Radical thought, you see, was instilled early for Marx. Following his university studies in Berlin, he became the editor of *Rheinische Zeitung*, a politically radical newspaper. By the end of his life, he found himself nationless and vigilantly waiting and watching for the next major paradigm shift in history to occur through a political revolution, as this was the crux to his political-economic theory (Berlin, 1978). Much like Sigmund Freud would later argue that all human energy centers around libido, Marx argued all societal interests center around economics. Wealth is achieved through social control over the means of production, and those who hold this capitalistic control were referred to as the *bourgeois*. Whereas, the *proletariat* referred to those exploited by the bourgeois, where this working-class's labor was unfairly being taken advantaged of at the hands of the power elite. The proletariat worked, keeping the bourgeois rich and powerful. Believing this exploitive imbalance of power could never be sustained indefinitely, it was only a matter of time before the working-class would rise up and topple the bourgeois, resulting in a single social class of *communism* where there would be great wealth surplus and everyone's needs would be satisfied. Marx, in his *Communist Manifesto,* sets forth the Marist's rally cry, "WORKMEN OF ALL COUNTRIES, UNITE!" (Marx & Engels, 1964, p. 116).

When first introduced to the ideas of conflict theory, too often there is a sort of knee-jerk intellectual response causing the student to recoil, assuming all sociologists suggesting any analysis whatsoever from this point of view are, in turn, subtly engaging Marxists indoctrination. The concern is no different from a fanatical cult member simply offering a sandwich and a place to rest to a wayward teenager as the first step towards complete allegiance and indoctrination into the cult. For conflict theory, this is not the case. To see the social dynamics of the world occurring through a conflict perspective is not part and parcel to agreeing with communism, mainly when applied to political ideologies. Today, Marxist social theory, which does apply a more literal and historically socialistic application of Karl Marx is but just one small sub-theory within the broader scope of conflict theory. To substantiate this point, consider the university admissions scandal which started playing out during the spring, 2019 when US prosecutors held a press conference to announce indictments were soon following for parents who had falsified application credentials for their children in exchange for large sums of money in return. In simple terms, a pay-off. Applicants in some cases were being awarded seats at prestigious schools through the athletic recruiting process, although the applicant never participated in the sport. In other instances, assistance was given in mastering the SATs by correcting the candidate's test, which is nothing more than a fancy description for *cheating*. This was apparently occurring at some of our nation's top-ranked institutions like Yale University and Stanford University. The scandal captured our attention, not just because it included known Hollywood actors, but such behaviors abrasively run against our fundamental values arguing we are all created equal, and earning a seat at a top tier school ought to be based on work and effort. A student scoring 1600 on her SAT, graduating valedictorian from high school with a 4.0 GPA, and having engaged in countless hours of civilly minded volunteering in her community's homeless shelter, should have the same shot at admission to Stanford or Yale. Parents' payouts of hundreds of thousands of dollars, should never recalibrate the criteria upon which admissions are based.

Had this scandal revolved around who had the first opportunity to purchase first-class tickets on a flight from New York to London, there would not have been much notice taken, but college admission is an altogether different animal, inherently understanding graduation from a top-ranked school opens doors that are otherwise firmly locked an inaccessible to the rest of us. Education is one of the means by which social mobility becomes possible. A college degree provides a fair shot for grasping a hold of the middle-class rung of the socioeconomic ladder, but a degree from the ivy league elevates us way up to possible access to the socioeconomic status of our society's elites. From a conflict perspective, the elite's interest embracing societal *values* as it concerns human equality or even merely playing by the rules does not exceed beyond their *interest* to ensure their child gets that seat at the ivy league. Social elites use the tools most readily at their disposal to exploit the process to their advantage: money. Finally, this vignette may have the same visceral reactions for those readers whose personal politics align firmly to the left as well as to the right on the spectrum, as conflict theory is apolitical at its core. It is merely an analytical lens that provides a means to see the ebb and flow of social dynamics.

Figure 3.1, Karl Marx's theory on Dialectic Materialism[5]

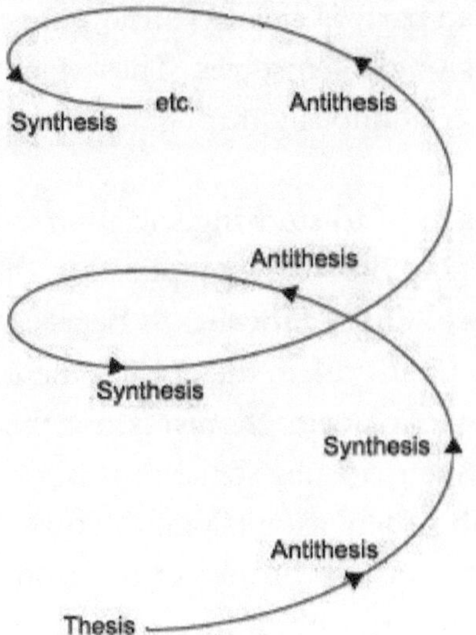

Symbolic Interactionism. Finally, *symbolic interactionism* (SI) determines the nature of meaning through the process of social interaction by looking at the meaning flowing out of everyday life though close

---

[5] Karl Marx saw the progression of human history resulting from the changing ideas on how people organize themselves around limited resources. In primitive history, there was no social classes, as the accumulation of wealth was not possible yet. Once it was possible to hoard resources, ideas on who should own and control these resources began (thesis), which was met with competing ideas (antithesis), and then resulting in a new idea (synthesis). At some points in history, Marx argued there existed several social classes all organized around society's wealth. For example, during the Middle Ages, there were social classes such as nobility, clergy, and surfs. Again, Marx saw his current historical period consisting of only two social classes: proletariat and bourgeois. The next antithesis would result in a new utopian social order of communism where there was no social class distinction and abundant wealth to be shared amongst all for the common good.

analysis of human exchanges in social settings such as work, school, and family. SI places emphasis on identifying the use and social exchange of symbols. In other words, the goal is to understand how meaning is communicated through body language, expression of feelings, and how biographies are articulated and negotiated between social actors. Moreover, SI takes the position the social world is dynamic and always in a state of ongoing change. Thus, one's biography is still somewhat unstable and never fixed. What it means to be a mother, physician, or a member of the republican party is always shifting, suggesting humans are not isolated islands unto themselves. These fluid elements of our biography are revised continuously through the process of social interaction.

When applying the sociological lens of SI to studying social problems, *labeling theory*—referring to a specific theoretical application of SI—has taken on significant importance. Often Howard S. Becker's *Outsiders* (1963) is acknowledged as a seminal work in the development of labeling theory. Here, he argues the act of being *deviant* is not the result of engaging in any specific act which violates social norms; rather, it comes about from those who label them as outsiders. In other words, deviance is not determined by the quality of the act but from the social consequences determined by others within the community. Even today, for example, a student observed smoking marijuana on a campus bench may be viewed by others who happen to be walking by as deviant, but an elderly woman smoking marijuana to alleviate the adverse effects of her chemotherapy while in a hospice may not be viewed in a similar light.

In the immediate years following Becker's *Outsiders*, labeling theory was applied to studying the labeling of patients, with emphasis on identifying how the identity of the patient role was assumed by those labeled and continuously renegotiated through the process of hospitalization. This was especially the case with psychiatric patients, as the criteria for a mental illness is much more subjective than that of a medical illness. In fact, some went as far as to suggest—through labeling theory—mental illness did not exist. The act of labeling the patient as being mentally ill was a process of socially constructing the concept of mental illness. Proponents supporting this perspective make up the anti-psychiatry movement. Psychiatrist Thomas Szasz, following the publication of his *The Myth of Mental Illness* (1974) soon became identified as one of the leading proponents of this *anti-psychiatry* movement. In this book Szasz argues referring to mental illness in terms of a medical disease is simply mistaken since actual medical diseases are the result of a "lesion" of the body; there is something wrong with the body that can be empirically detected in either bone, blood, or flesh. Whereas, with mental illness, there is nothing that can be identified as corrupt with the physiology and anatomy of the person. Moreover, Szasz goes on to argue, what is referred to as mental illness is better understood as merely "problems with living." But, whose problem?

For those aligned with the anti-psychiatry movement, the fault lies in the culture and a profession willing to assign a label to those who do not conform to the expectations of the culture. As David Cooper, who actually coins the term "anti-psychiatry," explains:

> I have been concerned with the question of violence in psychiatry and have concluded that perhaps the most striking form of violence in psychiatry is nothing less than the violence of psychiatry in so far as this discipline chooses to refract and condense on to its identified patients the subtle violence of the society it only too often represents to and against these patients. (1967, p. xii)

In so doing as sociologist Erving Goffman (1959) elaborates, the psychiatric patient does not experience any real care or treatment. Instead, what the patient receives is *re-socialization* where his or her true self becomes reoriented, polished down through a process of institutionalization. Here the patient comes to understand the real objective is to become "dull, harmless, and inconspicuous" where, in turn, the true self has eroded, resulting in a chronic state of mental illness.

Critics of the anti-psychiatry movement are often quick to sweep such ideas under the rug, suggesting such folks are nothing more than religious zealots, leftist political radicals, or ivy tower idealists who have never actually been present with an anguished patient in the clinical consultation room. It would simply be hubris to witness psychological pain in another human being only to suggest its etiology is merely a "myth" cloaked in social fabrication. Nevertheless, it is an error to assume anti-psychiatrists do not acknowledge the realities of human suffering, and they are willing to forgo all concern for such suffering all to pursue radical political fights over the intellectual ownership of mental illness. Proponents of the anti-psychiatry movement are concerned with addressing the needs of mental illness through patient-direct treatments. As Jacoby explains, "…there is no such activity as radical therapy—there is only therapy and radical politics… There is no shame in aiding the victims, the sick, the damaged, the down-and-out. If mental illness and treatments are class illness and treatment, there is much to be done within this realty" (1975, p. 139). Those who align themselves with the anti-psychiatry movement, and work professionally with patients, tend to cultivate approaches focused on acceptance, establishing friendships, and ensuring the clear exchange of communication even if the patient was not expressing him or herself by using correct language. For instance, Scottish psychiatrist R. D. Laing established Kingsley Hall, a community care center in London that was free of restraint and use of antipsychotic medications. Clinical psychologist David Smail (2005) built therapeutic alliances with his patients by focusing on the cultivation of friendships with his patients, believing that what everyone most needs is to be liked by others.

Anti-psychiatry advocates often see the assignment of the mental health label resulting from an imbalance of power. There is an exploitation of the powerful at the expense of the weak. In any psychotherapeutic relationship, the weakest amongst us are children whose consent for care, at best, lies in the hands of the parents or, at worst, lies in the hands of the state. The concern when assigning labels of mental illness to children is the assignment is done so to serve the interests of parents, foster parents, teachers, and others at the expense of children.

Mental health is thrust upon the child solely for the purpose to restrain, increase academic performance, or demand social compliance.

A research study, partially funded by the National Institute of Mental Health released in 2007, clearly stated there had been a 400% increase in the prevalence of children who had been diagnosed with a pediatric version of bipolar disorder in just a decade's period of time (Moreno, Laje, Blanco, et al., 2007). Once considered highly unusual, it would seem that pediatric bipolar disorder was quickly transforming itself into a typical childhood mental illness. Moreover, although the population was different, the treatment was more often the same treatment prescribed to adults. Believing pediatric treatment ought to model adult treatment for the same condition, children were regularly prescribed off-market atypical antipsychotic drugs (Chang, 2007); yet, there was no research to point to noting neither the effectiveness of using such drugs with children nor the safety risks associated with such drugs for such a young population.

The 2007 study acknowledges the possibility that, unless an epidemic had gone unnoticed and was being grossly underdiagnosed, there was a real possibility this young population was being "misdiagnosed." As subsequent research suggested, the symptoms of bipolar disorder did not present in the same way for children as symptoms did for adults. Perhaps clinicians were mistaking pediatric bipolar for something else. As Spittler explains, some of the most commonly reported symptoms, including "distractibility, pressured speech, and irritability" were overlapping with ADHD (2007, p. 23). While, others argued the differences in symptoms were rooted in developmental differences between children and adults (Chang, 2007); although, the disorder was the same. Being mindful 60% of children being seen by a physician when the precipitating factors for the office visit were symptoms of pediatric bipolar disorder were leaving with prescriptions for multiple drugs (The Brown University Child & Psychopharmacology Update, 2014), addressing this concern is vital.

With the release of the *DSM-5*, a new childhood disorder now appears for *disruptive mood dysregulation disorder* (DMDD). At the core of the new condition is "chronic, severe persistent irritability" (American Psychiatric Association, 2013, p. 156) manifesting in "temper outbursts" and prolong mood states of agitation or anger. Bipolar disorder is now considered an inappropriate diagnosis for a child between 6 and 18 years of age. Although the diagnostic label has changed from bipolar to DMDD, not much else has changed. Children are still primarily treated with atypical antipsychotics as the drug of choice. Changing the name of the diagnosis still does not address the 400% increase for diagnosing these children (Moreno et al., 2007) with this new label.

Anti-psychiatry advocates see the creation of the DMDD label as a means for controlling children's behavior and abdicating parental responsibilities onto a fictitious disorder. The DMDD label justifies medicating, thereby sedating the child making behavior more compliant and easy to manage. For instance, children in the foster care system were reported to be as much as eleven times more likely to be prescribed psychotropic drugs than those children not part of the foster care system (dos Reis, Zito, Safer et al., 2001). Fontanella, Hiance, Phillips et al. (2014) found for children the likelihood of being prescribed a psychotropic drug also increased when the child was male, disabled, and eligible for Medicaid.

Essential Skills for the Sociologist

Are you an advocate for domestic violence, supporting a man's inherent right to beat his partner to a pulp with absolute legal immunity? I would hope not, and now I have gone ahead and interjected my personal biased belief: I do not care much at all for those who inflict physical, as well as psychological harm on their partners. Now, let us say you agree with me, and you too do not like these "beaters" at all; actually, you despise them! This discussion on the topic has now actually steered you away from any future profession in sociology, now preferring to pursue a career in medicine. One Friday night years from now, it happens a man comes into your emergency room with a broken hand. "How did you break it?" you ask. He replies, "by punching my wife in the face." He then asks for you to do an especially good job setting the bones because he hopes to make a proper fist once again in the future. What is your treatment plan? If you are not going to do your best job in meeting the medical needs of your patient which will require you to put your personal beliefs aside, perhaps medicine is not the right field for you either. Doctors treat their patients, even the ones who are despicable; this is—in part—what it means to be a professional. Personal bias never compromises professional ethics. The same holds for sociologists.

Picture 3.1, Vandals paint #MeToo

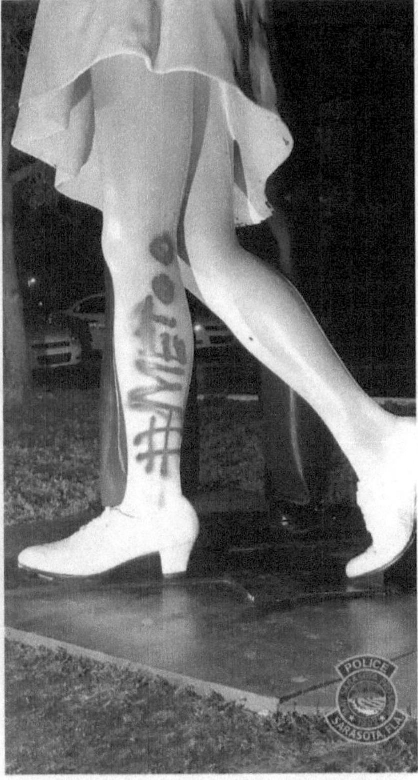

Picture 3.2, The V-J Day kiss[6]

<hr>

[6] The photo was taken by Alfred Eisenstaedt on August 14, 1945 who had taken notice of a sailor kissing random women as he participated in a makeshift parade in Times Square. Eisenstaedt saw a woman in a nursing uniform just ahead; he waited for the sailor to approach and snapped the picture (Verria & Galdorisi, 2012).

We have already identified a couple of essential skills for a sociologist which includes a degree of statistical and methodological savvy. That is correct: math is a requisite skill! As well, sociologists need to be familiar with the range of theory existing in the field and be able to apply such theory critically to a social phenomenon. Such analytic skills are also requisite. In addition to theory, one must also be able to employ the use of the *sociological imagination*, which C. Wright Mills argues is the sociologist's ability "to grasp history and biography and the relations between the two within society. That is its task and promise. To recognize this task and promise is the mark of the classic social analyst" (1959, p. 6). Absent the use of the sociological imagination, the theory remains two-dimensional, but its use adds both depth and perspective.

Consider, for example, recent events taking place within the #Me-Too movement. In the spring of 2019, a statue in Sarasota, Florida depicting the iconic photograph taken in Times Square (1945) showing George Medonsa[7] and Greta Friedman kissing was defaced with red spray paint with the words "#MeToo." Although # movements, like the #MeToo movement, lack clear elected leadership, several women were interviewed the following day across the litany of cable news networks, suggesting the statue was commemorating an act of sexual assault, and celebrating it is wrong. One commentator suggested the graffitist did not go far enough, meaning the statue should have been brought down to the ground and destroyed. Greta (then 21-years-old)—you see—had not given George (then 19-years-old) her consent to be kissed. George was in a movie theater with his fiancé when the film was stopped to announce the news: World War II just ended. Everyone ran out into the street to celebrate. George saw a young woman in a nurse's uniform, grabbing her in an embrace, and kissed her. A photographer happened to capture the image. In all the years which passed, Greta never once referred to the incident as an assault or violation. Today, should a 19-year-old run out into the street and plant one on an unsuspecting lady without first obtaining her explicit consent, leaving little doubt, the incident is an assault.

---

[7] George Medonsa passed away the day prior to the statue being vandalized.

Sociologists need to employ the sociological imagination by stepping outside of his or her cultural skin to evaluate a given phenomenon. To do so is referred to as *cultural relativism*, where the cultural norms and values for that specific society or time period is used to analyze the event. Once again, in Greta's case, she did not see it as an assault, nor did the millions of others who connected emotionally as well as psychologically to the photograph. Greta referred the incident as "a jubilee moment," as perhaps did most of the rest of a nation. The alternative is to use the perspective of *ethnocentrism* by evaluating norms and values through one's cultural standard. Therefore, if it is wrong for any man at any age to kiss a woman without her consent today, this also means it was wrong to do so 75-years ago. Moreover, it will continue to be as wrong to do so 75-years from today.

Sociologists do their best to avoid imposing their personal beliefs, norms, and values on their assessment of a social phenomenon, and doing so requires the cultivation of *professional distance*. Sociologists avoid making it personal. Keep the focus on the subject and situation. One's emotions tend to cloud our perspective much as cataracts impose fog on vision. For many sociologists, it is a difficult skill to acquire, requiring much deliberate effort, will, and time. For example, consider the case of social policy and Hurricane Katrina used earlier in this chapter. A lack of communication between federal and state agencies was cited as the basis for identifying the social aftermath as a *social problem*. The discussion, however, was apolitical. Readers who hold strong partisan beliefs and identification with a political party may have unconditionally barked out loud for a moment. To what extent was this *social problem* the result of a democratic mayor neglecting to carry out his sworn duties to ensure an evacuation plan was in place addressing the use of all of the city's public and school buses be used to evacuate hospitals and nursing homes, or a republican president appearing emotionally disconnected and unmoved by the tragedy unfolding beneath him while looking at Katrina's devastation on New Orleans through the window of Air Force One?[8] Quickly, as well as unproductively, the discussion divides into one of partisan politics. Essential in our operationalization of a *social problem* is the belief that something can be done to improve the problem. As we will explore in the last chapter, political advocacy is one such tool which can be used to this end, but firmly grabbing onto the political tool first before engaging in sociological analysis, is like grabbing hold of the point of the sword and thrusting the handle at the enemy first. Sociologically, the problem with political remedy is that these sorts of solutions are dichotomous, polarized, and two-dimensional, meaning they lack depth.

Picture 3.3, President George Bush looking down at a devastated New Orleans from the window of Air Force One

---

[8] President Bush explains: At some point, our press team ushered photographers into the cabin. I barely noticed them at the time; I couldn't take my eyes off the devastation below. But when the pictures were released, I realized I had made a serious mistake. The photo of me hovering over the damage suggested I was detached from the suffering on the ground. That wasn't how I felt. But once the public impression was formed, I couldn't change it. (Bush, 2010, p. 318)

Lastly, sociologists study societal behavior and sometimes do so by studying individual behavior as it relates to the societal. Even when working with individuals, sociologists are working with subjects, never patients. Sociology is not a clinical vocation with either the primary or secondary intent of helping to fix people as is the case with similarly related professions like social work, counseling, and marriage and family therapy. When working directly with subjects, sociologists take more than they tend to give. A sociologist who is studying the effects poverty has on the quality of parenting may interview dozens of parents. Perhaps, the sociologist's research may result in the suggestion of better parenting behaviors or be used by a legislature to direct more community funding to the needs of poor parents in another state, but it is unlikely the subjects interviewed will ever directly benefit from this research.

Again, sociologists take more than they tend to give to those who they directly study, and they tend to take from those who are more likely socially vulnerable. Liazos points to this fact in his classic article, "The Poverty of the Sociology of Deviance: Nuts, Sluts, and Perverts," where he explains, "In fact, the emphasis is more on the *subculture* and *identity* of the 'deviants' themselves rather than on their oppressors and persecutors" (1972, p. 108). Sociologists are far more likely to have at their disposal for study and investigation the socially weak and vulnerable amongst us, like "nuts, sluts, and perverts." Whereas, those who fall into the upper tiers, making up the socially powerful are far less likely to be the primary source of sociological study. Therefore, subjects require much care and respect.

Sociological work must occur ethically! To this end, the American Sociological Association (ASA)[9] maintains a robust code of ethics, always keeping this aspiration in crisp focus. For example, research with subjects is never carried out without expressed informed consent from the subject, meaning he or she is apprised of all the risks and possible

---

[9] The American Sociological Association (ASA) first founded in 1905 as the American Sociological Society (ASS) soon changed the organization's name realizing they were being mocked and referred to as "those ass-es." Their current code of ethics was last revised in 2018.

benefits before first consenting to the research. Sociologists maintain the confidentiality of their subjects. The ASA strives to ensure all its members practice professional competence, integrity, scientific and social responsibility, respect for people's human rights, as well as people's right for dignity (ASA, 2018).

Social Problems Are Ameliorable

Sigmund Freud (1856-1939) considered the *Father of Psychoanalysis* profoundly influenced the Twentieth and current Centuries with his theory suggesting our personalities are forged early in life through conflicts erupting over inner sexual fantasies (Liebert, 2017). We burry these conflicts deep into the unconscious mind, with our neurotic behaviors the only hint to their existence. As Andre' Malraux explains in *Man's Fate*, "man is not what he thinks he is; he is what he hides" (1934). Freud later applies a sociological application to his theory of psychoanalysis in *Civilization and Its Discontent* (1961), proposing all social adversity results from the ongoing quarrel between our desire to satisfy our internal carnal lusts and society's demands for conformity. "Much of the blame for our misery lies with what we call our civilization," says Freud (1961, p. 33), suggesting civilization exists for the express purpose of enhancing our safety and happiness, but the sacrifices required to do so, in turn, lead us inevitably to a state of unhappiness. From this perspective, social problems are as natural and enduring as water and air, which there is nothing that can be done to alleviate any social problem.

This socio-analytic idea, however, is contrary to the perspective taken by most sociologists in the pursuit of studying social problems, rather assuming the point of view there is something which can be done to improve or even possibly resolve social problems. Once again, a social problem originates from either an individual or society, and too often its true etiology centers around an incongruence of one's inalienable rights (i.e., life, freedom, and happiness), as well as the societal drive towards social values and needs. Sociologists, unlike Sigmund Freud, tend to be an optimistic lot believing when reasonable argument prevails, individual and social behaviors can realign. We will return to this discussion later, as it serves as the basis for the final chapter in this book.

Looking Ahead

The chapters which follow do not conform to a traditional textbook quality of discussion where there is an encyclopedic depth to the discussion suggesting undisputed facts, where the expectation of the reader is to memorize, and if being used in the context to support a course on social problems, the expectation is to regurgitate this memorized information on the exam. True, there are points made in this book, leaving little if any room for challenge. For instance, there is little to no debate: Auguste Comte is the *Father of Sociology*, and correlation studies can never argue for causation. Yet, when scaling back and looking at this book from a distance, the chapters which follow engage to some extent in speculation. These chapters identify what I consider to be emerging social problems, meaning social problems that are on the brink of maturing into the mainstream within the sociological community or which have been present all along but hiding in plain sight. Some may disagree with these speculations, including both those new to the subject of social problems as well as veterans in this field of study.

Statistics and science will be used in every social problem discussed in subsequent chapters, as the use of empiricism has already been identified as an essential element in differentiating a social problem from other sorts of social phenomena. Nevertheless, science cannot prove anything! Although an experiment looking at the connections between, let us say, smoking and cancer may conclude smoking *causes* cancer, this is not the same as saying we can *prove* smoking causes cancer. The best science can ever say on any topic is that the phenomenon is *robust*, meaning it is a pointless waste of time, energy, and economic resources to do even one more study as the science to date has yielded all that it possibly can yield; more research will not add any more to the current knowledge base. Do not forget, statistics has an element of subjectivity to it.[10] For example, suppose there still exists out there a state that has not enacted a mandatory seatbelt law up until right now. This state's legislation just passed the law. "Click it or Ticket," the campaign now reads. You are opposed to believing it is not the business of state legislators to mandate seatbelt use. A year later you want to show what a blunder this new seatbelt law has turned out to be. You do research looking at the rate of serious injuries sustained in car accidents. Your research will logically show in the subsequent year that significant accident injuries have substantially increased, suggesting seatbelt use elevates the risk for injury in a car accident. Of course, this would be the case! Had folks not been wearing their seatbelts they were more likely to have died in the accident, but now they are just severely injured.

Finally, although every attempt has been made to approach the following discussion apolitically, it is impossible to sterilize this aspect entirely. Many of the social problems to be discussed in this book are already, to one degree or another, a part of the political debate. There will be times where it appears I may be siding with the left, and there will be times where it seems that I might be siding with the right. Nonetheless, it is never the case that I am attempting to sway the reader towards a specific political perspective. Politics is but one tool that may be employed to ameliorate a social problem, but it is often not the essence of the problem, especially once removing a few rings of the onion.

In other words, any perspective, argument, or suggested truth which follows is still open for debate. The discussion which follows is not to suggest the final word on the topic. This is my primary intent with this book: to encourage ongoing debate, discussion, and expand

---

[10] Remember the old joke. There are three kinds of liars. There are liars, damn liars, and statisticians!

critical thinking. Any study on social problems required rigorous debate. Such debate is not personal and never challenges the essence of one's character. Such debate is academic. The moment when opposing viewpoints suggest one is a fool we have tumbled out of the intellectual dialogue. The academic explains why the idea is foolish while the rest intently listen while they consider the rebut.

Alas, the primary objective of this chapter was to provide an objective definition for social problems, to distinguish how these problems are different from all the rest of the concerns that capture our attention. Yet, there is more to be said. The next chapter takes a closer look at both the scope and depth of social problems, by identifying those attributes which provide context, differentiating one social problem from the next.

4   **Emerging Social Problems**

The approach typical to books attempting to identify the extent and depth of social problems existing across the social landscape is to identify these problems as they objectively reveal themselves through social institutions. Just about every textbook on the topic has chapter titles, beginning with the same three words: "Social Problems of…", followed by various social institutions such as "…sex and gender, …social class and economy, …race and ethnicity, … health and medicine, …environment, …crime and deviance, …family, …population and immigration, …education," and so forth. Moreover, the typical approach goes on to operationalize the social problem through objective measurements. For example, some sociologists may contend adolescent depression is a rising social problem, as we have seen a spike in the data suggesting a 29.88% increase in rates of adolescent depression in recent years (Mojabai, Olfson & Han, 2016). The problem is then further conceptualized by more data looking at how these numbers are even more dramatic for females than for males, and how we are not seeing any changes in the overall proportion of adolescents who are receiving any mental health counseling or other types of treatments to turn the tide and ameliorate this concern. Quickly, one is snow-blinded by data, failing to ask the essential question: why?

To this end, this book is different in that social problems are not identified merely based on being potentially "harmful" to people or because the concern impacts "a significant number of people" in some undesirable way, which is supported based on statistical evidence. Instead, this book purses a more subjective approach. In the previous chapter, a social problem was defined as "a dynamic connection... between the societal and the individual." Moreover, it is from the resulting friction between these elements from which social problems emerge and enter into social and personal life. Pointing out there has been, in fact, a 29.88% increase in adolescent depression rates, the statistic will be taken to represent—more or less—a symptom pointing towards the presence of a more profound sociological condition where the social problem is emerging, making itself known through such social-symptoms.

Figure 4.1, Degree of social problem severity

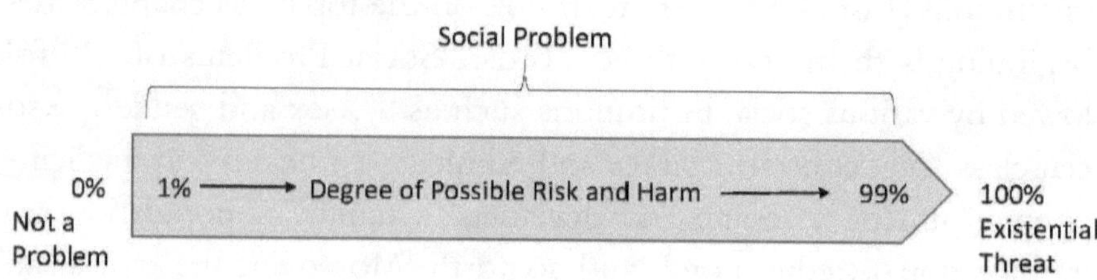

Social problems by their nature threaten the inalienable rights of individuals and our societal values. Although social problems pose a risk, not all risks emanating from social problems share similar degrees of potential harm, where some may sting us sharp like a wasp while others bite at us hard like a dog. In the first chapter, our attention focused on operationalizing social problems by differentiating what social phenomenon meets the necessary criteria for being identified as a social problem from that phenomenon which does not satisfy such criteria. In this chapter, we will begin to evaluate social problems across a continuum of severity, serving as the fundamental basis used to draw out and identify those specific social problems we will be discussing in the following chapters of this book.

Moving forward, four qualities absorbed into the fabric of social problems provides context to assess the degree of severity inherent in any social problem. An in-depth explanation for each attribute follows, but for now can be summarized as follows: first, social problems vary in their degree of ethical alignment between respective positions of morals and values, where *values*, refer to those things people genuinely care about, and *morals* refer to those ways motivation for our behavior bonds to shared human emotions and experiences. As the degree of congruency between these two ethical attributes increases, social problems take on less severity. In turn, the more these two attributes become incongruous with each other, the more socially risky the problem becomes. Second, as attention is misdirected away from the societal interests to various positions about a social problem, possible risk and harm to society increase, especially as the degree of involution increases whereby the social problem is entangled with multiple layers of complexity in the many different positions taken. Instead, sociological attention is best when redirected away from a particular position and focuses on social interests instead. Third, when the free, open, and reciprocal exchange of communication is present, the severity of risk decreases but will otherwise remain high when debate falls upon deaf ears indignant to acknowledging any other possible alternative position. Finally, as aegis authority increases, so too does the inherent risk associated with social problems. In other words, when a few sources of social authority maintain control over the social problem, the level of social risk rises.

Social Problems Vary by Degree of Ethical Alignment

Imagine that a week from next Tuesday while standing in line at Starbucks for your daily fix of a non-foam soy latté, you spot an acquaintance from work sitting off in the corner alone with red eyes and tears running down their face. Feeling moved emotionally, you join them and ask what is wrong? "You will not judge me, will you?" "Of course not," you reply. Your acquaintance proceeds to unload their emotion baggage, explaining how they left their physician's office earlier that morning. Without a moment's hesitation explains, the doctor diagnosed the symptoms necessitating the visit as gonorrhea and prescribed an antibiotic, which should clear up the problem in a week or so. Wishing you had decided on Dunkin Donuts for your java fix on this particular morning as you think to yourself, *TMI! I'm not their best friend!* Instead of sharing your actual thoughts, you try offering a supportive comment by explaining, "Well, now you know what the problem is and have a treatment to resolve it!" The acquaintance now leans in across the table towards you, "But, that's not what is upsetting me." *So, telling me you were just diagnosed with gonorrhea was just an icebreaker,* you think to yourself. "My doctor then went on to berate me, telling me I was immoral and a disgusting person to be behaving that way. Dirty! Dirty! Dirty! He just kept saying that over and over again. Wagging his finger at me, he went on lecturing, saying I must be absolutely stupid, no smarter than a sack of hair to be having unprotected sex. I started to cry. He almost laughed, saying that was good because it looked like I was finally listening, as my parents—who must also be of bad immoral stock—must've never properly educated me. I just grabbed the prescription out from his hand and bolted for the door." You chug the last of your latté in a single gulp and ask the name of the physician to store away for future reference, finally reminding your acquaintance, "Gotta go now! There's a budget meeting in ten minutes!"

To the point, is this physician a "good doctor?" He did examine his patient, diagnose the problem, providing effective treatment for it, and did not even bill for the additional lecture. Nevertheless, I suspect you would be telling friends and family never to go to see this physician, as we expect for our doctor to treat us, not parent us. The physician clearly allowed his personal moral beliefs to intrude into his professional role as a physician and contaminated otherwise quality-based medical care.

So too is the case when morality seeps into the equation on discussing social problems. The more that moral principles become influenced by the assessment, the more challenging and problematic the social problem becomes. Instead, sociological focus ought to be kept on societal values, including human values of inalienable rights. To start, it is all right that for the moment we drop the use of the phrase *social values* and apply our focus on the concept of *values,*[11] referring to those things people genuinely care about. These are the things that matter most to us, both at an individual level and at a societal level. Values are what motivates, determines our behavior, and frames our judgments regarding the rightness, wrongness, and the degree of desirability connected to such behaviors. Values are what matter most to us! Values flow into all social institutions, just as melted butter does into all the nooks and crannies of a Thomas's English muffin: science, economics, religion, family, sports, and so forth.

Social and personal *morals*, on the other hand, differ from values. Morals refer to those ways that motivation for our behavior bonds to human emotions and experiences. Once again, referring back to the above vignette, you decide to blast a scathing diatribe of this physician on Facebook, as well as to lodge an anonymous complaint to the Medical Ethics Board, all in an attempt to put this doctor out of business. It is your emotions which are preceding these behaviors and provide the rationale to determine the judgments made by both you as well as others as to the degree of rightness or wrongness, which connects to them. In other words, moral behavior is an outward way in which we operationalize our beliefs. It is through the psychological expression of empathy that we bridge the gap between the personal and the societal. *Empathy* refers to the ability to share and experience the feelings and emotional states of others; it is the sociological glue that connects us.

The distinction between values and morals can quickly become tricky waters to navigate merely by using definition and description.

---

[11] The philosophical study of values is called *axiology*, which examines the metaphysical and epistemological nature of values.

At such times it is always best to walk such concepts through a case study. Let us consider art. Our society attaches high value to art, as it falls under one of our inalienable rights: free speech. The United States Constitution grants us the right to share our ideas through the use of words and symbolic actions,[12] regardless of their popularity.

Moreover, society recognizes the inherent benefits to art, as it permits us to connect most directly with the human condition by building skills in empathy, creativity, and offers the opportunity to explore together ideas for problem-solving through the use of safe fictional spaces. Behaviorally, we encourage the patronage of the arts and financial support, as is too often the case, artists are not able to always support themselves from their work alone. As a social value, but perhaps not your value, we as a society do not believe in censoring art.

In the summer of 2019, an 83-year-old mural painted on the walls of a local San Francisco high school became a swarming controversy, as the city's democratic officials debated on destroying it. Victor Arountoff, a Russian immigrant, had been commissioned as part of the Works Projects Administration formed under President Roosevelt to paint the mural. Arountoff used this opportunity to depict images across the walls showing the uglier side to George Washington's life. The uncomfortable truth of his ownership of slaves and indifference to Native-Americans were on display for all the world to see. In 2019, attention and concern were now redirected towards the emotional, psychological pain and suffering the mural was argued to be causing students of color who had to be exposed to these images daily. Mark Sanchez, vice president of the school board and a third-grade teacher, said, "students who must walk past the mural during the

---

[12] The First Amendment to the US Constitution states: "Congress shall make no law respecting an establishment of religion, or prohibiting the free exercise thereof; or abridging the freedom of speech, or of the press; or the right of the people peaceably to assemble, and to petition the Government for a redress of grievances." There are exceptions to free speech of course. This right is not absolute. As is often used to exemplify this point, one cannot scream "fire" in a crowded theater. Moreover, one cannot claim photographic images in their possession depicting explicit child pornography represent art.

school day do not have a choice about seeing the harmful images. Painting it over represents not only a symbolic fresh start, but a real fresh start" (cited in Maldonado, 2019, n.p.).

Picture 4.1, Debate over George Washington mural

Political controversy over the censorship of art is certainly not a new public debate. Only months earlier in January, 2017, controversy sored yet again when 18-year-old David Pulphus' painting depicting a pig wearing a police uniform while brandishing a gun at African-Americans in the streets was removed from the United States Capitol at the request of the Republican Speaker of the House, Paul Ryan based on the argument the artwork violated the rules for social etiquette. Pulphus' painting was the winner of the William Lacy Clay congressional art competition. Following the removal, Democratic representatives rehung the picture, which was followed again by being removed and again being rehung. Over the subsequent week, much like a soap opera love affair, the painting was on-again and off-again from the wall. Democratic Representative Clay said of the controversy that it was "pathetic" for Republican members who "constantly refer to themselves as constitution conservatives not to apply fundamental free speech rights" to this young artist (cited in Tatum & Klein, 2017, n.p.).

Picture 4.2, Debate over David Pulphus' painting

It was intentional to provide two examples on opposing ends of the political continuum, where the first argument is from proponents led by democratic officials, followed by those advocates who were republican officials. In neither instance, was anyone arguing art is void of value and school walls, as well as canvas, looks better if left blank. No argument suggests either image is incapable of building skills in empathy, creativity, or identify realities on the human condition. Instead, personal emotions are in each instance, connecting empathically to those who are having a negative experience with the art. Police officers throughout the country expressed disgust over an image depicting police in such a vilified manner, which should not be hanging in the United States Capitol. It was the juxtaposition of the image with the building that ignited rebuke in the fictional space which art is supposed to create. Yet, is such an image unsafe? In the case of

Arnoutoff's *Life of Washington*, the same question can be posed: are images depicting, what has been referred to as our nation's greatest sin, unsafe for the viewer's eye? In each instance, the answer is a moral answer. Should a sociologist be studying these two cases, as well as the many other instances of possible art censorship in an effort to determine the degree to which this may or may not be a social problem, the assessment ought to be predicated on those actions that confront our societal values concerning art and free speech, not one's personal moral stance on the issue.

The sociologist bridges the gap when he or she allows their moral stance to seep into their analysis. I think of the iconic movie action hero, Dr. Indiana Jones teaching his class while wearing spectacles, bowtie, and tweed jacket later exchanges them for the whip, leather jacket, and fedora when going out into the field. Dr. Jones maintained a clear boundary between professor versus archeologist, so too should the sociologist between professional versus advocate, whereby *advocate* I mean *moral advocate*. Sociologists should avoid the call to action, preferring the analysis and sharing of ideas that come from the academic process. Sociologists, like Dr. Indiana Jones, can disrobe themselves of their spectacles, bowtie, and tweed jacket and head on out to the polling booth to vote, the rally to march, and tweet out their disdain regarding the city council's unanimous decision to tear down a historic building, but to do so while in spectacles and bowtie is a misuse of their professional role. The classroom is not the proper space to offer students extra credit for marching in the gay pride parade or showing support for removing the historical statue from campus by canceling the class to storm the administration building with these demands. A sociologist's moral compass does not point towards a finer degree of righteousness than that of the plumber or mail-carrier. Instead, sociologists research and teach on the state of social problems, like those falling under the topics of homosexuality or appropriateness of confederate statues, by informing students and the public on the extent human and social values have been impacted by the phenomenon. After that, some students will leave the classroom and head out to the polling booth and vote republican, while some will vote democratic, all the while democracy thrives.

Interest Over Position

Nineteen-year-old Nikolas Cruz is alleged to have walked onto the campus of Stoneman Douglas High School on Valentine's Day, 2018 bringing with him a semi-automatic assault rifle, which he used to murder seventeen students and staff members and injuring seventeen additional victims. He fled from the high school but was soon found and arrested by police. Cruz's killing spree is the deadliest school shooting to date in US history. At this time, Cruz nor his attorneys have offered any motivation for the attack. Nevertheless, the killing spree has once again unleashed a national debate on implementing effective measures for keeping schools safe by ensuring such massacres do not occur again in the future.

Lori Alhadeff, who lost her daughter Alyssa in the shooting, has started "Make Our Schools Safe," which is a national non-profit organization committed to "protecting students and teachers at school… [by improving] the safety of schools, research and test best practices, as well implementing those protocols by creating model schools…" fortified with bullet-proof glass, clear-plastic book-bags, guards at all entrances, and metal detectors. Still, much of the debate has polarized around the gun debate. On March 14, 2018, demonstrators organized, referring to themselves as "March for Our Lives" (MFOL, 2018). An estimated two-million people turnout for this event and descended on to Pennsylvania Avenue in Washington, DC, demanding their legislators take notice and respond to this ongoing threat by restricting gun access by such means as requiring universal background checks on all gun sales, closed gun show loopholes, increasing the federal age to 21 to be legally permitted to purchase a firearm, and place an outright ban on the sale of high-capacity magazines as well as bump stocks. On the other end of the debate are those who advocate the opposite position:

arm the schools, by pointing out the Second Amendment to the United States Constitution[13] was intended to ensure citizens have the right to shoot back. Having armed security or police officers stationed at every school may be insufficient, as critics have pointed out the school's resource officer at Stoneman Douglas High School failed to enter the building and even directed responding officers to stay out of the building where Cruz was believed to be. Moreover, establishing schools as "Gun Free Zones" is not shown to be an effective strategy for deterring school shootings, but a would-be shooter may be deterred if he or she knew members of the faculty and staff are both trained and armed to effectively respond.[14]

The above perspectives vary greatly on specific strategies and positions to effectively ameliorate gun violence from occurring in our nation's schools. Alhadeff argues for fortifying schools, MFOL argues in reducing legal access to deadly weapons, and NRA advocates suggest arming teachers. All of these divergent points of view are still united in sharing a common interest: reduce gun violence in schools. Unfortunately, the media, as well as many politicians, polarize the debate suggesting such interests are not expressed accurately, as the real agenda lies elsewhere. The NRA does not care about the fate of children. Left-wing organizations want to eradicate the Second Amendment and confiscate all guns. Sociologists should strive when addressing social problems—such as school violence—to avoid falling into univocal analytic arguments. Rarely do we find remedies to social problems by choices

---

[13] The Second Amendment to the United States Constitution states, "A well regulated militia being necessary to the security of a free state, the right of the people to keep and bear arms shall not be infringed."

[14] It so happens one of my former faculty at Florida Southern College where I attended undergraduate school was, now Sheriff Grady Judd. He taught a course on policing, which I was able to use as an elective for my sociology major. He recently rose to the national spotlight following the Stoneman Douglas shooting by proposing a new program whereby he would train teachers and college professors in tactics to effectively respond to school shooters. Judd told a television host, that before one of the Stoneman Douglas teachers was fatally wounded, he "would have shot the active shooter had he had a firearm [and] would have saved his students" (Peters, 2019, n. p.).

made on just one side of the argument any more than we find the problem intensifies by choosing the option on the other side of the continuum. Social problems are complex, confounding phenomenon. It just may be easier to count every hair on all ten of sasquatch's knuckles than it is to isolate the complete tangle of threads that weave a social problem together.

Unfortunately, this is a drawback when addressing social problems through politics, which tend to move us towards answers by taking either right and left steps, making the process look much like the sixth-grade homecoming dance. Consider, bump stocks which essentially convert a semi-automatic weapon into an automatic weapon. If outlawed, what is the effect on our inalienable right to life as guaranteed to us in the US Constitution, which ensures "the right of the people to keep and bear arms [which] shall not be infringed?" What is the degree to which such a compromise differs in degree from the right to own a tank, rocket launcher, or hand-grenades which are already deemed illegal to possess? Clarify the actual concern with training and arming teachers. Is the concern that all teachers are armed versus only some teachers? What if only those teachers who consent and pass the training are armed? What about teachers who had prior military experience or were former law enforcement? Is the cost of X-ray machines cost prohibitive versus the requirement of clear-plastic book-bags?

Such arguments polarize us into taking a *position*, meaning we take a side which, in part, is defined by its opposition to opposing positions. The debate, using this example of school violence, becomes defined by these various positions. Better for the sociologist to reorient the focus back to the interests which the social problem centers around. The risk with allowing a discussion on social problems to become bogged down in competing positions is for possible solutions to emerge in the form of compromises, which more or less ensures neither side gets completely what they want. By addressing our interests, the significance of what is determined to be important within the dialogue may be achieved by both sides of the debate. Keeping it simple, suppose my wife wants to go out to Chili's for dinner on Friday night, but I want to go to the Outback Steak House. We argue; I tell her that I hardly ever get to choose the restaurant (my position), she banters back that I rarely make wise choices (her position.) We compromise on Red Lobster,[15] and neither of us really get what we want. Instead, I ask her why she wants Chili's; to which she explains, she hates waiting for a table, and the line is shorter at Chili's, and maybe we would get out of the restaurant in time to see a movie (her interest.) I share with her, I wanted the Outback because I am hungry for a ribeye steak (my interest.) My wife tells me they have ribeye steaks on the menu at Chili's. Now we are both able to fully satisfy our respective interests.

Discourse and Debate

On the morning of December 30, 2018, Chuck Todd, host of NBC's *Meet the Press* went on-air announcing, "We're not going to debate climate change, the existence of it. The Earth is getting hotter. And human activity is a major cause, period. We're not going to give time to climate deniers [on this show]. The science is settled, even if political opinion is not." The problem, however, with Todd's declaration is that the scientific community is not unanimous in their opinion on Climate Change, especially as it relates to human activity being the chief culprit. Moreover, not all of those who disagree with a substantial proportion of the scientific community are "climate deniers;" some folks actual refer to themselves as being agnostic on the science. Regardless, Todd is proclaiming that moving forward, *Meet the Press* will not permit any alternative viewpoint to be heard on this show.

---

[15] This may be an excellent example to differentiate between *interests* and *positions* but may not serve as a practical suggestion for husbands wanting to ensure a healthy marriage. Here's how it should work in a marriage: many years ago, my wife and I decided we wanted to adopt a pet. I wanted to adopt a dog, and my wife wanted to adopt a cat. We compromised and got the cat.

Picture 4.3, Images of Rachel Dolezal

This unwillingness to entertain opposing points of view is not just limited to the political television talk shows where viewers can change the channel if offended. It is also increasingly taking place on the college campus, as well. In a 2017 survey, 58% of college students agreed with the statement: *it is important to be part of a campus community where I am not exposed to intolerant and offensive ideas* (cited in Lukianoff & Haidt, 2018, p. 48). Moreover, the college campus is witnessing a sharp increase in those instances where aggressive, intimidating, and even using violent behavior for shutting down a guest's presentation. This was the case in February 2017 when protestors at Berkeley University erupted, preventing conservative speaker Milo Yiannopoulos from delivering his lecture. Perhaps even more disturbing, this intolerance to opposing viewpoints has even bled into the science of academic research. Assistant Professor of Philosophy at Rhodes College, Rebecca Tuvel in 2017 published a piece in *Hypatia: A Journal of Feminist Philosophy*, essentially taking the position that our society tended to embrace Caitlyn Jenner's identity as a *transsexual* but was less accommodating to Rachel

Dolezal's[16] claim of being *transracial* (see Picture 4.3). The response from many in the academic community was harsh, accusing Tuvel of demonstrating a lack of concern, and these words could be harmful to women of color. The critics demanded the article disappear from the journal (Lukianoff & Haidt, 2018).

At an escalating rate, folks will not listen to someone else who holds an opposing point of view. Once the position was: *those are good people who happen to have some wrong ideas that—for their sake—we need to talk about this*, but increasing the default position is: *these are bad people because they have some bad ideas, and there is nothing else that needs to be said*. Such a stance is the common practice these days with our politicians, but reeks of contempt for the academic process within the halls of the academy. The goal of education is not knowledge; rather, it is the cultivation of those skills which promote critical thinking and problem-solving. As Gladwell explains, "the key to good decision making is not knowledge, it is understanding. We are swimming in the former. We are desperately lacking in the latter" (2005, p. 265). Sociologists are only able to fully conceptualize the true nature and extent of social problems if tirelessly listening to opposing perspectives. Listen as if you might be wrong. The ability to articulate an opposing point of view will never tarnish and corrupt one's moral footing. The further we move away from such dialogues the distinction between another person and his or her perspective blur and start to appear as if the same. Ideas can be foolish, wrong, bad, intellectually stale, and so forth, but those who attempt to explain such positions are never fools, bad, or stupid.

Aegis Authority

I use to live in a condominium in downtown Tampa, right near the Amelia Arena where the Tampa Bay Lightning play.[17] On Fridays, if I

---

[16] Rachel Dolezal was a former chapter president of the NAACP who had deliberately modified her physical appearance to appear to be African-American, although she is Caucasian.

[17] Go Bolts!

were coming home a little early, I often noticed city workers preparing for a hockey game or concert driving slowing setting out orange cones symmetrically straight down the centerline of the road. The next morning when I was out for a run, I would see the same city truck slowly working down the road picking up each cone. Why? If adding orange cones adds some additional safety, why not leave them out all the time? I suspect the city workers would not be too happy with a decision which reduces their job responsibilities. Now consider those folks along with the organizations they may be associated with tasked with the direct responsibility of working to address, ameliorate, or put an end to a specific social problem. There may also be an element of the organization that benefits from having the problem perpetuated, which may include factors such as employment, money, or social power.

The case of psychoanalysis as aegis authority. There are those instances where, even in the face of hard evidence and mounting empirical support, the social power structure is resistant to change and to revise its perspective. Consider, for example, by the 1980s, the ideas proclaimed by Sigmund Freud on psychoanalysis had been essential determined to be nearly as effective as witchcraft (see Eysenck & Wilson, 1973). Lying down on the couch as one's analysist listens from behind interpreting the symbolism all in an attempt to dislodge childhood memories long lost into the unconscious abys was at its least ineffective and at its worst invalid as a clinical technique. One such technique Freud argued for was *repressed memory*, where the ego facing a profoundly traumatic event buries the content into the unconscious mind, only to be freed back into conscious awareness as a *repressed recovered memory* once the ego's integrity is capable of managing the psychological implications of the truthfulness of the memory. Freud elaborates on this phenomenon in his case of Lucy R., who came to him complaining of an olfactory hallucination. She kept smelling burnt pudding. Through the process of free association, the cause for her hallucination was discovered as repressed sexual feelings for her boss.

"From this I concluded that Miss Lucy R. merged into that moment of hysterical conversion, which must have been under the determination of that trauma which she intentionally left in the darkness and which she took pains to forget" (Freud, 1912, par. 24).

Cognitive psychologist Elizabeth Loftus' research has called into question the factualness of repressed recovered memories. There might be a better explanation for why someone could wake up one morning to find a memory long ago forgotten now on the cognitive forefront of their consciousness. As the 1980s moved past the hump closer to becoming the 1990s, Loftus had already established for herself a long and successful career as a professor, memory researcher, and expert witness.[18] Early on in her career, she conducted research demonstrating the malleability of memory, showing how the details of memory quickly morph as if squeezing a ball of clay into new shapes. By merely suggesting to another, details like a stop sign remembered at the intersection of the accident scene morphs into a yield sign, or the neural static representing a masked bandit all of a sudden shift into a memory of a fully bearded man. A police officer interviewing asks, "how fast was the car traveling before *smashing* into the parked car?" This word, *smashing*, renders an account of a higher speed because the word *hitting* was not used instead by the police officer.

Loftus' career made a shift, of sorts, during the summer of 1990. This followed the arrest of George Franklin. Loftus discusses her experience serving as an expert witness during Franklin's murder trial (Loftus & Ketcham, 1994). Nearly twenty years earlier, a horrific murder occurred. The body of Susan Nason was discovered in a wooded area in Half Moon Bay, California. Susan was only eight years old, and tragically the murder case went cold, this is until Eileen Franklin, George's daughter, now an adult and mother herself, went to the police in 1989 telling them her memory of witnessing her father murder her school friend. Eileen told the police how she remembered her father

---

[18] Dr. Elizabeth Loftus also served as an expert witness in the trial of serial killer Ted Bundy. She was an expert for the defense. She says, "That's before we knew Bundy was Bundy," many years later in an interview with Laura Slater (2004). Loftus discusses this case as well as others in her book, *Witness for the Defense* (1991).

decided to drive her to school one morning in his van. Along the way, the two saw Susan walking to school; they stopped and offered her a ride, but they never made it to school that morning. Because George drove his van into a secluded wooded area and Eileen watched as her father assaulted her friend, smashed her skull in, and covered her lifeless body over with a mattress. The ordeal ended with George threatening his daughter to never speak to anyone of the day's events.

Twenty years later, however, Eileen was now speaking. When asked why she never came forward sooner, she explained she only recently recovered the memory. This memory, according to Eileen, had been "blocked out" (Loftus & Ketcham, 1994). She had experienced a repressed recovered memory. However, there were problems with Eileen's memory of these events. For instance, the errors in her memory seem to be consistent with the errors reported in the newspapers. Loftus' shared with the jury her research on the malleability of our memories, which did not prove to be helpful to George Franklin. "The prosecutor, attempted to persuade the jury that my studies," Loftus explains, "had little or nothing to do with Eileen Franklin's repressed memory. You study normal memory and forgetting, but so what? Her questions implied. What does that have to do with extraordinary memory?" (Loftus & Ketcham, 1994, p. 62). Although Loftus had empirical research showing how the details of memory can go awry, there was no empirical evidence to challenge the Freudian claims for supporting recovered repressed memories. George Franklin was found guilty for the murder, although "not one piece of forensic or scientific evidence connected George Franklin to Susan Nanson's murder" (Loftus & Ketcham, 1994, p. 59).

Loftus was now determined to substantiate Freud's fallibility scientifically, at least, as it related to repressed memory. The challenge was to devise a study that would demonstrate the inability to cast away memories to the unconscious. This proved to be complicated. What was possible in a laboratory setting, however, was to demonstrate the creation of a *false memory*, referring to an actual memory of an event that never occurred. A false memory is not "a lie;" although it is be-lieved to be as factual as any other memory, there is no factual basis for it. Loftus and colleagues devised a study where her students volunteered to be part of a memory study. The study involved getting information from each of the students' parents identifying historical events about her students' childhoods. All the events were accurate but one: being lost in the mall as a child. These historical events were noted in a memory-book where her students were asked to recount every detail they could remember about the event. If they could not remember the event, the student was told to simply write, "I do not remember this event." When flanked with factual events, the suggestion of having been lost in the mall was falsely remembered about 25% of the time (Loftus, Coan & Pickrell, 1996).

Although Loftus now had research findings suggesting the fallibility of repressed memory, meaning such memories might be false memories, at least 25% of the time, Loftus' research met with harsh criticism. Appreciate, beginning in the 1970s and throughout the 1980s, there was a proliferation of sorts with recovering repressed memories taking place in the offices of psychotherapists. Many psychotherapists were regularly witnessing their patients recover repressed memories of childhood sexual abuse. Many believed questioning the validity of re-covered repressed memory is akin to rubbing salt into the wound of a victim. Suggesting a recovered memory of childhood sexual abuse might be false and is perhaps a false memory is just another form of assault. Moreover, Loftus' claims implied psychotherapists were some-how at fault, too. The *Hippocratic Oath* guiding the provider to first, *do no harm to your patient* was violated, and it was now appearing psycho-therapists had been mistakenly suggesting a false account to their pa-tients. Lofts' research findings—as well as the possible legal implica-tions for establishing *reasonable doubt*—were met with hostility by both the lay and professional community, including hate mail, death threats, being assaulted on an airplane, and requiring the services of profes-sional bodyguards (Loftus & Ketcham, 1994). Nonetheless, any proper study of social problems requires an analysis to see if there may be an extent to which those who, not only worked with survivors of sexual assault but also held social control over the means to validate these claims did not want to lose their authority.

This was also the case in the 2018 US Senate confirmation hearing for Judge Brett Kavanaugh's appointment to the US Supreme Court. Psychology professor Christine Blasey-Ford brought forth allegations of prior sexual assault taking place decades earlier in the 1980s. The sociologist, once again, maybe listening carefully to the evidence presented, but should also be as interested in the debate taking place in the public square, and there were lots of words said. Some who said: *I believe survivors*[19] (Pressley, 2018).

As aegis authority increases, so too does the inherent risk associated with social problems. In other words, when fewer sources of social authority maintain authority and control over the social problem, rather than many, the level of social risk rises. Moreover, this sort of control and authority is vested within social bureaucracies. Max Weber, one of the *Three Fathers of Sociology,* was the first to look at how these large organizations use to divide up the division of labor. One inherent characteristic of bureaucracies is that they have the authority to act. In this example, Loftus' research was a challenge to the authority our society entrusted in the mental health system to place victims of assault into their care. To what extent is the social system defending itself, resisting potential loss of their authority, and place within the social order? A study on social problems cannot overlook this question.

---

[19] In this context, *I believe survivors*, does not refer to the belief in the allegation; rather, it refers to the confirmation as to the fact. She (or he) is a survivor, meaning she (or he) was—in fact—the victim of abuse. The statement now becomes a challenge to due process which ought to be the logical next step following a believable allegation. However, in this instance, due process is not necessary since the statement confirms the truthfulness of the event.

Looking Ahead

A social problem has been defined "as a dynamic connection… between the societal and the individual." Moreover, it is from the resulting friction between these elements from which social problems emerge and enter into both social and personal life, not through the analysis focused on objective ways the problem impacts individuals and social institutions. Moreover, four qualities provide context when identifying social problems. First, social problems vary in their degree of ethical alignment between respective positions of morals and values, where *values*, refer to those things people genuinely care about, and *morals* refer to those ways motivation for our behavior binds to shared human emotions and experiences. As the degree of congruency between these two ethical attributes increases, social problems take on less severity. In turn, the more these two attributes become incongruous with each other, the more socially risky the problem becomes. Second, as attention is misdirected away from the societal interests to various positions about a social problem, possible risk and harm to society increase, especially as the degree of involution increases whereby the social problem is entangled with multiple layers of complexity in the many different positions taken. Instead, sociological attention is best when redirected away from a particular position and focuses on social interests instead. Third, when the free, open, and reciprocal exchange of communication is present, the severity of risk decreases but will otherwise remain high when debate falls upon deaf ears indignant to acknowledging any other possible alternative position. Finally, as aegis authority increases, so too does the inherent risk associated with social problems. In other words, when a few sources of social authority maintain authority and control over the social problem, the level of social risk rises.

One of the goals for this book is to challenge the reader to consider a social problem, not simply as a phenomenon that has infiltrated into the social system, but as a systemic phenomenon emerging from the point of connection between the individual and the societal. To this end, social problems are considered as *emerging social problems* and center—more or less—around an existential framework, which represents that portion of the equation the individual contributes to the mix. In the next chapter, the existential aspects of social problems are explored.

I believe I have a right to enjoy the use of the community swimming pool in my neighborhood; after all, I pay the monthly HOA fees. I realize as well, so do most of my other neighbors, meaning they have the right to enjoy the pool too. We have to coexist in the pool together. *Norms* are established, referring to rules for social behavior in order to accomplish this objective. At the entrance, there are some rules posted, which include no glass containers, eating food in the pool, and abstaining from the use of giant inflatables. The rules also suggest we exit the area at sunset. Yet, there is a litany of unspoken rules also regulating behavior that never made it onto the sign. Do not indiscriminately splash people. Do not play your iPhone loud enough for others to hear it, especially if listening to Katy Perry! Be kind enough not to linger around the steps where people are attempting to enter and exit the pool. These behavioral expectations do not need to be added onto a sign unless you happen to have been raised by a pack of wolves. *Folk-ways* refer to those social expectations that have low social significance when violated but reflect necessary social conformity and expression of goodwill towards others. Moreover, holding someone underwater until they lose consciousness and nearly die because they happened to be listening too loudly to Katy Perry does not need to be added to the sign either, as there are already laws on the books regarding attempted homicide. Try drowning one of the kids in the neighborhood pool, and serious social disdain follows from violating such *mores*.

I have been referring to our legal rights, as the government grants such authority. If violated, there is an established process to rectify any grievance. If I am getting bashed around in the community swimming pool by a dozen kids riding recklessly on large unicorn rafts, I can go to the HOA and complain they do something to put an end to the behavior. If my Ring-Doorbell captures video images of some porch-pirate stealing a package from me, I will notify the police, and I expect them to try to apprehend the creep stealing my stuff! We look to governing authority to ensure access to our legal rights.

Moreover, the same legal authority can change a prior law. For instance, the HOA may now permit reckless unicorn rafting in the pool! That is the way the law works.

On the other end of the spectrum, there are *inalienable rights,* suggesting these are not dependent on laws or government for experiencing their direct benefits. These rights cannot be forfeited by another authority simply because they were not previously bestowed upon us from the government. Inalienable rights slice across all governments and cultures, as they are universal. Traditionally the source of inalienable rights has suggested one's creator endows them. Those who may find this idea uncomfortable may, in turn, refer to these rights as *human rights*[20] or what John Lilburne, the Seventeenth Century thinker called *freeborn rights*. Regardless if origins are believed to be derived from the divine or embedded in the core of the human fabric, much like a set of kidneys or lungs, philosophers have considered deeply on the topic. We see such ideas emerge within the *Reformation Doctrine* challenging papal authority in the Sixteenth Century by Martin Luther, who said:

> …every man is responsible for his own faith, and he must see it for himself that he believes rightly. As little as another can go to hell or

---

[20] I'm old-school and much prefer listening to Led Zeppelin over Justin Bieber any day of the week! I'll also use the term inalienable rights over human rights but do not do so to encourage readers to adopt a religious basis for the term for themselves.

> heaven for me, so little can he believe or disbelieve for me; and as little as he can open or shut heaven or hell for me, so little can he drive me to faith or unbelief. Since, then, belief or unbelief is a matter of every one's conscience, and since this is no lessening of the secular power, the latter should be content and attend to its own affairs and permit men to believe one thing or another, as they are able and willing, and constrain no one by force. (1523)

In the Seventeenth Century, John Locke referred to such rights as being life, liberty, and property. Moreover, these rights could not be relinquished simply by surrendering them over to the state's authority; their conservation was sufficient grounds for political rebellion. As George Mason makes clear in his draft of the *Virginia Declaration of Rights*, "all men are born equally free ... [and have] certain inherent natural rights, of which they cannot, by any compact, deprive or divest their posterity" (cited in Maier, 1933, p. 134). Furthermore, we see this idea embedded into our *Declaration of Independence*, that "We hold these truths to be self-evident, that all men are created equal, that their Creator endows them with certain unalienable Rights..."

If Ralphie was unable to convince his mother on the virtues of a Red Ryder B.B. gun as a gift in the classic movie, *A Christmas Story*,[21] it is unlikely I will convince the reader we do have inalienable rights. Regardless, moving forward, the assumption is that we do have such rights. Moreover, when infringing upon these rights occurs—either by self-infliction or from outside authorities—we suffer as a result. For example, suppose your best experiences in high school were the English classes you took. Even when you got stuck with the old teacher who had a sever body odor issue, and nobody could understand her when she spoke due to ill-fitting dentures, you loved the class. You could barely think of anything else that last semester your senior year

---

[21] Little Ralphie tries to convince anyone who will listen to why the "...official Red Ryder carbine action, 200-shot, range model air rifle with a compass in the stock..." would make for the perfect Christmas gift. They made some great movies back in the 1980s!

when taking creative writing, and it was at that moment your life's calling bit you on the butt. You would have wanted nothing else from life than to be an English teacher, but there is one problem: your parents who are both math teachers have told you your entire life you can be anything you want to be in this world, except a teacher! You can be anything you want to be in this world, but they would prefer that you become a nurse. A dozen years have now gone by, you are married, have a mortgage, a student loan, two children, and have been working as a nurse now for the last eight years. Describe your sense of happiness, keeping in mind that you have a wonderful spouse, beautiful children, and an income that pays for that lovely house with little to no economic worry. Was accepting your parents' influence, accepting their authority, and foregoing your choice to pursue a teaching career the right choice? Is there a cost at a personal, psychological level for making a choice, perhaps better stated as "foregoing your choice?"

Existential Psychology

Tethered theoretically to traditional European existential philosophers like Søren Kierkegaard, Friedrich Nietzsche, Jean-Paul Sartre, and others, by the mid-1900s, the new school of *existential psychology* began to emerge starting with psychiatrists Karl Jasper (1883-1969) and Viktor Frankl (1905-1997), suggesting psychological angst is deeply rooted in the patient's struggle with the existential givens of human existence which include death, freedom, responsibility, and establishing meaning in life. This idea represents a radical departure from the assumed doctrine of Sigmund Freud's psychoanalytic theory, which was prevalent at this time. Freud argued that mental illness results from instinctual conflict with one's deepest libido wishes while at the same time being pressed up against societal demands resulting in anxiety. The individual must address the anxiety, so he or she employs the use of a defense mechanisms and becomes *neurotic* as a result (referring to a functional expression of psychopathology) which keeps the patient from dropping off into the abyss of complete and total *psychosis* but, nevertheless, Freud fails to offer the patient an opportunity to achieve a state of wellbeing through either personal growth or insight. As psychiatrist Irving Yalom explains, existential psychology differs from those ideas of Sigmund Freud, in that "Freud's sequence begins with 'drive,' whereas an existential framework begins with awareness and fear… The therapist has far more leverage if he or she views the individual primarily as a fearful, suffering being rather than as an instinctually driven one" (1980, p. 10).

To be clear, validating the existence of inalienable rights occurs through reflection on the "givens" of existence. The existential psychologist takes the position when a person fails to consider the givens (e.g., death, freedom, responsibility, and establishing meaning in life) of human existence inherent to those inalienable rights, healthy psychological wellbeing decompensates. Thus, the primary concern for the existential psychotherapist is providing an opportunity for the patient to be aware of fears over their human plight. "Wisdom does not lead to madness, nor denial to sanity: the confrontation with the givens of existence is painful but ultimately healing" (Yalom, 1980, p. 14).

Death. Just before his death, Tolstoy's terminally ill character Ivan Ilyich who lived the life of a sour, meaningless bureaucrat confronts the ultimate truth on how we face the end: "he is dying badly because he has lived badly" (1960). Humans have the capacity for knowing this inevitable truth about life: it ends for us all. "There is a remedy for all things except death," Don Quixote tells us (Cervantes, 2013).

Place spiritual belief aside for the moment, the act of dying is both certain and true. Religious faith may offer belief as well as a solace on what lies for us on the other side, but it does not bypass the physical act of dying. "Death is the condition that makes it possible for us to live life in an authentic fashion" (Yalom, 1980, p. 31). Knowledge of death brings intensity for us in this *here-and-now* for this moment in life.

Carpe diem![22] Consider as an example of how so many teenagers believe in their specialness and invincibility as the one person who as ever lived that will never grow old and die. As we know, teenagers—especially males—too often engage in reckless, dangerous behavior as a result. Suppose, however, now in the first semester of college; he receives a text message from his girlfriend that she has met someone new, and their relationship is over. This happens just an hour after learning he failed his first class and will have to repeat algebra next semester. He becomes psychologically distraught and borderline suicidal. The psychological reaction is completely out of proportion to the losses of the day, but unconsciously his belief of invincibility has been devastated. He now knows the truth: *if someone can end a relationship with me, and I can fail a class, then I am just like everyone else. I am just as mortal as everyone else then too.*

Freedom. We desperately want to know we are at the helm freely able to direct the course of our lives. We are not merely a caged rat enclosed within the *Skinner box* running to and fro, pulling at levers for the food that follows because we have no choice but to do so. The circumstances of life may be thrust upon us taking the form of unemployment, jilted by our lover, imprisoned by our state, or debilitated by an injury. Regardless, the one *freedom* which can never be taken away, explains psychiatrist and Holocaust survivor Viktor Frankl (1959), is our freedom to choose our attitude to life's circumstances. Freedom, however, attaches to it a cost: *responsibility.* "To be aware of responsibility is to be aware of creating one's own self, destiny, life predicament, feeling and, if such be the case, one's own suffering. For the patient who does not accept such responsibility, who persists in blaming others—either other individuals or other forces—for his or her dysphoria, no real therapy is possible" (Yalom, 1980, p. 218).

---

[22] A Latin phrase meaning "Seize the Day!" I'm also keen on *Sine Metu,* which means "without fear." The latter phrase happens to appear under the family crest of John Jameson who bottles a particular beverage I enjoy now and again.

Once again, going back to the existential question posed to you a few paragraphs back, as that 30-year-old nurse rather than a 30-year-old English teacher, how much regret—what is often referred to as *existential guilt*—do you bear over those life choices made? Unhappiness and lack of career satisfaction, in this case, is the result of one's own choices, as parents cannot control the choices we make at 18-years of age any more than they do when we are 32-years-old. Even if parents were right; they had the wisdom and foresight to see the entire educational system would soon be revolutionized placing teachers out of work, replaced with artificial intelligent (AI) online moderated public education or nursing really was a better individual fit for your interests and personality, is their imposed joy and pleasure actually pleasant and joyfully experienced now that you are a little older and wiser?

Isolation. This idea of isolation refers to the physical act of being set apart from others where there is an actual geographic barrier. Consider those years when the Berlin Wall existed, and families who were sometimes just yards of distance away nevertheless were estranged from all physical contact; there was no phone, no mail, no seeing, and no touching, just a feeling of loneliness. *Existential isolation* is similar but profoundly different too. Consider Mel Gibson's character William Wallace in the movie, *Braveheart* (1995), who at the end of the movie is tortured to death amongst a cheering crowd. He focuses on the image of his dead wife, perhaps a ghost walking through the crowd, but their voices are not as loud now, and their faces are out of focus. It is as if only two people are existing at this moment, sharing a deep connection with each other. Existential isolation is much like this experience, but there is not any connection to another, rather one is alone. It refers to isolation where there is "an unbridgeable gulf between oneself and any other being. It refers, too, to an isolation even more fundamental—a separation between the individual and the world. 'Separation from the world'" (Yalom, 1980, p. 355).

Assuming the existentialists are correct, and we are both free and responsible for the authorship of our own lives, then we are to this degree alone in this world. We come into this world dependent but alone, and it is so that we leave this world alone too. Psychoanalyst Erik Erikson (1949) argued this was the primary motivation for securing a mate; it is not for satisfying the physical needs of intimacy or companionship; instead, it is for satisfying that deep psychological itch for emotional intimacy. We need to attempt to emotionally connect to someone who might know the uniquely special person we know ourselves to be. Consider Judith Guest's character Calvin Jarret from *Ordinary People* (1976) who is emotionally isolated from his histrionic wife, Beth, in his grief over the tragic death of their 18-year-old son. The couple still makes love routinely—and perfunctory—on Saturday nights, but there is no connection of the souls, and the pain plays out within the family dynamics. Without an emotional, human connection to others, we are left adrift in a sea of depression and anxiety. As the psychoanalyst Eric Fromm explains:

> The awareness of his aloneness and separateness, of his helplessness before the forces of nature and of society, all this makes his separate disunited existence an unbearable prison. The experience of separateness arouses anxiety; it is indeed the source of all anxiety. Being separate means being cut off, without any capacity to use my human powers. Hence to be separate means to be helpless, unable to grasp the world—things and people—actively; it means that the world can invade me without my ability to react. (1956, p. 7)

Meaning. Viktor Frankl's (1905-1997) work is referred to often as the "Third Viennese School of Psychotherapy." Where Sigmund Freud introduces us to the unconscious mind, and Alfred Adler places emphasis on individual psychology, it is Viktor Frankl who unites a philosophy for human existence with an original approach to psychotherapy. This approach Frankl calls *logotherapy,* referring to a psychological approach centered on finding and creating the experience of personal meaning in one's life.

Frankl's ideas on meaning confound with his biography; understanding one without understanding the other makes little if any sense. He shares in his autobiography (2000), along with Adolf Hitler's rise to power came to a growing certainty; his fate would soon follow many of his other Jewish neighbors living in Vienna. He, along with his family, would be round-up and sent off to concentration camps. Unlike Freud who lacked clarity failing to grasp the magnitude of the hostile climate towards Jews in Vienna, Frankl fully understood. He had applied and just received a visa to immigrate to the United States, but the visa only offered passage for just he and his wife, not his parents or siblings. He knew that leaving his parents behind would mean he was leaving them in the hands of the Nazis and certain death. Not knowing what to do, he went for a long walk and found himself at the steps of a church. Although Christianity was not his faith, he entered the cathedral, believing it offered a quiet place where he might pray, asking God for what he referred to as "a hint from heaven." After about an hour, receiving no "hint," he left. Once back home, Frankl found a shard of marble sitting on the family's dining room table placed there by his father who recovered the chunk of debris from a synagogue just destroyed by the Nazis. He picked it up, recognizing a single letter carved out. It was at this moment his father spoke to him, saying the letter was from one of the Ten Commandments. Which one, Viktor asked? His father replied, "Honor thy father and mother, that thy days may be long upon the land which the Lord thy God giveth thee." Viktor believed he had just received his "hint from heaven." He stayed in Vienna, but in 1942, along with his entire family, he was sent off to the concentration camps.

At Auschwitz, it was Dr. Josef Mengele who first sorted the new arrivals into two lines: those who would go off to the work camps and those who were immediately doomed being dispatched right off to the gas chambers. Mengele tapped Frankl on the left shoulder, sending him off to join the line to the left. Frankl while waiting in line recognized a couple of colleagues standing in the right line and stepped over to the other line to join his colleagues not realizing until later he had initially been standing in the line for the gas chamber.

It was during these years spent enduring the daily horror of life in the camps where ideas for logotherapy were finalized. A thought transfixed me: for the first time in my life I saw the truth as it is set into song by so many poets, proclaimed as the final wisdom by so many thinkers... I understood how a man who has nothing left in this world still may know bliss, be it only for a brief moment, in the contemplation of his beloved. In a position of utter desolation, when man cannot express himself in positive action, when his only achievement may consist in ensuing sufferings in the right way—an honorable way—in such a position man can, through loving contemplation of the image he carries of his beloved, achieve fulfillment. (Frankl, 1959, p. 48-49)

Other than one of his sisters, Frankl was the only one of his family to survive the Holocaust. Later he learned the murder of his wife Tilly occurred upon her arrival to the camps. It was in the years immediately following his liberation he wrote *Man's Search for Meaning* (1959), first telling his account surviving the Holocaust, explaining how his experience informed his thoughts on psychotherapy, then outlining his theory for logotherapy.

Picture 5.1, Victor Frankl

The most significant departure for *logotherapy* away from psychoanalysis is the belief in one's capacity to exercise individual freedom, what Frankl refers to as *freedom to will.* Our history may exist, but history need not exert any influence on the present. Frankl abandons all arguments favoring psychic *determinism*, meaning our past experiences determine our immediate choices in life. This is what makes all existential theories, including logotherapy, an *open system theory*. People can influence their environments, as well, as the ability to permit environmental forces to influence the development of their *self*. Still, it is the person who suffers—but in this instance—not because of any unconscious conflict; rather, suffering stems from the "existential frustrations" in exercising free will. "A man's concern," Frankl explains, "even over his despair, over the worthwhileness of life is an existential distress but by no means a mental disease" (1959, p. 108). The rise of aggression, compulsive addiction, depression, and a general state of overwhelming purposelessness results when we are unable to identify a sense of *meaning in life*.

Dropping the idea of psychic determinism, Frankl adds the concept of *meaning*. The nature of the human condition necessitates a force from within to embrace a state of meaning for our life. This *will to meaning* requires us to have a sense of meaning, direct experience of meaning, and to seek out behaviors leading towards the acquisition of *meaning in life*. We are all directed by an inner pull to experience such meaning. This fundamental premise serves as the basis for logotherapy's two other core concepts: *freedom of will* and *meaning in life*.

We are not merely reacting organisms shaped by the external environment. There may be some limitations placed upon us by our biology and social conditions, but we are still capable of exercising some degree of self-determination. "What he becomes—within the limits of endowment and environment—he has made out of himself," Frankl reminds us (1959, p. 135). For example, consider the actions adopted by Civil Rights advocates under the guidance of Dr. Martin Luther King, Jr. during the 1960s. In the face of degrading behavior, discriminatory actions and physical intimidation, young people responded not in like manner, but in a manner demonstrating courage, respect, and peace as they sought to undo a social system bound in segregation.

Though one is treated like a dog, one does not have to respond like a dog.

Logotherapy does not offer any generic prescription to achieve meaning in life. "One should not search for an abstract meaning of life. Everyone has his own specific vocation or mission in life to carry out... [and] everyone's task is as unique as is his specific opportunity to implement it" (Frankl, 1959, p. 113). Instead, Frankl suggests that meaning in life is achieved by exercising freedom of will in three different ways. First, meaning is experienced through the creation and expression of a work of art. Writing a story, painting a picture, or performing a dance offers one the opportunity to experience meaning in life. Second, meaning in life can be achieved by committing to another person, especially in the act of caring for children, the ill, or the elderly. Finally, meaning in life can be experienced through the attitude freely chosen in the face of unavoidable suffering. A terminally ill cancer patient may consider suicide but instead, choose to adopt an attitude of acceptance to serve as an example for her children and other loved ones on how to face death when their time comes. "In some way, suffering ceases to be suffering at the moment it finds a meaning, such as the meaning of a sacrifice" (Frankl, 1959, p. 117). As Ray Bradbury explains from *Fahrenheit 451*:

> It doesn't matter what you do, he said, so long as you change something from the way it was before you touched it into something that's like you after you take your hands away. The difference between the man who just cuts lawns and a real gardener is in the touching, he said. The lawn-cutter might just as well not have been there at all; the gardener will be there a lifetime. (2013)

Existential Sociology

This chapter so far has placed a weighted emphasis on the psychological, much at the cost of ignoring the sociological. The psychological perspective suggests one's angst and despair is the product of the disconnection he or she makes by avoiding the existential "givens" of human existence. One fails, for instance, to acknowledge the realities of death and as a result, death anxiety erupts. Perhaps this is due to the existentialist's emphasis on one's ability to exert free will and not merely being left completely adrift and influenced by various social currents. For example, we might say to ourselves: *it was simply inevitable he would be arrested for committing such a crime. After all, look at the neighborhood he lives in, and look at the family he lives with.* The existential psychologist, while ignoring the influences of these social institutions always appears steadfast to point out the free will we can rely upon. However, it is the existential sociologist, while not discounting the presence of a free will, nevertheless acknowledges those social forces which do exert potential influence upon us. These social forces tug at us much like the currents do the swimmer who purposely directs their efforts towards a destination.

Social institutions have substantial influence over all aspects of us. The most influential of these Erving Goffman (1961) refers to as *total institutions*, as such places have complete and absolute influence over one's life. The total institution tends to oversee the weak and vulnerable in our society (i.e., nursing homes), where segregation from the dominate society is preferred, and its members may be expected to do specific types of work (i.e., military service). The total institution has complete control and influence on its member's day-to-day schedule, telling one when it is time to eat, sleep, and relax. Additionally, one's physical identity is at the will of the institution by issuing uniforms and shaving heads. Quickly, one begins to be socialized and absorbs the institution's norms and values.

Again, we have addressed those ways in which individuals may be adversely affected at deeply personal levels when attempts to engage our inalienable rights through existential self-engagement are either thwarted, denied, or infringed. We now move to the other side of this equation: the sociological connection. Thus far, the term *dynamic* has been used referring to a reciprocal connection binding together the individual and the societal. The word infers a sense of force and power, reflecting a clear, forceful intent. Too often it is the case sociologists do not effectively recognize this powerful connection, preferring to focus attention on the many ways the societal effects the individual. The purpose of this section is to turn our attention to the side of this dynamic exchange where the individual effects the societal. When the individual experiences existential angst and despair, it is potentially infectious to the societal as well. Social institutions can reciprocally absorb such despair too.

Social institutions connect us. Recently I taught a Study Abroad course on Social Problems in Northern Ireland. We spent much of our time in two cities, Belfast and Londonderry. One morning the class was waiting for the traffic light to change and noticed someone also waiting for the light wearing a University of South Florida (USF) T-shirt. USF is the nearest state university in proximity to where I teach, and many of my students plan to transition over to USF in the near future. "You go to USF?" "You live in Tampa?" "What are you majoring in?" "Do you know any of my friends?" Instantly, there was a connection with my students and this stranger they stumbled upon in Belfast. Those social institutions we are associated with bind us to others through their culture.

Culture may reflect the various beliefs, behaviors, and material objects making up a people's way of life, but culture also provides for its members an essential tool: a means for survival. Animals rely on their instincts for navigating their behavior, especially those behaviors which advance the likelihood of survival. Humans, on the other hand, rely on their culture for survival through the use of *social cuing*. This refers to a highly refined attentiveness of cultural familiarity, especially those behaviors accepted by the group's majority. For example, researchers Darley and Latané (1968) conducted a study where a student believes he or she was alone in a room listening to other students through an intercom and heard a student through the intercom ask for medical help. The researchers were looking to see if the perceived size of the group would have any influence on the likelihood the student would leave the room to seek out help. Size does matter. When the student believed there was just one other student somewhere out there also listening, the likelihood he or she would go try to find help was about 85%, but when believing there were at least six other students out there also listening, the likelihood plummeted down to just 31%. Darley and Latané even did a version of this study where a student was asked to complete a lengthy application in a room along with other students. Within a few minutes, black smoke began to seep out from under a closet door. The other students knew the actual purpose of the study and were instructed to ignore the smoke, and the actual subject only left the room to report a possible fire about 31% of the time but did so most of the time when he or she was alone in the room.

Social institutions provide guidance and direction for our thoughts, feelings, and behaviors. They tug at us, and in doing so, we nudge back, all the while confirming to both ourselves and others within the culture this is the way we ought to be thinking, feeling, and behaving. This, too, is the case for the existential "givens;" culture directs and influences their ebb and flow, too. Such is the case for associating ceremony and ritual to significant life events such as weddings, graduations, and funerals, suggesting life has meaning associated with it, and upon reflection, we may see and perhaps experience such meaning. A funeral may remind us we need to engage in our own life as this experience we have on Earth is finite. Additionally, social institutions set and define the norms which guide and navigate human interactions. Feelings of isolation might erupt for a university student who decides this semester to take all her classes online rather than inside the brick and mortar of the institution.

Literature as a sociological tool. Take notice of how regularly literature (as well as cinema) was used in the previous section for this chapter to lock-down various existential ideas discussed (e.g., Tolstoy, Guest, *Braveheart*, and Bradbury). This is typical for both philosophical and psychological existentialists. Albert Camus wrote using stories to express his philosophical ideas (e.g., *The Stranger, The Plague,* and *The Myth of Sisyphus*). This is typical for the existentialist, as literature becomes a natural medium for stripping away the dense use of nonfictional language that can frequently create barricades between us with no less difference than using a statistic to convey the emotional depth to one's suffering. Stories connect us by using feelings as their muse.

Perhaps Rene Descartes' most remembered for his proclamation: "I think; therefore, I am." But, he could have just as well uttered: "I feel; therefore, I am conscious." Feelings by their nature refer to the self-awareness of our emotions (Damasio, 1999). As Frosh (2011) points out, the act of experiencing a feeling is the very recognition of one's existence. No consciousness is not self-consciousness. Thus, social scientists are inherently interested in the subject of feelings. As many young men struggling with writing a love letter can attest, feelings can often be evasive and brutish to capture accurately with words. One's verbal intelligence does not positively correlate with one's range, depth, or capacity to be emotionally self-aware. In this sense, words merely provide a means by which we hitch our feelings to a linguistic, cognitive context.

Incorporating the use of literature to facilitate self-awareness, encourages us to, not only be aware of feelings present within our consciousness, but to engage in deeper self-awareness by acknowledging, perhaps for the first time, feelings we are not even aware we are feeling. As Frosh explains, "people can only allow themselves to feel things only when they are safe enough to face the consequences" (2011, p. 66) of their feelings. In such instances, literature can offer safe harbor by allowing our feelings projection on to literature. Consider for a moment, Maurice Sendak's (1963) classic children's story, *Where the Wild Things Are.* The story of Max and his mystical journey to the island where the Wild Things live has been read to children, grandchildren, and now great-grandchildren since first published in 1963. In these simple ten sentences, we find a story on how children deal with their feelings of anger at parents or in this case, a mother. We connect with the story; it resonates with us across the generations because we can identify with Max's emotional plight.

Feelings also serve as a form of sociological adhesive by connecting us to other people. "Feelings are social: they pass through people, infecting each other" (Frosh, 2011, p. 13). Sharing one's feelings is an act of intimacy. "How are you doing?" may be the most human question we can ask another person. Literature is a means by which we mutually tether our feelings to while in the company with others. With literature, we can share an emotional experience. It is even possible to argue that stories are the fundamental building block for any civilization (Liebert, 2013).

Literature provides a means for the exploration into the depth and application of social theory, as such concepts can be analyzed and manipulated in ways nonfictional writing cannot lend itself to provide. The pioneering German sociologist, Max Weber (1949) argued in an effort to make valid and precise observations of our social world the social scientist is wise to employ the use of *ideal types,* referring to a hypothetical construct based on extracting just the pure characteristics of the phenomenon being studied, in this instance, feelings. Literature may serve as an ideal type for exploring, comparing, contrasting, classifying, and measuring sociological theory. Consider William Golding's (1954) *Lord of the Flies*; the allegorical story not only serves as a demonstration of conscious-unconscious interaction with the reader but directly addresses Sigmund Freud's (1990) theoretical discussion on Thanatos, showing how our inherent death instinct will inevitably serve as our downfall. "Maybe there is a beast... maybe it is only us" (Golding, 1954, p. 80).

Additionally, literature can serve as the basis for which sociological theory is drawn and refined. Again, case in point, literature significantly influences Sigmund Freud's psychodynamic ideas on gender acquisition and fixation during the phallic stage of development. "The myth of King Oedipus, who killed his father and took his mother to wife, reveals, with little modification, the infantile wish, which is later opposed and repudiated by the barrier against incest, Shakespeare's *Ham-let* is equally rooted in the soil of the incest-complex, but under a better disguise" (Freud, 1961, p. 51). As acclaimed story writer Chuck Palahniuk explains:

> Stories have always been our way of dealing with social issues that we can't address directly because we'd just fight resolution. Horror stories give us a way of exhausting our emotions around social issues, like a woman's right to an abortion, which I always thought was the core of *Rosemary's Baby*, or the backlash against feminism, which I always thought was the core to *Stepford Wives*. (2008, n.p.)

Literature is often the preferred tool for the existentialist because it serves as a conduit for a dynamic exchange for feelings. This ability to share, understand, and experience the feeling that someone else is feeling refers to *empathy*. At those moments, when establishing the connection of empathy, one is listening and understanding another. Empathy is a profoundly intimate act.

Summary

The intent for this chapter has been to offer up a basis to support the claim we all carry within us inalienable rights. We have the right to life, liberty, and the pursuit of happiness. Existentialism provides a means by which we engage these inalienable rights. For instance, the degree to which one is *free* one is *responsible*. Moreover, when these inalienable rights are ignored, hindered, or denied, we suffer. This suffering may extend no further than just a single person and merely reflect a *social trouble*, as discussed back in Chapter 2. Such suffering may be broadly experienced by many others as well and be absorbed within the fabric of societal institutions, placing at possible risk the continued functioning of such institutions.

It is from this perch of existentialism we will now go on to identify and explore four emerging social problems. *Chapter 6: Free Will and*

Thinking[E] explores the possible societal and individual effects technology is now imposing on our most succinct inalienable rights: freedom of thought. Human neurological functioning naturally processes information though uses of schemas and heuristics in predictable ways in which search engines are now beginning to influence. Moreover, technology has now begun to alter and influence our other most valued freedom: debate and free speech by relocating the public square to virtual platforms that do not support free speech for all.

Chapter 7: The Melting Middle-Class addresses the social problem of economic inequality—not through an analysis looking at the assorted range of inequality occurring between the group who has the least contrasted against the group who has the most—through the effects a redistribution of the center rung of the socioeconomic ladder by pushing these folks into either higher or lower rungs is levying on society today. Happiness is an inalienable right achieved, in part, by securing purpose and meaning in life. Achieving actual meaning in life is compromised when lifestyle including the ability to have and afford to raise children and earn an affordable higher education leading to a certificate of value is no longer in reach for many in our society today.

Chapter 8: Social Isolation explores emerging social problems stemming from technology's anti-socializing effects. Human intimacy through ample societal opportunities to connect is essential. As more schools encourage online classes over face-to-face classroom experiences and social networking platforms inhibit real opportunity for actual physical, synchronistic contact with each other, society is witnessing an epidemic incidence of mental illness the likes of depression and anxiety along with increasing suicide rates. This chapter also examines the effects of decreasing marriage rates in favor of alternative lifestyles like cohabitation is having on intimacy and happiness.

In *Chapter 9: Social Meaning*, we again return to the issue of happiness and the existential need to experience purpose and meaning in life. The proliferation of marijuana's legalization in states across the country in recent years proposes some social problems may not be widely considered alarming or even be considered benign, but are—in fact—verrucous.

6   Free Will and Thinking[E]

Freedom of thought represents our most succinct inalienable right. The state may place necessary regulations and restrictions on our behaviors, but not our ideas. Even the ugliest and vilest of thoughts are permitted free range in our personal cognitive spaces. Shakespeare reminds us, "We are such stuff as dreams are made on, and our little life is rounded with sleep" (1998, Act 4, Scene 1). Imagination is the essence of freedom, yet this may no longer be the case. Moreover, even the ability to share and debate on our ideas in the public square is increasingly under attack. Restriction of freedom of speech is an emerging social problem.

On February 14, 2018, when a gunman attacked Stoneman Douglas High School, Kyle Kashuv was then 16-years-old. At the time of the shooting Kyle was in a different campus building, and he survived the tragedy. He went on to add a distinctly conservative voice to the gun debate which immediately followed, including his criticism for the *March for Our Lives* rally, actively supporting Ron DeSantis' (R-FL) successful campaign for Florida Governor, and speaking at the NRA convention held in April 2019. Kyle has not been shy about his identity as a political conservative and that he had been accepted to attend Harvard University starting in the fall of 2019, but his university plans ended following the release of screenshots taken of posts Kyle made a couple of years before the attack at Stoneman Douglas High School. The comments, which Kyle claims were intended to be private exchanges between just himself and friends, were racist and anti-Semitic. These words were vulgar. Following the public release of the screenshots, Harvard University rescinded Kyle's offer of acceptance into the 2019 freshman class, but not before Kyle tweeted out words of apology:

> I have recently been made aware of screenshots circulating that include offensive comments former classmates and I made a few years ago, long before the shooting. I want to address this with honesty and transparency.
>
> We were 16-year-olds making idiotic comments, using callous and inflammatory language in an effort to be as extreme and shocking as possible. I am embarrassed by it, but I want to be clear that the comments I made are not indicative of who I am or who I have become in the years since.
>
> This past year has forced me to mature and grow in an incredibly drastic way. My world, like everyone else's in Parkland, was turned upside down on February 14th. When your classmates, your teachers, and your neighbors are killed it transforms you as a human being. I see the world through different eyes and am embarrassed by the petty, flippant kid represented in those screenshots. I believe those I have gotten to know since know that I am a better person than that.
>
> I can and will do better moving forward.
>
> (Twitter post made 6:00 AM, 17 June 2019 by Kyle Kashuv)

We all have made mistakes in life and may have found ourselves at one time or other regretting prior behaviors and reaching out for forgiveness. Even better, we have learned from our mistakes and evolved into a wiser person. Keeping all this in mind, what are your thoughts about Kyle? Before answering the question, take a moment to identify the many confounding layers to Kyle's narrative which provides form and shape in crafting your opinion: he survived a tragic event where some of his friends and teachers did not; he was a child when these events occurred; he is publically acknowledging what he said was wrong; he is asking for forgiveness with the pledge he will "do better" as he moves forward in life. Concerning Harvard University, does the school have a right to rescind the offer of acceptance; to what extent is Harvard's motivation based on Kyle's political leanings; are some words unforgivable? You certainly have an opinion on the matter, as do I. Perhaps we can tussle over our respective opinions to see which one is most vibrant and robust, declare a winner, and then move on to the next social controversy. Suppose, first, we were to dissect our debate, cut it up like it were a frog laid out on the slab in a high school biology lab. I suspect we would find something when we start to analyze the thinking which has just taken place. Thinking about thinking, what psychologists call *metacognition*, looks closely at the factors which come into play as we engage our cognitive tool and ponder about it.

Picture 6.1, Kyle Kashuv presenting at the NRA conference

Both biological, as well as social factors, influence our thoughts. While reading Kyle's plight, if you are 15-years-old, your brain cannot work the neurological cogs and gears with the same slick efficiency as a 21-year-old whose brain has matured a higher degree of capacity for abstract reasoning. We know brains continue to develop cognitive capacity into one's twenties. Life experience comes into play, as well. You may feel differently if you have ever been the direct target for such racist vulgarity or if you have ever pleaded for your forgiveness for a much-regretted act. Thinking, to be clear, is not merely a neurological act occurring somewhere between the ears involving the currency of neurotransmitters snapping across the synapse. The environment influences both what we think and how we think. It is to this point that a social problem is now brought up for discussion and debate. Outside social forces are influencing our ability to think freely and engage in an open exchange of ideas today. Thinking is too quickly becoming *thinking*[E]. As it may turn out to be the case, your willingness to extend forgiveness to Kyle Kashuv may be preempted to Google first extending out a hand offering to forgive.

This is a radical claim to toss out there. Respectfully, the idea requires we first lean into it a bit before taking the claim head-on. In the sections which follow, the set limit for these cognitive skills (i.e., intelligence) will also be shown to be under some degree of environmental influence. Additionally, the process of cognitive development will be explored, explaining how the human brain typically interacts with the environment and, in turn, develops ever-increasing cognitive abilities. Third, we will explore the development of using our primary cognitive tool: language. After that, the problem of thinking[E] will be addressed head-on.

Environmental Influences on How We Think

William Golding, author of *Lord of the Flies* writes, "It was a particular moment in the history of my own rages that I saw the Western world conditioned by the images of Marx, Darwin and Freud, [who are] the three most crashing bores of the Western world," (1982, p. 186-187). No doubt Golding is right as to the first assertion: regardless if their claims are correct or not, the ideas of these three men have had a profound influence over Western values, beliefs, and norms. As to the second contention, I tend to disagree, especially when contrasted against competing claims. Darwin, for instance, composes a brilliant proposition when he asserts we are the biological sum of our species' best attempt to ensure the highest likelihood for passing along our genetic selves to the next generation. However, it is the juxtaposition of Darwin's claim against the simple but as profound suggestion that we are instead the product of the "conditioned reflex" as Ivan Pavlov proposed several decades later. It is through the associations we make in our environments that shape, motivates, and directs behavior. It is through the clash of these two opposing points we are presented with the alternative debate of *nature vs. nurture*, asking to what extent are we biological manifestations or environmental ones. We debate if the answer is best determined somewhere on the continuum of these two extreme opposing points or if it just might be the result of a diathetic predisposition where the biological erupts over a specific environmental encounter. Listen to any social scientist long enough, and the discussion inevitably takes shape around the implications of nature vs. nurture.

Intellectual Development

It is challenging to go ten minutes watching traditional television without being confronted with a 23andMe commercial touting all the benefits to knowing your individualized genetic profile. The company reports access to 125 specific individualized reports which can be prepared to share the biological essence of who you are with yourself, (or whoever else the report's details happen to be shared with). The assumption is that your DNA defines you. It not only sets you apart from the rest of the herd as a unique original but suggests the boundaries setting personal limits.

23andMe indeed represents a new technology that is readily available to the masses, offering insights into the core of the self in ways that were simply unimaginable just a few years ago, but this idea for identifying a simple test with the ability for revealing something true about one's self is not new. Science has long attempted to offer the recipe for determining those ways we each set ourselves apart from the herd. During the 1950s and 1960s, for instance, science had set its sights on *intelligence*,[23] typically defined as a person's overall capacity to understand the environment and adapt to it based on available information. Several decades earlier, Stanford University psychologist Lewis Termin established the formula still used today: intelligence quotient is equal to one's mental age divided by their chronological age and multiplied by 100 to provide a whole number ($IQ = MA/CA \times 100$).[24]

---

[23] Yes, I'm passing over this potential conflict just as I would avoid waking up a sleeping rattlesnake napping underneath my front door all curled up against today's Amazon package. The topic of intelligence and efficacy of intelligence testing continues to be a highly contentious debate in the field of psychology today. Lewis Terman retrofitted the *Simon-Binet Scale* that measured for just Mental Age (MA). Binet and his colleague Simon authored the assessment to assist with determining student grade assignments in France during the turn of the former century. Students were to be assigned an appropriate grade-level based on their MA rather than their chronological age. MA was conceived as a single phenomenon made up of various attributes such as memory, judgment, language, and analytic abilities. In other words, intelligence was seen as a single event that just happened to be made up of those attributes which are valued in school-based settings. Is there more to intelligence which takes us outside the academic setting? Harvard psychologist Howard Gardner (1983) speaks to this in his groundbreaking book, *Frames of Mind*, suggesting the possibility for multiple intelligences (e.g., linguistic, kinesthetic, interpersonal, and so forth). Moreover, personal endowment with one type of intelligence does not argue association with other types of intelligence. For instance, a clinical psychologist may demonstrate a strong skill-set with interpersonal capacity (i.e., the ability to be aware of the emotional experiences of others) but struggles with finding the right words to express her feelings (i.e., intrapersonal intelligence). These are the debates which social scientists continue to wrangle over: we devalue those attributes demonstrating exceptionality that lie outside the classroom-based arena. Moreover, intelligence is seen as a single, composite event rather than being made up of many discrete abilities where one such ability does not influence any of the others.

[24] IQ scores fall along the *normal curve*, meaning scores falling outside the mean average score still tend to be close to the mean. Scores falling farther and farther away

Schools were routinely assessing students' IQs in an attempt to determine absolute academic capacity for each student based on the belief a student cannot engage in school curriculum, which exceeds his or her intellectually set limit as determined by their IQ. I am six-feet and four-inches tall. My wife is only five-feet and six-inches tall. Unless she stands on a step stool, she will never be able to reach the coffee mugs resting on the top kitchen shelf in the cabinet. No matter how she feels about it, the number of vitamins she takes, or even if she commits to daily sessions of goat-yoga, her height sets the limit to her reach. This was the agreed-upon belief in these prior decades: one's IQ sets the limit to intellectual reach. School psychologists filled out the hours of the school week calculating their students' IQs so teachers would know the boundaries and possibilities for each student's potential learning ability. Harvard psychologist Robert Rosenthal and San Francisco Super Attendant of Schools, Lenore Jacobson (1966) raised the question

---

from the mean do so based on even distribution. Most people have an MA that is equal to their CA; in other words, the most typical IQ is 100. About 68% of the population has an IQ score falling somewhere between 85 and 115, which is referred to as the *average range*. About 95% of the population has an IQ score ranging between 75 and 130, with 75 to 85 referred to as *low normal* and 115 to 130 being referred to as *high normal* scores. *Exceptional scores* refer to those whose IQ is higher than 130, correctly referred to as *gifted*. Those exceptional scores falling below 75 are typically explained using diagnostic language to explain the intellectual deficit (e.g., traumatic brain injury, Alzheimer's disease, or Down's syndrome).

Figure 6.1, IQ and the normal curve

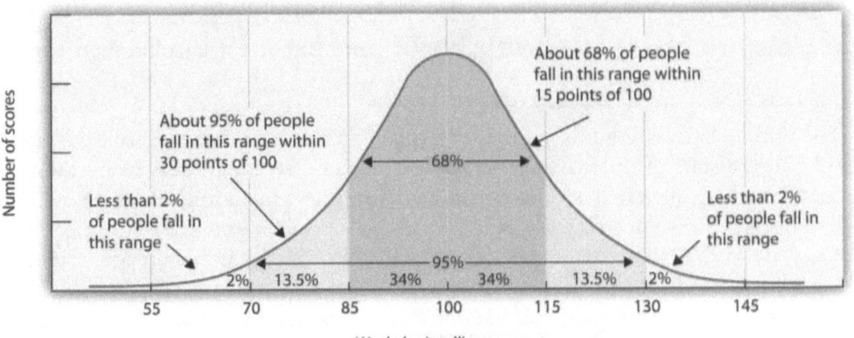

to this once held belief when they conducted their study on the *Pygmalion Effect*.[25]

Just before to the start of the school year, Super Attendant Jacobson called all the teachers together at one of her elementary schools to introduce the exciting new psychological instrument just developed at Harvard University by Rosenthal, who explained to the teachers how this new psychometric instrument was able to predict *Academic Bloomers!* In other words, this newly developed test would be able to indicate and "show unusual intellectual gains during the academic year" (1966, p. 115) that was about to unfold. It was a test to predict academic blooming, rather than identify those who had already bloomed. The test was planned to be administered to every student, grades one through six at the start of the new academic school year.

To be clear: no such test which predicts academic blooming exists. What Rosenthal and Jacobson have told these teachers is nothing but a lie, or what academics prefer to describe as *deception*. Each student was given an IQ test at the start of the school year. Nevertheless, teachers throughout the school were given the names of students in their classrooms, identifying them as *academic bloomers*, but these names had been chosen at random. Towards the end of the school year, the same IQ test was once again administered to every student throughout the school. The findings were especially apparent for the lower grades: those students identified as *academic bloomers* were shown to have experienced higher IQ gains over the academic year. Rosenthal and Jacobson suggest these IQ gains were influenced by "the favorable expectancies of the teachers" (1966, p. 118), meaning teachers believing these *academic bloomers* were capable of pushing their intellectual limits

---

[25] The term is based on a play entitled *Pygmalion*, written by George Bernard Shaw (1913). At the start of the play, we see two gentlemen, both members of London's social elite taking shelter from the rain along with others including Eliza, a flower girl who speaks in such a manner as to immediately reveal her lower, working-class status. One of the two gentlemen suggests with a little social and language training he could pass her off "a duchess." Eliza, overhears the two men and eventually takes up the offer and the self-fulfilling prophecy ensues, and we also learn the actor Kevin Bacon was not the first to star in a romcom.

further were treated in ways which supported the belief, in turn, resulting in a sort of self-fulfilling prophecy. We do more when the expectation is for us to do more. In this case, Rosenthal and Jacobson are pointing out that IQ is not a rigid number that defines and sets the limits to our capacity where we are unable to exceed beyond our IQ threshold.

To be clear: the use of IQ as an indicator of intellect is not being discounted here in this current discussion, tossed aside like an old and worthless VHS recorder. IQ may account for as much as two-thirds of explaining why some succeed, while others fall short of the same challenge (Neisser, Boodoo, Bouchard, et al., 1996). Instead, the suggestion here is to take into account those attributes which appear to be able to storm the gate of IQ, pushing through the IQ limits towards goal attainment. Duckworth, Peterson, Mathews, and Kelly's (2007) research suggests these attributes include creativity, vigor, emotional intelligence, charisma, self-confidence, emotional stability, physical attractiveness, and perhaps others as well. Angel Duckworth (2018), who has gone on to write a national bestselling book, *GRIT: The Power of Passion and Perseverance*, explains:

> My research focuses on two traits that predict achievement: grit and self-control. Grit is the tendency to sustain interest in and effort toward very long-term goals… Self-control is the voluntary regulation of impulses in the presence of momentarily gratifying temptations … On average, individuals who are gritty are more self-controlled, but the correlation between these two traits is not perfect: Some individuals are paragons of grit but not self-control, and some exceptionally well-regulated individuals are not especially gritty. (2019, n.p.)

Duckworth is a professor at the University of Pennsylvania and CEO of Character Lab, a non-profit organization whose mission is to "advance the science and practice of character development (2019, n.p.). Moreover, Duckworth has developed a psychometric test measuring for these qualities,[26] suggesting one can influence their score when committed to doing so. The score can also be influenced much in the same way Rosenthal and Jacobson were able to do through a quasi-Pygmalion effect of its own.

Cognitive Development

A discussion on cognitive development even still today centers around the contribution made by Jean Piaget (1896-1980). His life's research suggests we are born with a drive to know our world by understanding how and why it works as it does. We want the world to make sense to us, and this requires we continuously engage our environment, thereby encountering more confusion, and again compelling us to engage the cognitive machine to adapt and overcome (Boeree, 2018).

Picture 6.2, Jean Piaget

Early in his career, cognitive psychologist Jean Piaget worked as a test-grader in France for Alfred Binet who had developed one of the

---

[26] You can take Angela Duckworth's test in order to measure your own grittiness at: http://angeladuckworth.com/

first psychometric tests to assess for intelligence, what Binet called *mental age*. The test focused on measuring children's verbal, memory, analytic, and reasoning skills, believing these were the essential attributes comprising intelligence. Those who scored higher on the Binet-Simon Scale were assumed more intelligent than those children who scored lower. The young Piaget was charged the task for marking-up the tests to determine the score, which sounds rather dull. Thank God for the creation of scantron machines and number two pencils! Yet, over and over again, Piaget began to observe children who were of about the same age tended to miss similar questions on the test. Moreover, these children tended to also supply the same consistent wrong answers as other children of similar age. This observation intrigued Piaget who came to the idea that perhaps these children were not missing the questions on the tests due to a lack in their intelligence; instead, these children were missing these questions because they had not yet acquired the cognitive ability (referring to the ability to engage the neurological machine) to handle the test question. This experience guided Piaget into a life-long pursuit of studying the cognitive development of children. *Cognitive development* refers to the age-related changes in learning, memory, perception, attention, thinking, and problem solving, which occur as a natural process of maturation and experience (Singer & Revenson, 1997). There are just some cognitive tasks younger children cannot complete but, perhaps, in just a few more months, they can complete such tasks.[27]

---

[27] Many years ago I was asked to conduct what is called a dependency evaluation which parents might use when petitioning the court to reestablish parental rights after a state agency may have removed children from home for cause. In this case, a mother brought her two children to my office: a young girl who was about four-years-old and her older brother, about six-years-old. I asked to interview the girl first and requested the mother and brother wait outside. Hearing this, the girl became nervous and grabbed onto her mother's leg. This *stranger anxiety* and *separation anxiety* is normal and healthy behavior for a child of this age. I said I would leave the door cracked, not that confidentiality was of concern. Still, she was anxious. I started with several questions that should be of interest to her in an attempt to *warm up* to me, as this is also an indicator of healthy development. I asked her if she happened to have any brothers, to which her face lit up and a smile beamed! She absolutely loved and adored her big brother. He was so cool and even rode a bus to

Piaget proposed that cognitive development takes place in four stages beginning in infancy and ending with adolescence. However, to gain a full appreciation of Piaget's stages of cognitive development, it is first helpful to address the core assumption Piaget is suggesting, which is simple and clear. The central and primary goal of all children is for their world to make sense, which Piaget refers to as *equilibration*, suggesting a world which is in a state of harmony with the environment. The world makes sense to us when everything has a place, and everything is in that place. To accomplish this end, often, we will employ the use of *schemas,* meaning knowledge clusters. Consider, for example, Little Joey, who has constructed a schema that *all animals with four legs and a tail are doggies.* By employing the use of this schema, Joey can maintain a state of harmony or equilibration in his world every time he confronts an animal scampering about with four legs and a tail. However, one-day Little Joey's mother takes him for a ride out in the countryside. While looking out the window, he sees an animal matching his schema in a field chewing on grass. Joey jubilantly yells out while pointing to the animal, "Look a doggie!" His mother corrects him saying, "No! That's a cow." Now at this point, Little Joey's world is no longer experiencing a harmonious balance. Equilibration has slid into a state of *disequilibration.* At this point, Joey cannot continue to live in a world in which not all animals having four legs and a tail are always doggies. The original schema for Little Joey is no longer working. He now must engage the use of a *function* that helps to readapt to this new environment due to this conflicting information. There are two types of *functions.* With *organizational functions*—the first type—individual schemas are integrated into larger, more organized schemas. For instance, early reflexes such as rooting and sucking, become *organized* into

---

school! Then I simply asked if her brother happed to have any little sisters, to which her eyes crunch for a moment before saying, "no." From the room right outside my office, the mother gasped saying, "Oh my God! She's mentally retarded!" Absolutely not. At four-years-old she was not able to cognitively engage the principle of *reversibility.* Children cannot flip around the facts. If 3+2 =5, then 2+3=5, but a four-year-old would have to start counting on their fingers again. Piaget is right!

a schema called eating. This approach, however, will most likely serve to be unhelpful to Little Joey's current plight. It is now likely Little Joey will employ the use of *adaptational functions*, whereby there is an attempt to modify the cognitive ability to meet the new demands imposed by the environment. There are two types of adaptational functions. The first type, *assimilation,* occurs when the child incorporates new information into an already existing schema. For instance, in the past Little Joey may have been confronted with big dogs and little dogs with each still working within the framework of the original schema: all animals with four legs and a tail are doggies. The second type, *accommodation,* occurs when the child makes a change in the original schema to make room for new categories. For instance, now Little Joey has accommodated his original schema to add that *all animals with four legs, a tail, and go "woof" are doggies.*

The above represents the foundation upon which cognitive development occurs, according to Piaget. It is a result of this internal drive to maintain a state of equilibration in the face of disequilibration, which causes children to move through four stages of cognitive development. Children are forced to push past the current limit of their cognitive machine to resolve the challenge, thereby expanding cognitive capacity.

In the first stage of *sensory-motor stage* (roughly occurring over the first two years), children learn about their world as a result of doing. There is a lack of symbolic representation. Objects are whatever those objects can do. During this stage, children also are unable to recognize the concept of *object permanence*; in other words, when an object is absent from the child's senses, it ceases to exist. The object is gone, showing that the child cannot hold a symbol in their mind's eye. There must be a direct experience with the object by seeing, touching, smelling, or hearing it. This first stage takes place roughly through the first two years of life. In the second stage (from about two to seven-years) referred to as the *preoperational stage*, children are better able to employ the use of symbolism. They can now pretend a doll-baby is a real baby.

Figure 6.2, Egocentric thinking during the preoperational stage[28]

Figure 6.3, Conservation challenged in the preoperational stage

Nevertheless, children in this stage continue to have difficulty with *egocentric* thinking where they have difficulty taking the perspective of another. For instance, a child calls his grandmother on the telephone on Halloween night dressed as a pirate, and when his grandmother answers the phone states, "Bet you can't guess who this is?" believing his grandmother will not recognize him in his costume over the phone. Additionally, in this stage, children have difficulty with the concept of

---

[28] Piaget developed the *three mountain task* for children during this stage. He would ask the child, "What does the doll see?" To which the child would respond, "She sees two mounts in front of one mountain."

conservation, referring to the fact that, although a substance may change its container, the amount of the substance stays the same. For instance, a child may watch as a glass of orange juice is poured from a short fat glass into a tall thin glass and believes all of a sudden, there is more orange juice now. The third of these stages is the *concrete operational stage,* occurring roughly between the ages of seven and eleven, where increased use of symbolism occurs. The child can now demonstrate the ability to manipulate concepts. Rule-based behavior becomes increasingly important, and logical thinking begins to occur. By about the age of eleven, the child moves into the final stage of cognitive development: *formal operational stage.* This stage for Piaget marks the completion of cognitive development. It represents the start of now being able to employ abstract reasoning where an idea that can only exist as an idea within the mind's eye takes shape. The young adolescent, for instance, can now start to see a world absent of all social problems. More recent research shows that formal operational thought continues to develop into one's twenties.

Central to this process of cognitive development is language. Consider George Orwell's *1984;* the novel takes us to the city of Oceania, a dystopian place somewhere off into the not so distant future where free-speech no longer exists; every action is now monitored by the government, thoroughly controlling humanity. Inalienable rights cannot exist for long if such an idea of a human right cannot first be conjured up into the mind's eye, and this can only be accomplished first by possessing vocabulary. Words breathe life into ideas. Oceania outlaws ideas that first do not come from the government, and the best prevention for any uprising of ideas is to take away the words.

> It is a beautiful thing, the Destruction of words. Of course the great wastage is in the verbs and adjectives, but there are hundreds of nouns that can be gotten rid of as well. It is not only the synonyms; there are also the antonyms. After all, what justification is there for a word, which is simply the opposite of some other word? A word contains its opposite in itself. Take "good," for instance. If you have a word like "good," what need is there for a word like "bad?" "Ungood" will do just as well — better, because it is an exact opposite,

> which the other is not. Or again, if you want a stronger version of
> "good," what sense is there in having a whole string of vague useless
> words like "excellent" and "splendid" and all the rest of them? "Plus-
> good" covers the meaning or "doubleplusgood" if you want some-
> thing stronger still. Of course we use those forms already, but in the
> final version of Newspeak there'll be nothing else. In the end the
> whole notion of goodness and badness will be covered by only six
> words – in reality, only one word. Do not you see the beauty of that,
> Winston? It was B.B.'s idea originally, of course, he added as an af-
> terthought. (Orwell, 1987, p. 54)

Language is an essential element in our capacity to develop increasing levels of critical thinking, as abstract thoughts do not exist in the physical world; they are only available to the mind's eye through the words attached to them.

Even more essential than cultivating robust language skills for intellectual and cognitive development to flourish is exposure to the right environments. Intelligence is not an innate ability one is born with fully intact. There may be an academic debate to the degree which environment contributes towards one's overall intellectual growth and development; nonetheless, the academic research supports the claim: environment matters.[29] As we have seen so far, the environment affects both intellectual opportunities and is essential for cultivating the requisite cognitive skills. In other words, there is a sociological factor influencing individual capacities for thinking and thinking in ways that society views as necessary. We have tasked several social institutions with some of this responsibility for cultivating these capacities. The most pervasive social institution for this purpose is the family. Our *family of orientation*, referring to the one we are born into, serves as our primary teacher throughout our lives. When we first become parents

---

[29] Thomas Bouchard and colleagues (1990) at the University of Minnesota have done extensive research on this topic by looking at monozygotic twins (i.e., identical twins). They measured the correlation between IQ scores for twins raised apart from each other in separate households against those who were raised together in the same household. The degree of similarity suggests 78% of intelligence is rooted in our biology, with the remaining 22% attributed to the environment. The environment may not be the most significant factor explaining intelligence, but it matters!

ourselves, we reflect on our experience of being parented as we settle into our own techniques for doing the job. Even in those later years, we look to how our parents navigated their final steps towards the grave, as our time now begins to approach. The social institution of education runs, perhaps, second to the institution of family in the overall degree of influence for cultivating these cognitive and intellectual abilities, but we will look at this social institution of education elsewhere in this book. It is the social institution of the *public square* that now captures the focus of our attention moving forward.

The Public Square

The *public square* refers to that open space where public exchange and debate occurs. Knowing *how* to think is of utmost importance but falls only second to know *what* to think. The homeostatic relationship between securing our inalienable rights while, at the same time, ensuring social stability, which is fundamentally necessary to survive as a collective people is carried out best in the public square. It is the primary means by which this essential footing is achieved, ensuring *what* we think drives from somewhere within. German sociologist, Jürgen Habermas, argues the public square (which he refers to as the *public sphere*) is "conceived above all as the sphere of private people [who] come together as a public; they soon claimed the public sphere regulated from the above [politicians] against the public authorities themselves, to engage them in a debate over the general governing relations in the basically privatized but publicly relevant sphere of commodity exchange and social labor" (1989, p. 30). To be clear, Habermas argues the public square's purpose is to carry out public debate; it is not the place for compromise and settling on common ground. Rather, it is a place to sound the alarm as a sort of social-problem-detector capable of sniffing-out emerging societal concerns, especially when our politicians are telling us there is no concern, "nothing to see here; move along!" The public square is not the place for expressing *everyday civility*.

The public square is a place carved out within a free society for confrontational debate.

Picture 6.3, Jürgen Habermas

I am an early riser and always the first to arrive to the office, but on this particular morning, one of my students was waiting for me at my door. "Can I please talk with you Dr. Liebert?" I let the student into my office, and before I could even find my seat, he opened the floodgate. "You can't believe how much you disturbed me with that comment in class yesterday. I am so upset; I haven't been able to stop shaking." Knowing there was no chance first to arm myself with coffee, I asked, "What was it I said?" I saw a full breath of air going into his lungs, then it all came out. "That depression is not real. I am telling you it is real! Dr. Liebert, my mother, is clinically depressed. She has been treated in the hospital for it. She even tried committing suicide not so long ago because of it. Depression is real. It is real as I am this morning talking with you in this office." We talked for a solid hour exploring the point that there is no objective measure for depression (e.g., blood test) and how psychological pain is a factual experience for the one who suffers from it. At times, my student was nearly yelling, but always respectful, disagreeing with my previous comments, always referring to me as "Dr. Liebert," and not accepting any compromise. He was attempting all the while to demonstrate I was wrong, and I was attempting to keep my ground on the point. It was a robust debate! Nevertheless, he left the office believing depression is a disease where something has gone awry with either the body's bone, blood, or flesh, and I continued to hold my position the real plight has a deeper existential etiology to it. Debate can get a bit rowdy, but violence, force, and intimidation are never an appropriate means and are contrary behaviors within the public square.

The importance of the public square is essential in a freely functioning society but will continue to evolve, as is the case for all social institutions. Today the public square has quickly morphed in recent years to the virtual space. Twitter, Facebook, Pinterest, Instagram have emerged as the new location for public square engagement. These spaces also serve to fill the mind with senseless trivia, but they are also the spaces where essential debate sparks and ensues. For example, on July 14, 2019, President Donald Trump tweets: "So interesting to see 'Progressive Democratic Congresswomen,' who originally came from counties whose governments are a complete and total catastrophe… telling the people of the United States… how our government should be run. Why don't they go back and help fix the totally broken and crime infested places from which they came…" The nation captures onto the words "go back" and we debate the possible racial inferences. The debate on race, racism, and prejudice continues to be an essential conversation and debate, and the virtual platform can readily serve as the space for this debate to ensue.

This new virtual public square does raise a significant concern: "A handful of executives in Mountain View, California, has more power over humankind than a small group of people has ever had before," explains cognitive psychologist Robert Epstein (2016, n.p.). The virtual public square meets societal needs by serving as a neutral host for essential debate. The intentional censorship for participation in the virtual public square is dangerous to a free society.

Picture 6.4, The public square is essential for free speech

For example, in 2019, both Twitter and Pinterest shut down Live Action's account. Live Action is a pro-life organization, known for posting videos describing (not showing) abortion procedures, undercover clinic videos taken in Planned Parenthood, and other similar materials promoting a pro-life point of view. Alison Centofante, director of external affairs at Live Action, says "that their Pinterest account was removed permanently from Pinterest for 'harmful misinformation, [which] includes medical misinformation and conspiracies that turn individuals and facilities into targets for harassment or violence.' Also, Live Action says that Pinterest describes their content as having 'immediate and detrimental effects on [a Pinterest user's] health or public safety'" (cited in Scheer, 2019, n.p.). Live Action does not find themselves alone, now cast out from the virtual public square and into the bin of censorship. Conservative speakers Jesse Kelly, conservative cartoonist Ben Garrison, actor James Woods along with a host of others, find themselves keeping company with Live Action.

Consider that CNN was sued for $275 million in a defamation lawsuit filed by lawyers representing Covington Catholic High School student Nicholas Sandmann following CNN coverage depicting the student mocking Native American Nathan Phillips. The coverage of the event made it appear Sandmann, and fellow students rushed and intimidated Phillips, but as the lawsuit alleges, it was Phillips and others who rushed the students and hurled insults at them. This occurred in the same year Live Action was booted from the virtual public square on the grounds their posts had "immediate and detrimental effects on [a Pinterest user's] health or on public safety." If this is untrue, why then cannot Live Action fall in line with Sandmann and file a lawsuit? The answer is easy: the law does not permit them this remedy. Unlike a news organization like CNN now accused of libel or defamation of character, online platforms are virtually immune from similar claims, as online platforms fall under Section 230 of the Communications Decency Act, stating:

> No provider or user of an interactive computer service shall be treated as the publisher or speaker of any information provided by another information content provider… The Internet and other interactive computer services offer a forum for a true diversity of political discourse, unique opportunities for cultural development, and myriad avenues for intellectual activity." (cited in Altschul, 2018, n.p.)

In Google We Trust!

Time for a moment of nostalgia. You, youngsters, have it so easy today! Back when I was in college, writing a research paper first required a trip to the college library and hours spent flipping back and forth in large green paperbacks to cross-reference key terms to identify possible journal articles that might be relevant to my research paper topic. After writing down the reference, I had to trek upstairs to the second floor hoping the library just happened by chance to have those specific journals on the shelves, and some other student who was also writing their research paper on a Marxist interpretation of George Orwell's *Animal Farm* had not already liberated these journals from off the shelf. It was a tedious process, now replaced with two big thumbs smacking key-words on an iPhone immediately followed by a stash of relevant links and PDFs coming back at you in less time it takes a college sophomore to run-up to the second floor of the library while taking two steps at a time. However, soon, the world changed and quickly got much easier. By the time I was in graduate school, computer databases had replaced the card catalogs which *The Pottery Barn* immediately took possession of, retrofitting them into coffee tables by the thousands. The technology promised to deliver to us all the world's knowledge. Instantaneously, beckoning the truth to our monitors in ways Karl Marx never imagined, as real power is not rooted in economic surplus but access to knowledge.

At the rapid speed which only technology can travel, today what is becoming the single essential piece of criteria upon which we find answers to objective questions and form opinions to those more subjective questions is the first-page *list*. Ask Google what the capital of Florida is, and the answer generates more than 610,000,000 responses in about 0.49 seconds, spreading out over dozens of pages. However, the first answer that appears at the top of the list return is always the correct answer, which in this case is *Tallahassee*. Computers are always right, after all! We have been conditioned to look at computers as impartial instruments delivering to us just the facts. However, there is a strategy for Google's process; moreover, this strategy is biased.

The answers Google gathers up to such a query as "what is the capital of Florida?" is based on generating an *algorithm* that refers to a systematic formula or cognitive strategy for solving problems that will guarantee to find an answer. For example, consider the following scramble letters: AINLF. If using an algorithm to solve this problem, you would systematically rearrange each letter until the word "FINAL" appears. As there are five letters, you might work through all 120 different letter combinations until the answer appears, which might require a bit of time to accomplish this task, and it is unlikely you would engage this process. More likely, you would engage the use of a *heuristic*, which refers to a sort of educated guess, not a random guess, but a guess that hones in on logic and commonsense. For instance, based on all your vast prior experience reading words over your lifetime, you have observed that typically the vowels are going to be flanked by the constantans. Do so in your mind's eye, and quickly enough, the answer just jumps out at you, "FINAL!" Google employs the same approach, although the heuristic aspect of the process weighs heavily on how others have responded to similar questions, believing the algorithmic output is correct. In other words, we trust the first topic returned in the list as the correct answer because others have thought so too. There is a sort of hive mentality taking place when zeroing in on the Google list.

Let us say you are now satisfied knowing Tallahassee is the capital of Florida and want to know the answer to a more subjective question, like "What is the best state to live in?" The Google return list yields about 4,880,000,000 responses in about 0.65 seconds. The first return on the list says, "The fifth best place to live is in New Hampshire…" Using the same algorithmic strategies, this process permits—and perhaps evenly purposefully ensures—bias gets infused into the formula. I know this because New Hampshire would be my fiftieth choice of states where I would ever like to reside.

Google spokeswoman Susan Cadrecha explains the company's goal is not to do the thinking for its users, rather it is "to help you find relevant information quickly and easily… We encourage users to understand the full context by clicking through to the source" (cited in Nicas, 2017, n.p.). Psychologist Robert Epstein, however, disagrees. In his testimony before the United States Senate Judiciary Subcommittee on the Constitution (2019), Epstein suggests Google adopts intended strategies to manipulate the list, and thereby manipulate the way we think, feel, and behave, what he refers to as *Search Engine Manipulation Effect* (SEME). Epstein does not parse his words, "SEME has proved to be one of the most powerful and dangerous effects ever discovered in the behavioral sciences. It is powerful because of the big results it produces, and it is dangerous because it is virtually invisible as a source of influence" (2016, p. 20).

How dangerous might SEME be? Epstein and colleague Ronald E. Roberson (2019)[30] have published researching show how this approach could be used to swing an election. They state, "specifically we show that biased search ranking can shift the voting preference of undecided voters by 20% or more, the shift can be much higher in some demographic groups, and such ranking can be masked so that people show no awareness of the manipulation" (n.p.). Today, elections tend to fall to the razor's edge, followed by legally required ballot recounts as the margin is too close because the population is nearly evenly divided on political ideology. Epstein and Roberson are suggesting SEME can be the single factor that pushes the candidate off the edge and into the political office as the designator winner.

Close Only Counts in Horseshoes and Hand-Grenades. Before moving forward, take your iPhone and search the name, *Anita Hill.* What did you learn about her from the results yielded from your search? I am suspecting much of the information centers around her testimony in the US Senate's 1991 confirmation hearing of Clarence Thomas to the US Supreme Court. In other words, if you were assigned to write a 1,000-word report and the only single piece of information provided was her name, nothing else—likely—most of your 1,000-words would be spent on the topic of her claims of sexual harassment when she worked for Clarence Thomas at the Department of Education. Yet, in the decades that have followed since the early 1990s, Anita Hill has gone on to have a distinguished career as a professor at Brandeis University. She has been the recipient of many prestigious academic awards and authored many journal articles and books. I would suspect a few if any of your 1,000-words focused on any of the content from her 2011 book, which focuses on the topic of race and gender equality.

---

[30] Epstein and Roberson's (2019) research on SEME began well before the nation's attention to the 2016 Presidential Election which followed by accusations of Russian meddling, political conspiracy with foreign governments, and weaponizing federal agencies like the FBI to obtain FISA warrants to spy and contrive baseless conspiracy theories. In other words, simply what we refer to as *Political Theater.*

The first page matters! It is reasonable to say the first-page list is all that matters in the overall list results, as we rarely move on to the second page of the list results. One study even shows there is a 140% likelihood We will review the last item on the first page of the list over the first item on the second page from the list (Chitika, 2013). Did you review any of the material on pages 2, 3 or beyond from the list return on Professor Hill? And, what you will remember most from your Google list is found on this first page. Some of the earliest research in psychology on memory concludes we tend to remember what we see first in a list and last in a list; it is the information in the middle we are more likely to forget (Ebbinghaus, 1913).

Those who want to sell their product or get buy-in for their perspective or position are willing to pay vast amounts of money to secure representation on that first page list, after all Google is a business and profits are the driving force for any business, and paid advertising is the most used SEME strategy for manipulating the list. Search Google for the term "Sneakers," and the first three results are paid advertisements. It is subtle, but underneath the first return entitled, "High-Quality Running Shoes" is the word "Ad" finely outlined in a box. It would be expensive, but still possible for the first result in Professor Hill's list to be an advertisement for her most recent book; in doing so, "A Refresher on Anita Hill and Clarence Thomas: NPR" appearing at the bottom of the list would get bumped to the top of second page of the list, rendering it as obscure as Justin Guarini's last album.

SEME occurs both in overt and subtle ways. Concerning the latter, Epstein and Roberston (2019) argue this manipulation in thinking occurs through *autocomplete*, which is a search feature predicting the rest of the word or phrase, and the user can easily accept the search suggestion or continue typing in the rest of their intended phrase. For example, start with the word, *abortion*, and immediately the following words dropdown to complete the search phrase: *...pill ...clinics ...laws ...statistics*. Visual cues quickly direct our eyes to the top of the list, psychologically preferring the top of the list over the bottom list options. Moreover, subtly influence abounds by a sort of electronic peer-pressure where the internal voice inside our head suggests most people are interested in *abortion pills* over *abortion clinics,* as the latter seems to be the path least taken by everyone else out there searching the subject.

If you attempt to search the word *suicide* using Google, the results yield 540,000,00 answers in about 0.53 seconds, and at the top of the list appears information for the National Suicide Prevention Lifeline along with a toll-free number intended for those who are in the midst of crisis. Google made a deliberate choice to manipulate their search algorithm by including a suicide prevention resource because doing so aligns with their corporate and social ethic to be responsible and "do the right thing" (Scherr, Haim & Arendt, 2019). Like most everyone else out there, your moral ethic probably aligns with the choice made by Google to offer help to those who may be amid great angst and despair. Nonetheless, where is the line drawn between a widely shared public concern, a far less held moral belief, and the intentional attempt to manipulate the public's thinking and behavior?

In 2016 Google rolled out its new *Global News Initiative* (GNI) which streamlined the algorithm to favor results to some news organizations over those of other organizations. As Google explains, GNI "is our effort to work with the news industry to help journalism thrive in the digital age" (n. d.); nonetheless, preference now may be given to those news outlets who have a monetary edge over others and who may also align more closely to Google's corporate and social ethic. There is a "lack of clarity regarding how content is being evaluated by the algorithms," explains Sean Gelles, "as well as the susceptibility of these platforms to political pressure, they run the risk of eliminating a lot of content that simply does not conform to the dominant disclosure regarding specific topics." Gelles goes on to say, "the danger is that this kind of censorship will limit the public's ability to consider the issue thoroughly and make the best decisions for themselves and their communities" (2018, n.p.).

What is so Bad About Group Think. Recently one of the economics faculty in the department took ill and had to undergo emergency surgery. He is fine now, but this occurred the night before final exams. I had to step in and proctor the economics exam, grade them, and submit final grades for him. Economics is "not my wheelhouse!" I do not have a degree in economics. I only ever earned two C's in college: *tennis for beginners* and *macroeconomics*. Although I had a copy of the professor's exam, I did not have answers to any of the questions. I wrote the answer-key by taking the answers from the first ten students who finished the exam. The answer chosen by the majority was the one I used to construct the answer-key. Several weeks later the economics professor casually mentioned in the faculty lounge that I "aced" his exam, and wondered how I was able to do that, as many of his questions came from the lectures and would have been very difficult to find in the textbook. *The power of We is always stronger than the Me!* But, is this the case?

Going back again to Google's algorithm, which incorporates a sort of groupthink into the formula, the likelihood of results is based mainly on the way others have similarly responded. Consider first, *groupthink* refers to the process by which the group tends to align their thinking with conforming to the others in the group. We seek social harmony by yielding individuality of thought towards collective thought. This desire to conform results in a "mode of thinking that persons engage in when concurrence-seeking becomes so dominant in a cohesive in-group that it tends to override realistic appraisal of alternate courses of action" (Janis, 1971, p. 45). Google is different from the other virtual vendors we have discussed in this chapter in that Google holds itself out as a means for searching the internet to find relevant information, not as a public platform to debate on the issues. Habermas' (1989) argument does not seem to apply here. Earlier, I said, "Knowing *how* to think is of utmost importance but falls only second to knowing *what* to think." Diversity of thought ought to cultivate from within, rather than being shaped from outside, originating somewhere else in the environment. What might such an algorithm look like? The mere suggestion to propose an answer would demonstrate nothing shy of hubris. Still, I wonder if such a discussion might not take us back to our earlier discussion of Kyle Kashuv, which started this chapter. In the years that are to follow, Google search his name as will most certainly be the case for future lovers, prospective employers, and nosey neighbors, and what Google will deliver back in under 0.5 seconds in the return list will be the racial and anti-Semitic statements, and Harvard University rescinded his admission. Google captures what might just be our worst day, ignoring all the days that are to follow. How might forgiveness be included in the formula?

An Emerging Social Problem: Thinking[E]

This chapter addressed an emerging social problem, referred to as Thinking[E]. The topic acknowledges each of the four criteria necessary for identifying an emerging social problem as such. First, there is a significant degree of ethical incongruence found between moral and value perspectives. It is likely to assume, for example, staunch supporters favoring legalized abortion would, at first approach, cheer online platform providers like Twitter and Pinterest for ridding the public square of pro-life rhetoric. However, upon further consideration, realize the societal risks such silence may cause by stifling debate. It is easy for the reader to take the bait: *abortion is so wrong/right. Yes, Twitter did the right/wrong thing in this instance.* It requires some degree of deliberate effort not to become derailed and divert attention away from the universal social value which this chapter has argued is in play: free speech within the public square.

Additionally, arguments centering around this social problem emphasizes position over interest. The government needs to step in and do some good old fashion *trust-busting* with Google or Twitter, and the like should no longer abuse their protection under Section 230 of the Communications Decency Act. What at first appears to offer quick and easy solutions, upon the second inspection proves to be confounding in their possible outcomes. Should Twitter, along with the other public platform companies, be seen as news outlets who are afforded no longer the legal protections Section 230 provides, what then becomes of the public square? Replace Google's moral position with whose position? Is it even possible for a corporation to be directionless as it applies to a moral compass? Moreover, when speaking of aegis authority, I return back to Epstein's words: "A handful of executives in Mountain View, California, has more power over humankind than a small group of people has ever had before;" moreover, if his research is correct, then Google would have the ability to actually shape our respective positions over this debate by directly modifying their algorithm.

7   The Melting Middle-Class

Every society has established a *stratification system*, a ladder of sorts, that differentiates and separates the population in degrees of distances from each another. *Inequality* refers to extent of these differences, and the primary basis for determining the range of inequality and gradation of rungs within the range is determined by socioeconomic status based on indicators of wealth, income, education, and occupation. *Wealth* refers to the total amount of assets one has (i.e., stocks, bonds, gold coins hidden in the sofa cushions, or real estate), and *income* refers to the amount of money one is earning at the moment. Other factors, to a lesser degree, also help to determine where one finds himself or herself positioned on this social ladder (e.g., education and vocation). For example, the community's minister may have earned an advanced graduate degree, have a high level of social prestige within the community, but not have much of an annual income nor any accumulated wealth and still find himself with a higher social ranking than a bail bondsman who has no college education, but has a large annual income. The typical rungs on the American ladder include the *upper-class* (i.e., Jeff Bezos) which holds the majority of wealth; the *middle-class* who tend to have higher levels of education, annual income and some accumulated wealth (i.e., physician, accountant or attorney); the *working-class* (i.e., secretary, store clerk, or factory worker) are considered to have little or no education beyond high school, work pay-check to paycheck, and have debt, not wealth. The *lower class* may experience hunger at times. These folks are considered to have not completed high school and work for minimum wage at undesirable jobs (i.e., janitor or landscaper).

The politicians keep telling us, "the rich are getting richer while the poor are getting poorer!" The only problem with this cliché, it is somewhat accurate but not entirely true. The real concern is the deterioration of America's middle-class, as the middle-class is now melting away. *The corrosion of the middle-class is an emerging social problem.* The middle-class functionally meet the necessary needs of our society. Without the middle-class, our society would transform into a different type of system, behaving radically unlike our current system.

Chart 7.1, Distribution of social stratification

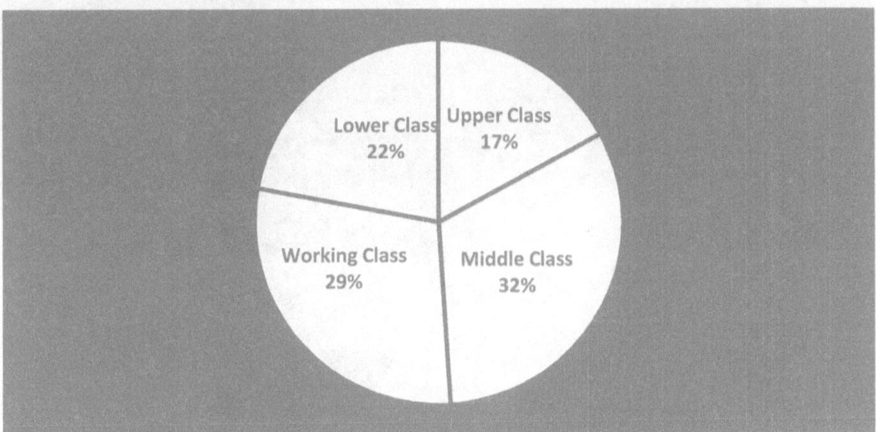

Every individual who is not rich may hold out that dream of becoming the next billionaire, but it is still the middle-class collectively we point to and champion for their contribution to the nation's success. It is the middle-class that addresses many of our society's basic needs. As the sociologist C. Wright Mills explains in his groundbreaking text, *White Collar: America's Middle-Classes*:

> It is to this white-collar [meaning middle-class] world that one must look for much that is characteristics of twentieth-century existence.

By their rise to numerical importance, the white-collar people have upset the nineteenth-century expectation that society would be divided between entrepreneurs and wage workers. By their mass way of life, they have transformed the tang and feel of the American experience. They carry, in a most revealing way, many of those psychological themes that characterize our epoch, and in one way or another, every general theory of the main drift has had to take account of them. For above all else they are a new cast of actors, performing the major routines of twentieth-century society. (1956, p. 1)

Picture, 7.1, C. Wright Mills

Too often, it is the values of the middle-class that capture the attention and focus when attempting to isolate their societal importance. To this end, the middle-class is said to possess an excellent work ethic making them dependable, motivated, honest, and self-disciplined. The problem with singling out the middle-class' values is the suggestion these values are somehow superior to those of other social classes like the wealthy or poor. We start to blur the lines between moral behavior and societal values. Nevertheless, the middle-class offers functional benefits to our society. The middle-class is not just the best argument against Marxist communism; they offer a tangible benefit to our society.

First, the middle-class consistently demonstrates a compelling interest in promoting sagacious strategies making government work better for everyone, poor and wealthy, alike. Unlike the wealthy who may have more social power and influence, the middle-class' fate is more likely knotted up in the outcomes of government policy. For example, if Social Security is expected to bankrupt by the year 2032, as several experts are suggesting, the middle-class will experience greater adversity from this failure than the wealthy who will not need to rely on Social Security in the years to come to support their retirement. The middle-class' collective insights on practical suggestions to ameliorate the problem may have more inherent value than what the wealthy may suggest.

Second, the middle-class has traditionally been that segment looked towards to replenish our population. The US Census Bureau (2018) reports that the national *population growth rate* is now at 0.6, which is the lowest since 1937[31]. "While the nation's growth rate varied through wars, economic upheavals, baby booms, and baby busts, the

---

[31] Footnotes are the place for distractions. Although the national PRG is 0.6, the global PGR is 1.07, according to data provided by the United Nations. In other words, the world's population has been exponentially increasing, while the US population is lagging in growth. Most of the population gains have been occurring on the African content with India and China still representing the densest populations. Most of these gains have been the result of two confounding factors: life expectancy and infant mortality. The ability to provide essential healthcare and immunization has resulted in increased life expectancy, especially during the first year of life. Infant mortality rates—referring to the number of live births that survive past the first year—have dropped significantly, yet many in these poorest regions of the globe continue to have high birth rates. Where in the past, many of these children did not survive, and parents had to have many children in the hopes a few would survive to adulthood. Combine this with increasing life expectancy, referring to people living on average longer; the net result is surging population growth in particular regions of the world. The United Nations estimates this surge will begin to level out around the year 2050.

current rate reflects a further dip in a trend toward a lower level of growth—below 0.80 percent—registered since the Great Recession of 2007-2009," as suggested in Figure 7.1 (Frey, 2018, n.p.). Traditionally, the wealthy have not contributed to high birth rates; instead, it has been those in the middle-class and lower classes. This means immigration may be seen now as a primary means for increasing the national population as baby-boomers are dying in more significant numbers, and the middle-class is choosing childless lifestyles at unmatched rates (see Figure 7.1; Frey, 2018). Immigration is now contributing to overall population growth at nearly the same rate as natural population growth and is predicted to exceed natural population growth, serving as the primary means for the nation's population growth by the year 2030, as suggested in Figure 7.2 (Frey, 2018).

Figure 7.1, US population growth from 1991 to 2018

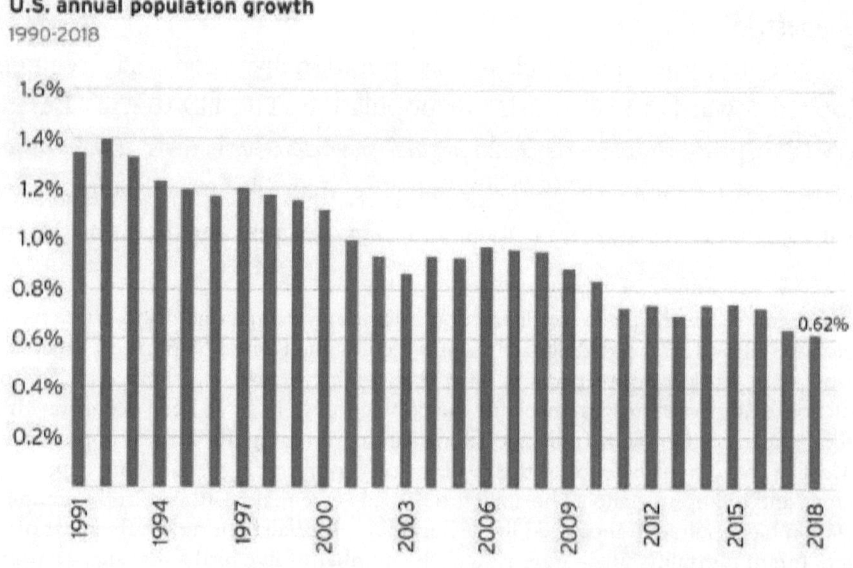

Figure 7.2, Immigration and natural population growth from 2001 to 2018

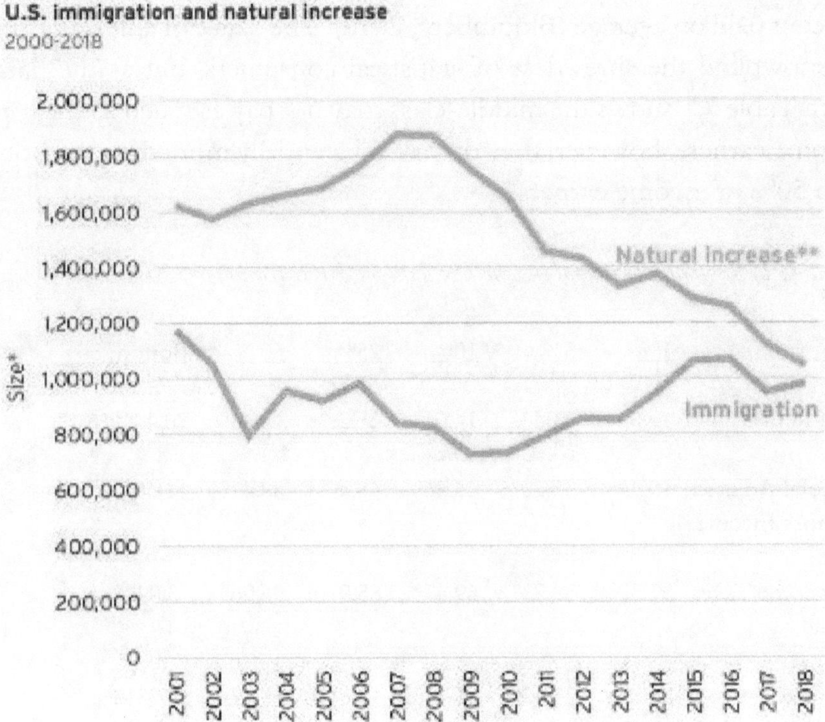

Finally, the middle-class has traditionally served as a substantial basis for tax revenue. The money families pay in federal income taxes represents the federal government's single largest source of revenue. An estimation for this figure for the fiscal year 2018, is about $1.7 trillion (McClelland & Werling, 2018), which is a substantial increase from 2016, which was $1.4 trillion (Bellafiore, 2018).[32] The individual income tax system is designed to be progressive, meaning those who earn more in income pay a higher rate in federal income tax. The steepness of the progressive curve is more apparent at the highest levels.

---

[32] To be fair, economic experts are still speculating on the effects associated with the changes made to the tax code in 2017.

The average tax rates paid for the very wealthiest have fallen in recent years from a peak of 24.1 percent in 2013 to 22.9 on 2016 and was a full four percentage points below the 26.9 percent that the top one percent paid on average (Bloomberg, 2018). The data can quickly begin to snowblind the shrewdest of statistical consumers, but as the data from Table 7.1 shows the middle-class may not pay as much as the top income earners, however, they do pay substantially more than the bottom 50% of income earners.

Table 7. 1, Summary of federal income tax data for 2016 (Bellafiore, 2018)

Top →	1%	5%	10%	25%	50%	Bottom 50%
# of Returns	1.409	7.04	14.01	35.22	70.44	70.44
% Total Adjusted Gross Income	19.72%	35.20%	46.56%	68.43%	88.41%	11.59%
% Income Taxes Paid	37.32%	58.23%	69.47%	85.97%	96.96%	3.04%
Average Tax Rate	26.87%	23.49%	21.19%	17.84%	15.57%	3.73%

* Reported in Millions

Social Stratification and the Middle-Class

Any analysis of the stratification system within a society entails a *macrosociological* perspective. It is a study of the entire society, rather than an analysis of particular facets or niches within the society (i.e., an analysis of social factors promoting cohabitation within a society). At its core, stratification refers to the ways people within society interact and relate to one another. Moreover, inherent within these social interactions amongst peoples where varying degrees of inequality exists, the basis for defining the boundaries between one status and the next may be identified, the conditions necessary—when possible—to move from one status to the next is discovered and to identify the exclusionary strategies used by groups to maintain their status may also be revealed.

Since World War II, the United States has traditionally held a healthy and vibrant middle-class. Unions were influential during this era, guaranteeing members sufficient wages to support a family by working in factories, especially the likes of the auto industry. The GI Bill and relatively low tuition costs at state colleges and universities ensured access to degrees, which would lead to white-collar jobs along with white-collar incomes. For example, during the 1960s, a new community college was opening its door at the rate of about one each week. Community colleges also embrace the idea of *open access* to college; unlike other schools restricting access to those who may have lower admission scores (i.e., SAT or ACT), the community college provides access to the college classroom. Such ideas embrace an American stratification system that is an *open system*, meaning there is a possibility for social mobility within the rungs of the social ladder. While other societies have a *closed system* (i.e., caste systems), where there is no opportunity for social mobility, this is not true for Americans. We love our *rags to riches* stories of folks like Jeff Bezos, who takes a company that first started in his garage at home and built it into one of the most successful businesses ever known. We tell our children they must study hard in college, and they will end up thriving as a result. The middle-class is often referred to as one of the nation's pillars of strength, mainly as it represents economics and values.

Nevertheless, the recent trend for the middle-class has been to either fall into the ranks of the lower rungs or—more likely the case—absorbing into higher rungs of the socioeconomic system. A 2016 Urban Institute study found that 38% of American families defined as middle-class in 1979, and today that number is 32% (Pethokoukis, 2018). Although a 15.80% change in the difference may not sound like very much, the actual difference is substantially more. Walking around outside in the summer when it is 100 degrees is an entirely different experience when doing so out in the desert of New Mexico versus the Florida marshlands. The above statistic is misleading on two levels: Relative standards and the middle-class as a false positive.

Relative standards. The standard of living for the 1970s is much different from the standard of living for today. Gregg Easterbrook (2003), refers to the *progress paradox* where Americans today are benefiting from a higher standard of living but also appear not to be as happy as previous generations. The square footage of our homes has increased, there are more cars on the driveway, we let the drycleaners press our shirts, and we enjoy summers inside with air conditioning. The mistake with Easterbrook's analysis, however, is confusing *wants* with *needs*. What might be taken as a luxury back in the 1970s is argued now as a necessity for us to have today. For instance, "two generations ago in the United States, most families lacked a car; by our parents' generation [of the 1970s], most families had one car while the two-car lifestyle was a much sought ideal; today a third of American's families own three cars or more" (Easterbrook, 2003, p. 16). Easterbrook is suggesting the second car is a luxury or a *want*, as families were able to make due in the past. Consider the data presented in Table 7.4 (US Department of Education, 2011), which shows the increase in higher education earned by women within two generations period of time. Women have been earning more education for a purpose: to compete in the job market. The dual-parent working family is the norm today. Whereas, in the 1970s, the *traditional family* where the father was the breadwinner, and the mother stayed home to care for the children was the more typical arrangement. It would seem rational to suggest a car is a necessity when employed full time.

Table 7.2, Women's share in higher education.

	1985	2009
Bachelor's degree	51	57
Masters' degree	50	60
Doctorate degree	34	52

There are no charts to show the number of iPhones per household from the 1970s until today, but a similar argument can be made for the necessity over luxury for owning a smartphone. Perhaps not a fair practice, nevertheless, we need to stay connected to the office (our middle-class meal-ticket) after hours and over the weekend. The boss expects an email sent out Friday at 7:00 pm read before we enter the office on Monday morning at 9:00 am. The client expects her real estate agent to answer the phone on Saturday at 11:00 am. If not, she will find another agent who will. Technology, in many instances, is not a luxury; instead, it is a necessity to own a laptop, subscribe to a Wi-Fi provider, own a smartphone, and have a car in the driveway.

Moreover, if the norm today is dual-income earning families, the most valuable commodity becomes time. Sending shirts out to the drycleaner is a luxury when there is a stay-at-home-spouse otherwise able to iron them. Running through the drive-thru to pick up dinner for the family at 6:20 pm is not a luxury over pulling the gizzards out from a chicken and cooking a home-cooked meal on a Tuesday evening. Two cars are more expensive to own than one car; drycleaners are more expensive than replacing an iron every three years; takeout is more expensive than home cooking. However, these expenses become necessities in the dual-income-earning family.

Image, as it relates to social status, is vital as one attempts to negotiate the rungs on the socioeconomic ladder. Can a real estate agent compete as successfully when touring prospective clients around neighborhoods shopping for homes in the $500,0000 range in a five-year-old Honda Civic versus last year's Jeep Grand Cherokee? What would the boss think of an employee who wears the same three shirts day after day? To suggest social image and socioeconomic status are discrete phenomena is to embrace to one degree or another apparent naivety.

Moreover, unlike the 1970s, the *technical divide* is a sustained reality today. It can be expensive to compete on a level playing field today.

Consider as an example of today's typical college classroom. The history professor has announced four weeks from now the term paper is due on Sunday night no later than 11:59 PM. Students are also reminded they need to have their papers scanned for plagiarism and submit this report along with their paper. In other words, the term papers are to be submitted in the electronic drop box setup in the class' Learning Management System (LMS; i.e., BlackBoard or Canvas). The professor assumes that every student has reasonable access to a computer at home, along with Wi-Fi. Of course, those students who cannot afford such technology can use the computers in the library... once they become available, and these students will have to manage their time more efficiently since the library may close on Sundays. Again, today, the costs associated with expensive technology are not a luxury, but in many instances, it is a necessity.

The middle-class as a false positive. The middle-class was described above as a socioeconomic group with "some accumulated wealth." In other words, they are more likely than the working-class to have "toys," like a boat in the driveway, an RV parked in the backyard, or an aluminum-framed touring bike along with a few kayaks stored in the garage. Perhaps the RV is 25-feet long, but a 20-foot RV would have been a little more manageable with the monthly budget, or the aluminum bicycle was purchased interest-free based on three easy monthly payments. This month, however, the uninsured iPhone got dropped in the water while trying to snap a picture of an alligator on a recent kayak trip and now has to be replaced, making the third bicycle payment not so "easy." The fact those who make up the middle-class may—from time-to-time—find themselves having a financially tricky month, where a dinner or two out is replaced with a home-cooked meal instead on Saturday nights, a fishing trip altogether canceled or even discovering their new Audi is in the clutches of the repo-man, does not demote them from the ranks of the middle-class when operationalizing socioeconomic status by criteria such as income, wealth, education, and vocation. In the last decade or so we are finding a new social class, what I refer to as the *false positive middle-class* (FPMC). They satisfy the criteria for being middle-class, but in actual practice, they look and behave more like the working-class. This socioeconomic group is, what Quart (2018) refers to as being *squeezed*, "running furiously and breathlessly just to find themselves staying in place are a large and varied coterie" (p. 5).

Let us discuss as a case study an example of this FPMC phenomenon using a newly graduated and licensed clinical psychologist whom we will call Sigmund. According to a report conducted by the National Science Foundation (2013), the median annual salary for clinical psychologists is $80,000, with 57% of all psychologists earning an annual salary within the range of $60,000 to $120,000. This same report shows that psychologists who work in private practice earned about $97,000 annual, but it takes a bit of time to build up a successful practice. For this case study, we will assume Sigmund was not just smart but a little lucky too and within two years of practice is earning an annual income of $80,000, which is equal to the overall mean income for psychologists.

The two graduate degrees typically earned and necessary for the practice of clinical psychology are the Ph.D. (Doctor of Philosophy) or the Psy.D. (Doctor of Psychology). A typical question undergraduate students ask in an abnormal psychology class when discussing education requirements to practice as a psychologist centers around the difference between these two degrees: is one more marketable, easier to earn, or qualifies the practitioner to do more with patents. The actual differences are minimal; Psy.D. programs are more structured and focus more on clinical practice; whereas, Ph.D. programs place more emphasis on research. But, these differences are overall minimal. Thus, my reply gets right to the point: the only real difference between the two degrees is about $125,000. Graduate school is expensive. The average amount of debt for students completing a Ph.D. is about $75,000, whereas Psy.D. students' average rate of debt was about $200,000 (Stinger, 2016). Therefore, the only real difference between the two degrees is their cost. This is because most Ph.D. degrees are earned at state universities where students benefit from in-state tuition rates, and Psy.D. degrees are earned at private colleges/universities.

Moreover, most graduate programs—Ph.D. or Psy.D.—in clinical psychology offer students little to no opportunities for scholarships or other sources of funding to cover their expenses. Students pay tuition and other fees out of their own pockets, meaning most students borrow through federally-funded student loan programs the cost for their graduate training. Regardless, where one earns his or her degree, professional training in clinical psychology is expensive. Unfortunately, all too often, this piece of information is not discussed in undergraduate psychology classes. "The cost of education and the impact of student debt, particularly as debt is emerging as a new sociological category of poverty in the United States" (Doran, Marks, Kraha, Ameen & El-Ghoroury, 2016, p. 9). In the end, most degrees awarded in clinical psychology today are Psy.D. degrees, and for this case study, we will assume Dr. Sigmund earned a Psy.D. degree and borrowed a total of $200,000 in student loans.

This is the reality of becoming a clinical psychologist today; those new to the professional practice of clinical psychology find themselves saddled with a lot of student debt! A typical monthly student loan payment, based on 4% annual interest rate with a 30-year repayment plan would be about $950.00 per month. This means for the student who completes all their graduate work at the age of 28, he or she will be making a monthly payment of $950 until reaching the age of 58, at which time the total amount paid over the lifetime of the loan will have been $342,000. Despite such high figures, most students who are currently pursuing their graduate work as well as those who have recently graduated still say, if, given the option to choose a different career path, they still would pursue clinical psychology (Winerman, 2016). Sigmund, although happy with his career choice, does have a $950.00 monthly student loan payment. There is no dodging a federal student loan. The government will garnish Sigmund's bank accounts. Even if he retires at age 67, his Social Security checks will be garnished by the federal government. In almost all cases, student loans cannot even be bankrupted.

There is another crucial piece to Sigmund's life. While he was in graduate school, he became romantically involved with another student, Mary. She became pregnant, and in Sigmund's final year of school, he became a father. Mary, on the other hand, began to question her decision to become a clinical psychologist and decided to quit school, move to the Far East to study transcendental meditation, and left their baby in a whicker-basket outside Sigmund's front door just before leaving town. Sigmund has never heard from Mary ever again. Taking care of a newborn while balancing the demands of graduate studies was very difficult for Sigmund, but it was very costly too. Sigmund lives in Rhode Island, where by chance daycare for infants reflects the national average of $12,867 per year (Child Care Aware of America, 2015), although Sigmund can expect that cost to go down to about $10,400 when his daughter becomes 4-years old.

Sigmund has just left his accountant's office, who has prepared his annual federal income tax form. Sigmund is feeling a little down after looking at all these numbers and decides to stop off at a bar to enjoy one or two adult beverages. The bartender, Anna, happens to be an old friend of his from back in high school. Anna never went on to college, spent the last dozen years working at mostly minimum wage jobs, but has been working at the bar for the last two years. Anna is earning about $12.00 per hour, including tips. She is earning about $25,000 a year. Consider Table 7.3; how much better off is Sigmund over Anna economically?[33] When considering all the other expenses associated with raising a child beyond daycare, it might be nearly a wash economically. Sigmund and Anna are enjoying similar lifestyles, shopping in the same stores, living in the same neighborhoods and struggling with similar economic challenges, but Sigmund is still being defined within the ranks of the middle-class while lumping Anna into the working-class cohort.

---

[33] We will not consider the fact Anna gets free drinks at the bar!

Now let us suppose Sigmund finds himself stopping off at that same bar on those days he knows Anna is working. They start dating and a year later marry. Now, their combined annual net income is $58,133. There is more disposable income for the new family as monthly expenses (i.e., rent) are folding into each other. Based purely on economics, would it be a wise idea to have a second child? Now assume the case of Sigmund and Anna is not rare; there are lots of single adults, single parents, and couples out there sharing similar economic realities to the one portrayed in this case study. To the point: there is a growing segment of the population who appear to be in the ranks of the middle-class but experience a different socioeconomic reality. The two most substantial financial challenges prohibiting this group of people from legitimate access to the middle-class are the costs associated with childcare and higher education.

Table 7.3, Comparing case study incomes

	Sigmund	Anna
Annual Income	$80,000	$25,000
Income Tax	($17,600)	($3,000)
Student Loan	($11,400)	($0)
Childcare	($12,867)	($0)
Net Income	$38,133	$22,000

Higher Education: The Emerging Obstacle to Middle-class

"Much political rhetoric these days is devoted to the importance of broadening access to college—and there is plenty of evidence that a degree improves financial prospects—but ... today a good education may not keep you from hovering near the poverty line" (Quart, 2018, p. 35). According to the US Department of Education:

> For the 2016–17 academic year, annual current dollar prices for undergraduate tuition, fees, room, and board were estimated to be $17,237 at public institutions, $44,551 at private nonprofit institutions, and $25,431 at private for-profit institutions. Between 2006–07 and 2016–17, prices for undergraduate tuition, fees, room, and board at public institutions rose 31 percent, and prices at private nonprofit institutions rose 24 percent, after adjustment for inflation. The price for undergraduate tuition, fees, room, and board at private for-profit institutions decreased 11 percent between 2006–07 and 2016–17, after adjustment for inflation. (2019, n.p.)

The rate of tuition has vertically outpaced every other expense for which measuring inflation occurs. When I graduated from high school in 1989, the estimated cost of a four-year degree was $26,900 ($52,900 when adjusted for inflation), and today's cost for the same degree is estimated at $104,440, making student loan debt the single most significant type of debt held by families today (Maldonado, 2018).

The rising cost of college has reached a breaking point. Many families and students are questioning the economic value associated with investing in a bachelor's degree. To major in criminology, for example, intending as a goal to work in law enforcement following college, means a monthly student loan payment of $750 every month over the next thirty years. This is leading families and prospective students to question either vocational goals or the economic value to pursue a degree that leads to entry into lower or mid-range strata of middle-class employment. For instance, for many years now, there has been a glut of general practitioners working in the area of family medicine over that of board-certified specialists. Dr. Munshi points out, "In 1961, almost half of US physicians were general practitioners; by 2014, the fraction had declined to one third" (cited by Frances, 2016, n.p.). One of the driving forces explaining the trend has been the high cost of medical education. Medical specialists earn more than family doctors, and it is now necessary to enter medical school pursuing higher paying areas of medical practice in order to service the student loan debt necessary to earn the degree in the first place.

It is a fact: tuition costs have risen at a rate substantially higher than the cost of groceries, homes, cars, or a pair of khaki-colored chinos from the Banana Republic. We might be able to explain—perhaps even justify—the increase in the cost of a new car purchased off the dealer's lot today from the cost of a new car 50-years ago by pointing out the superior gas efficiency, air-bag safety features, and increased life-time mileage of cars manufactured today. The real cost of a car is more today, but there is more value to the car bought today. To this end, there does not appear to be a similar rationale to explain this dramatic increase in the cost for college today. As Quart points out, "at least 28 percent of households that used food stamps in 2013 were headed by a person with at least some college education. This proportion was 8 percent in 1980" (2018, p. 35).

Take a look inside today's college classroom; it does not reveal a space much different from that of 25-years ago. The ratios between student and faculty are nearly the same, as is the ratio between full-time faculty and adjunct faculty. There have been a few changes. Computer bunkers wired up to ceiling-mounted projectors beaming PowerPoint driven lectures have replaced the old transparency projectors that once beamed hand-written lecture notes on the same canvas screen. Final grades are now transferred efficiently to the Registrar's office through the Learning Management System (LMS). Students prefer to email their professor—if it is necessary to speak with him or her in the first place—over using the telephone. Many students prefer taking cell phone pics of the notes on the board over actually having to write them down. True, there have been some technological shifts in how the curriculum is delivered today in the classroom, but such expense does not come close to explaining the shocking rise in college costs. Even with those schools that have shifted more of their courses from the physical classroom to the virtual classroom, today's tuition expenses are not justified, as virtual classrooms are more affordable in delivering the curriculum than the traditional approach.

The radical tuition hikes are explained at first slowly, then as something seeming to occur all at once. Up until the 1980s, government grants primarily explained how higher education was financed outside of personal funds contributed by the student and family. Moreover, federal grants are not repaid; it is like a gift. Under the Reagan Administration, federal grants started to give way to federally subsidized loans. Students and families would take out a federal loan to pay the portion they were unable to pay themselves. Private banks would provide the financing, and while in school, the federal government would pay the interest on the loan. Private banks were the beneficiaries of a loan guaranteed by the federal government and interested paid by the graduate, once consolidated, over time, typically 10 to 30 years.

In 2010 the federal government sought to cut out the banks on the deal. The Student Aid and Fiscal Responsibility Act now eliminated the banks, and the government became the direct lender. Effectively, the price of tuition was between the university and the federal government. The university set the price; the government fronted the cost to the student, convinced this was the only means possible to secure entry into the middle-class job market. The pace of student loan debate now took off like a rocket, with the Federal Student Aid portfolio now accounting for "nearly ten percent of our nation's debt," according to Secretary of Education Betsy DeVos (US Department of Education, 2018, n.p.).

Now flush with cash, the universities spent their newly gained wealth on what Charles Sykes has called "academia's 'law of more'" (2016, p. 95). The money was spent on non-academic projects, which have included new layers of administrative bureaucracy in positions that had not previously existed before, such as Chief Diversity Officer, marketing officers, Vice Provost of Engagement, as well as many others. Building programs followed, including new sports stadiums, plush dorms, and Olympic quality fitness centers. As noted by the *New York Times*, the money appeared to be directed at "vast expansions and amenities aimed at luring better students: student unions with movie theaters and wine bars; workout facilities with climbing walls and 'lazy rivers'; and dormitories with single rooms and private baths" (quoted in Sykes, 2016, p. 109).

Final Remark

A social problem has been defined as a social phenomenon which is not merely limited to the experience of a *social trouble*, referring to an adverse event experienced by another. Rather, the reach of a social problem extends beyond the personal experiences of people by adversely affecting societal institutions. To this point, the melting of the middle-class presents as a social problem. It is easy to get emotionally caught up and focus distracted when confronted with the personal stories of folks—especially young folks—who are unable to secure entry-level jobs and incomes necessary to enter into the ranks of the middle-class and enjoy the benefits of marriage, family, and the many residual advantages that ought to follow after completing a higher education.

Moreover, social problems have been defined as a social phenomenon operationalized through the lens of empirical evidence. Again, the statistical evidence is clear: more Americans today struggle and endeavor endlessly to keep afloat in the middle-class, but are nevertheless being pulled down, unable to secure the basic trimmings historically afforded to previous generations earning similar degrees and working at similar vocations. The data is clear: the middle-class is not thriving; rather, it is perishing before our eyes.

A social problem refers to a social phenomenon which, either places at risk or compromises the sustainability of societal functioning or the inalienable rights of those impacted directly or indirectly by the social problem. To this end, the melting of the middle-class threatens both. The functional benefits of the middle-class are now being challenged. As a young generation begins to embrace political platforms based on socialistic ideas, will this generation apply the same sagacious contemplation ensuring our government works better for everyone, poor and wealthy, alike.

Although identifying the melting of the middle-class as an emerging social problem, it benefits our discussion to remind the reader when reasonable argument prevails, there is the belief that something can be done to ameliorate or even resolve a social problem. The middle-class can be reestablished and thrive within a stable socioeconomic system, but such resolution is not univocal; instead, it is complex and first requires rowdy and robust debate.

Harry Harlow (1805-1981), born Harry Israel, changed his name at the urging of his doctoral adviser, Lewis Terman, who believed Israel sounded too Jewish. Terman was the renowned intelligence researcher at Stanford University who devised the formula for measuring intelligence (IQ = MA/CA X 100). Terman, however, was not impressed with Harlow's intellect and suggested he should rest his hopes teaching at a junior college because he thought it would be the most Harlow could achieve. But, Harlow proved Terman wrong as he was offered an assistant professorship at the University of Wisconsin—Madison. With his Ph.D. fresh in hand, his dissertation research predicting a method for measuring the intelligence of rats now behind him, Harlow left Palo Alto for the cold north of Wisconsin. The year was 1930.

Once at the university, Harlow hoped to continue with his research on measuring rodent IQs but was horrified to learn he would be overseeing a rhesus monkey lab. Assistant professors too often have little say over such matters; so Harlow scratched out the word "rat" and replaced it with "rhesus monkey." Despite an obvious problem with alcohol, Harlow was a meticulous observer; although his focus was on his subjects' intellect, he began to see an odd behavior of sorts played out daily in the lab. When the monkeys' cages were cleaned up, and the cloth pads lining the bottom of the cages were replaced, the monkeys became distressed. It seemed to Harlow the monkeys had become emotionally attached to these cloth pads. Harlow faced a *rabbit trail.* Researchers, like Harlow, need to keep a narrow focus and avoid getting distracted by every observation presenting itself in the course of the study; investigating every new idea popping up during a study risks that nothing will ever get done. Nevertheless, Harlow abandoned the topic of intelligence and now moved on to study an even riskier topic: *love.* Psychologists prefer not to use the term love, preferring the term *attachment* instead. Harlow was interested in observing how baby rhesus monkeys form initial attachments to their mothers with the intent of understanding the nature of love in human beings.

For most social scientists, however, the topic of love did not require any further study. You see, Sigmund Freud had already explained the etiology of attachment. It was understood; love is based on *drive reduction.* The breast is not only the first erotic object; it is also the source that quenches the pain of hunger. As Freud explained, "Love has the origin in attachment to the satisfied need for nourishment" (quoted in Blum, 2002, p. 57). Perhaps, it was Harlow's sense of feeling marginalized by his former Stanford advisor or sheer indifference to the established Freudian majority, and he pressed on deciding to challenge Freud's drive reduction theory empirically.

Harlow's study required he separate infant rhesus monkeys from their mothers, who showed absolute anguish as their babies were taken from them. The baby monkeys were isolated from one another. In their cages, however, were two inanimate surrogate mothers. One was wrapped up in terry cloth; the second was constructed out of wire. The wire surrogate was also forged to hold a bottle, and it was the wire surrogate the baby needed to seek out for feeding. Quickly the monkeys became habituated to the presence of the two surrogate mothers. At which time, Harlow then proceeded to strike terror into these babies by having a wind-up bear-doll march through their cage while banging on a drum. When in a state of emotional terror, the baby monkeys would always seek out and cling onto the terry cloth surrogate, not the wire surrogate. The terry cloth had something to offer the wire could not, tactile comfort. An outcome that indeed calls into question the wisdom of drive reduction theory.

Picture 8. 1, Harry Harlow's study on attachment

Harlow's methodology was *observational*. He replicated the study, meaning he repeated it, over and over again, watching and taking note of the outcome. With predictability, Harlow could conclude the baby monkeys, when distressed, sought comfort from the object that could offer a soft touch, rather than the object that was hard, cold, and offered it nourishment. Although an observational method is based on a weaker analysis, it was superior to Freud's case study approach, and for Harlow, these findings set his career in motion. He quickly rose to a place of prominence in psychology, even serving as the President of the American Psychological Association from 1958 to 1959. Harlow's research, as it would turn out, offered a degree of support to the feminist cause. Freudian ideas supported the idea that in order to raise healthy, well-adjusted children, a mother needed to be present in the home. However, now children required touch, not just mothering. Harlow's research findings argued against the common notion that:

> Women should be housebound slaves. He had never taken fathers out of the parenting formula. There is evidence of that even in his APA presidential speech. After dismissing the food-equals-love approach, he pointed out that if love begins with just being there, with comforting and holding a baby tight, then "the American male is physically endowed with all the really essential equipment to compete with the American female on equal terms in one essential activity: the rearing of infants." (Blum, 2002, p. 235)

Amongst the applauses and acclaims, something unsettling started to occur. Those babies raised on touch became psychotic. These monkeys raised on cloth-mothers were far from thriving as the psychologically-intact, healthy adults Harlow promised they would become. Soon it all went sideways. During times of social play, the monkeys demonstrated violent and antisocial behaviors. "The females attacked the males and knew nothing about correct sexual posturing. Some of… [them] began to display autistic-like features, rocking and biting themselves, sores blossoming open on their arms, the blood rising through the fur-like bright pulp—infections set in. One cloth-mothered monkey chewed off its entire hand. Something, now he saw something had gone terribly, terribly wrong" (Slater, 2004, p. 144). Harlow had hoped to determine in later research what sort of parents they would become, but they could not mate on their own. With the assistance of artificial insemination, the females became pregnant but never were able to care for their young properly, or even worse; the mothers' killed their babies through neglect or merely taking the babies by their legs and smacking them against the walls of their cage. It soon became apparent to Harlow more than mere touch was required. Harlow continued to work his recipe for cultivating healthy attachment, finally resting on three ingredients: touch, movement, and socialization. This generation fared much better.

Within this triad of needs, Harlow acknowledges the vital importance of *socialization*. Our need for connection to others ranks right up there with our need for food, water, and shelter. We are nothing less than social creatures. Research suggests there is an association existing between human social interaction and our psychological and physical wellbeing. When we feel lonely, cortisol hormones increase, which over time, may lead to chronic stress that will—in turn—adversely affect our cardiovascular health (Sapolsky, 2004). Having fewer social connections has been linked to increased heart disease, impaired immune functioning, higher cancer rates, and slower recovery time following an illness (Umberson & Montez, 2010). We are more likely to be able to work through our grief when social support is made available (Liebert, 1998).[34] Even life expectancy is correlated positively with having higher levels of socialization (Berkman & Syme, 1979; Holt-Lunstad, Smith & Layton, 2010). Socializing more seems to benefit our brains, explains neuroscientists Hari et al., as "social interaction is

---

[34] I wrote my dissertation on this topic (1998). I did correlational research looking at non-residential spouses whose husband or wife had been admitted into a nursing home for long-term care due to dementia, typically of the Alzheimer's type. There was no expectation the residential spouse would ever return home. I observed that these non-residential spouses found themselves in a uniquely challenging position. Emotionally, they were grieving the loss of their marriage. Correct, they could visit their mate during visiting hours, but they did not eat meals with their partner; they slept in an empty bed. They existed in their home alone. Moreover, there was also a likely chance when they did visit their partner during established visiting hours their spouse did not even recognize him or her anymore due to dementia. I will repeat it: these non-residential spouses were experiencing a state of grief over the loss of their marriage. Typically, when a spouse passes, the widow also experiences an exchange of their social support networks. This might sound slightly horrible, but it is true; when a person becomes a widow, they then lose all their friends who tend to be married couples. This is because couples socialize with couples and singles socialize with singles. When one becomes a widow, they swiftly begin to socialize less with other couples and more with other widows. Except, I found when a marriage ends due to long-term nursing home placement, and the admitted spouse is unable to participate and manage relationships due to their dementia, the non-residential spouse starts this transition of losing their couple friends, but since their spouse is still alive, they do not establish new friendships with other widows. In essence, they are without meaningful social support networks, and this adversely impacts their ability to effectively managing their grieving.

among the most complex functions humans (and their brains) pre-form" (Hari, Heniksson, Malinen & Parkonen, 2015, p. 181). "Mammals are more socially connected than reptiles, primates more than other mammals, and humans more than other primates," Lieberman explains; "what this suggests is that becoming more socially connected is essential to our survival. In a sense, evolution has made bets at each step that the best way to make us more successful is to make us more social" (2003, p. 23).

Central to *Social Baseline Theory* (SBT)[35] is the belief that the human brain expects access to social relationships. We need such human interaction because it ameliorates possible environmental risks as well as decreasing the level of effort required to satisfy many of our personal goals and expected behaviors.

> This is accomplished in part by incorporating relational partners into neural representations of the self. By contrast, decreased access to relational partners increases cognitive and physiological effort. Relationship disruptions entail re-defining the self as independent, which implies greater risk, increased effort, and diminished wellbeing. The ungrafting of the self and other may mediate recovery from relationship loss. (Coan & Sbarra, 2014, p. 87)

In other words, socializing with someone requires we share to one degree or another a standard set of goals. For example, Mary and Susan are chatting over lunch:

M: I just can't stand Mrs. Alexander.
S: Worst history teacher ever!
M: Mean too!
S: That test on Friday is going to be a killer!
M: So much for hanging out at the beach this summer.
S: History and summer school are our destiny.

---

[35] *Social Baseline Theory* (SBT) integrates the study of social relationships with principles of attachment, behavioral ecology, cognitive neuroscience, and perception science.

Through the static, it is clear that both girls are worried about the upcoming test. By acknowledging their independent anxiety, it now converts into mutually interdependent anxiety. Additionally, they are now each aware they share the same goal of passing the history exam. Thus, the girls do not have to share the total cognitive weight for confronting the challenge which lies ahead. They each now perceive having more personal bioenergetic resources to draw upon, meaning their "social connection" with each other becomes a perceived resource.[36]

Getting back to the point, we need a human connection, and not just any old type of connection will suffice. Returning to Harry Harlow, it is worth pointing out the two surrogate mothers (one made out of wire mesh and the other out of terry cloth) both were present for the baby monkey, and the baby used them each for separate purposes: feeding and tactile comfort. Each was insufficient for cultivating a healthy state of attachment. To this end, both surrogate mothers failed, suggesting there is a special quality of socialization found in some types of interactions that are not present in other forms of interaction. Socialization is not a "one size fits all" phenomenon. For social interaction to be of value, addressing our existential awareness of isolation, socialization needs to connect at an intimate level. The term, *intimate*, may be used in reference to being sexual, especially if used today by folks who had once jumped out their bedroom windows to see Jim Croce live in concert. The term, however, is much more emotionally

---

[36]Although I like this example of Mary and Susan, who are worried about the history exam that I came up with on my own, sometimes two examples are better than just one. This one I did not come up with, rather belongs to Proffitt et al. (2003). A subject is walking and confronts somewhere out in the near distance a large, steep hill. It is obvious at first sight this is not going to be an easy hill to climb, especially while wearing a heavy backpack, feeling already physically tired, and being in a sour mood. The subject now sizes up the task, and in doing so takes note of the bioenergetic resources that will be required (e.g., strength, psychological commitment, insulin resources, hydration, and so forth). When asked by researchers to estimate the degree of difficulty in making the trek, the subject is more likely to estimate more energy and effort (e.g., bioenergetic resources) will be required when alone and less when hiking with a partner. In other words, the social connection is being included in the bioenergetic calculation as a resource that can be drawn upon.

rooted in its meaning. Intimacy refers to the degree to which one exposes themselves emotionally and, yes, even physically to another person where such exposure places the person at or near the same degree of emotional risk. Being intimate is being vulnerable; it is an exposure to those more profound parts of our psyche. Thus, we may worry about sharing with others those private dimensions of ourselves, fearing it will result in becoming dependent on another, losing the essence of our self or grinding the psyche down to lifeless particles of humiliation and degradation. In response, some avoid these risks by filling up the space and time of their day-to-day lives with the meaningless static of Instagram, Facebook, Netflix, eating, gaming, and so forth. We choose isolation over belonging. Nevertheless, what is left is once again what psychiatrist Irving Yalom calls the "unbridgeable gulf between oneself and any other being" (1980, p. 355). Albert Camus captures the essence of such a plight in his work *Death of the Soul*:

> Here I am defenseless in a city where I cannot read the signs… without friends to speak to, in short, without diversion. In this room penetrated by the sounds of a strange city, I know that nothing will draw me toward the more delicate light of a home or another cherished place. Am I going to call out? Cry out? Strange faces would appear… And now the curtain of habit, the comfortable tissue of gestures and words, wherein the heart grows sluggish, rises slowly and finally unveils the pale face of anxiety. Man is face to face with himself: I defy him to be happy… (2013, p. 83)

We are alone in this world to the extent that we are responsible for our own life. No one guards and protects us from those absolute realities of the world. No other person can step into the grave for us when our time comes. No other person can paint the picture consuming us to the same degree with the satisfaction of creating a work of art. No one can run those five miles for us, depositing the physical benefits into our account of health and wellbeing. We are alone, with the only solace being those moments of intimacy when another fellow traveler acknowledges my state of aloneness.

It is at this place of existential isolation we now turn our attention to another emerging social problem. Escalating quickly, we find social institutions closing down opportunities to connect, socialize, and share intimacy with others. This loss hurts. This chapter will address three instances where the pores of the social institution have constricted, making opportunities for intimate social interaction increasingly more difficult to experience. These three institutions include the rise of social media, marriage, and school.

Social Media Compounds Social Isolation

I worked in the electronics department of Mass Bros., which was an anchor store in the local mall when I was in college. Great job, since not too many people were interested in buying pricy consul television sets in what had the reputation of being a pricy department store, leaving me lots of time to peak at my textbooks when the manager was not looking. It also let me keep tabs on what some of my high school classmates were now up to. Mass Bros. was about 20 miles from my home and 50 miles from Florida Southern College, where I attended school. In the summer and back from their out of state schools, I would see familiar faces roaming around the mall. I had a reasonable sense of what became of the class of 1989! Moreover, there were no "filters" to make my situation look any better. I was financially broke and had to work; while they had their summers off, all funded by their parents.

Back around this time, the mall—like most malls around the country—was thriving. Sociologist George Ritzer (2009) coined the term *cathedrals of consumption*, pointing out how these retail edifices became the new locations where we worshiped our nation's newly discovered use of leisure time. Not so much anymore. Recently, my wife and I took a stroll through that old mall. Three of five anchors stores were boarded up; actually, many of the stores were without tenants, and I questioned the legality of the products sold in those stores that were open for business. Holding my arm tightly, my wife asked, "What happened here?" "*iGeners* killed it!" Amazon.com is now our new cathedral of consumption. Gone are the days when parents dropped their teenagers off at the mall to roam, mingle, and catch a movie located on the opposite end of the parking lot.

Developmental psychologist Jean Twenge (2017) refers to the cohort of folks born starting around 1995 who are now graduating from high school, who were that first group to be alive with the internet in place and received their first iPhone while an adolescent as the *iGen* generation, which sounds more rational of a name than whatever letter comes next in the alphabet. This is also the first cohort absorbed in virtual media. As Twenge points out, their increasing use of social media means less actual socialization. This cohort is less likely to go to parties, since binging on Season 2 of *Ozarks* is no less as enjoyable. They are less likely to go to the movies since it will be available for order up in about three months. They are less likely to engage in a dinner conversation with their parents while sitting at the table because all their friends are there, too, via texting. Through social media, today's iGeners have "friends" whom they have never physically met before, but they are still engaging frequently over ten hours a week with them over social media. There appears to be a rather substantial similarity between Harry Harlow's rhesus monkeys and today's iGen cohort: we need interaction with others, not screen time or surrogate time, but actual face-to-face time with others. Similar to those monkeys raised by the terry cloth surrogate mothers, those "teens who spend more time on screens are more likely to be depressed, and those who spend more time on nonscreen activities are less likely to be depressed" (Twenge, 2017, p. 82).

iDepression

We are witnessing an epidemic of depression striking our nation in recent years, especially hard hit has been the iGeners. *Depression* is a severe condition carrying with it potentially devastating consequences.

Although underlying symptomology tends to be shared (e.g., tearfulness, sleep disturbance, poor concentration, eating disturbance, pain, and suicide ideation) ranging in intensity and duration, there are several specific diagnostic types of mood disorders (e.g., disruptive mood dysregulation disorder, major depressive disorder, or persistent depressive disorder) according to the American Psychiatric Association ([APiA], 2013). For example, *major depressive disorder* (MDD) is often diagnosed by professionals when over a two-week period of time, consuming a person with feelings of hopelessness, expresses no interest in pursuing pleasurable activities (i.e., sex), has experienced a change in weight from over/under eating; has experienced insomnia/hypersomnia most days, fatigued, expresses/feels a high degree of worthlessness about himself or herself, cannot focus concentration on tasks like work or school, and experiences recurrent thoughts of death and/or suicide (APiA, 2013).

There has been a surge in the incidence rates for MDD amongst *adolescents* and *young adults*.[37] According to the National Survey on Drug Use & Health, there has been a 26% increase in MDD for adolescents and 11% increase for young adults since 2005[38] (cited in Mojabai, Olfson & Han, 2016), with adolescent girls witnessing a 27.6% increase and boys experiencing 23.5% increase over this period of time. What is also rather sobering about these figures is additional data flanking these numbers. Mojabai et al. point out that "the proportion of adolescence… who received mental health counseling or treatment in the past 12 months for their depression from any provider did

---

[37] Although these terms are often used interchangeably, in this instance, their use is more formal. An *adolescent* is referring to someone between the ages of 12 and 20-years old; whereas, a *young adult* applies to someone between the ages of 21 and 25-years old.

[38] This study is based on annual survey results taken between 2005 and 2014. The subjects may or may not have been diagnosed with MDD, but based on their responses to the questions on the survey, a diagnosis may be warranted. The report showed changes in adolescents rose from 8.7% to 11.3% and for young adults from 8.6% to 9.6%. For non-Hispanic girls, the statistical increase went from 13.1% to 17.3% but for boys, the changes were less dramatic, 4.5% to 5.7%; however, the percent difference is not too far apart: 26.6% for girls and 23.5% for boys.

not significantly change over the 2005 to 2014 period" (2016, p. 6). In other words, we know incidence rates for mental health diagnoses can be influenced by several environmental factors (i.e., the disorder is positively portrayed in a movie by a glamorous Hollywood star; Liebert, 2017). This data is based on undiagnosed symptoms, rather than in newly diagnosed cases. Moreover, the rise in these statistics is nearly consistent with historical differences we see between males and females. Females are diagnosed at higher rates with depressive disorders than are males. Even more alarming is the increase our nation is witnessing in suicide rates for this age group. Between the years 2000 and 2016, there has been a 30% increase in suicides for the overall US population (Hedegaard, 2018). Alarm truly sets in when analyzing this data based on younger age cohorts. Females between the ages of 10 and 14-years have experienced a 165% increase in suicide, and males in the same age cohort have experienced a 73% increase. The numbers are also striking for those between the ages of 15 and 24-years (females at 93% and males at 35%).

Table 8.1, Changes in suicide rates (Hedegarrd, 2018)

Age Group	Year 1999	Year 2017	Percent Increase
Female			
10-14	0.50	1.70	165%
15-24	3.00	5.80	93%
Male			
10-14	1.90	3.30	73%
15-25	16.80	22.70	35%

Although there has been much attention given to the claim mood disorders such as MDD along with other mental illnesses are the result of failed neurobiological factors, this claim is not empirically validated. To suggest the cause for depression is from a sort of disruption within the ebb and flow of neurotransmitters comprising our brain chemistry is merely stating a theory for which there are a host of other widely supported theories within the professions of psychiatry and clinical psychology. For example, *cognitive behavioral therapy* (CBT) rests on the assumption that depression is the result of faulty thinking. How one interprets an event mediates how one both feels and behaves. Such interpretations are ongoing and, over time, influence our day-to-day belief systems. The objective for the psychotherapist practicing CBT is to point out to the patient his or her dysfunctional cognitive beliefs, directly challenge it, and revise it by adopting a healthier cognitive point of view. For example, *dichotomous thinking* refers to such a faulty belief system; here, the patient sees no middle ground, and all positions fall onto the extreme sides. (e.g., *If I don't get any "likes" on this selfie I just posted in the next 60 seconds, I must be as ugly as a badger's butt!*) Another example of a false belief system is *mind-reading*, which occurs when the patient draws conclusions based on his or her belief on what others are thinking, feeling, or believing. (e.g., *If he doesn't ask me out to the prom, then he's not at all interested in me.*) Another example is *catastrophizing*, which occurs when self-evaluating minor challenges to the extreme, carry grave consequences. (e.g., *If I fail this trig quiz, I'll probably fail the entire class and will not get into a decent college and have to spend the rest of my life cleaning out portable toilets in the heat of the summer at construction sites.*)

Research demonstrates a host of factors influencing depression which lie far outside neurobiological boundaries. It is not merely an older generation that is out of touch or attempting to impose their 1980-90s standards on their teenagers and young adults when suggesting to disconnect from social media. Social media engagement does appear to be related to a lifestyle exposing younger folks to elevated risk for depression and suicide. Screen interaction is not actual socialization. Screen interaction does not improve feelings of loneliness and overall isolation. Non-screen time refers to healthier social interaction. Consider what is represented here in Table 8.2. The most significant risk factor associated with depression is having a negative school experience, and having parents who are less engaged with their children. Moreover, the data seems to suggest a positive correlation between actual socialization and human engagement and having a lower risk for depression.

Table 8.2, Analysis of MDD predictors (Lu, 2019)

Variable	Type	Percentage
Sex	Boy	5.4
	Girl	16.5
Age	12-13	6.4
	14-15	11.6
	16-17	14.1
Household Income	<$20,000	10.6
	>$75,000	10.5
Father in Household	Yes	10.4
	No	12.0
Mother in Household	Yes	10.7
	No	12.3
Race	White	11.4
	Hispanic	11.0
	Black	8.4
	Asian	9.5
	Other	12.5
Siblings in Household	Yes	9.9
	No	11.8
Authoritative Parent Style	High	8.9
	Low	21.6
School Experience	Positive	8.7
	Negative	22.3

The Problem of Marital Intimacy

The first attachments we form with our primary caregiver, which is often our mother, is vital. As Harlow observed, we enter into this world with a need to attach to another, and as Harlow's research demonstrates, in the absence of an actual mother, we will attach to just about anything, even a sock-doll monkey. This need for connection to another is innate. As Bowlby's (1969) research went on to suggest, when a healthy attachment is provided to us, meaning our caregiver is sensitive and responsive to our needs, we develop a sense of trust in our caregiver that she or he will be available to us when we most need their love and attention. Hazan and Shaver (1987) go on to argue that we take these good childhood experiences and project them onto our adult relationships when forming a trusting and loving bond with a mate. However, if these early childhood experiences have been poorly established, characterized by insensitivity, fears of abandonment, and rejection establishing healthy, significant relationships with another in our adult life may become compromised.

The committed relationship we share with our mate is the most intimate of all relationships, meaning it is the one genuine relationship that permits a degree of respite from the pain of our existential isolation. The novice to love initially falls into the trap believing *love*, or in this instance, being *in love* is the remedy to our feelings of loneliness, being misunderstood, and always vulnerable to this cold world. The poison tainted on the tip of Cupid's arrow peddles to us a promise to which no street drug dealer pushing their product in the 7-Eleven parking lot could ever begin to match. Falling in love results in a complete and total collapse of, what M. Scott Peck (1978) describes as our *ego boundaries*. This state of being *in love* now takes the form of a mystical juice that completes us. More than the psychostimulant offering the cognitive focus necessary to earn the grade on the exam, or the performance enhancement compound ensuring victory on the field, being in love now offers a state of permanence to those momentary sparks of insight we all have from time-to-time of Nirvana. The boundaries separating each of us from reality collapse, the entire world is now possible. *We do not need money to survive; all we need is each other! I do not need rehab to treat my addiction; I just need your love.* Alas, this description is not to belittle and trivialize these incredible feelings, if so fortunate, we have experienced. Falling in love is necessary for what is to come next. As Peck explains:

> The temporary loss of ego boundaries involved in falling in love and in sexual intercourse not only leads us to make commitments to other people from which real love may begin but also gives us a fore-taste of (and therefore an incentive for) the more lasting mystical ecstasy that can be ours after a lifetime of love. As such, therefore, while falling in love is not itself love, it is a part of the great and mysterious scheme of love. (1978, p. 97)

Love is not made in the bedroom; instead, love is made through the intimacy of trusted disclosure where our isolation exposes us to our mate. Again, consider the words of psychiatrist and Holocaust survivor Viktor Frankl:

> A thought transfixed me: for the first time in my life I saw the truth as it is set into song by so many poets, proclaimed as the final wis-dom by so many thinkers... I understood how a man who has noth-ing left in this world still may know bliss, be it only for a brief mo-ment, in the contemplation of his beloved. In a position of utter des-olation, when man cannot express himself in positive action, when his only achievement may consist in ensuing sufferings in the right way—an honorable way—in such a position man can, through lov-ing contemplation of the image he carries of his beloved, achieve fulfillment. (1959, p. 48-49)

Love results in a committed relationship with our mate as a result of deliberate effort and work. Harry Harlow was mistaken at first to con-clude all that is necessary for healthy attachment to occur is touch. He was mistaken to the same degree as anyone who believes good sex is all that is necessary to sustain a healthy, loving relationship between partners. Nevertheless, Harlow was not entirely wrong either; touch is important, sexual, and non-sexual touching alike. All forms of touch communicate intimacy, as this is the only tangible way we can connect to another person. Sex, of course, is the most intimate way we touch and physically connect to another person. This certainly explains why fidelity, trusted exclusive sexual commitment to one's partner, is an essential element to most paired relationships. Psychotherapists routinely explore sexuality with the couples they work with who are experiencing a crisis. Talking to couples about their sex is often an effective way of looking at the actual problems occurring with intimacy and trust, even if they are not seeking help with their sex life. St. Augustine referred to our eyes as "the windows to the soul." Yet, most married couples keep their eyes closed during sex. Only 43% of married couples prefer having sex with the lights on, stating feelings of uncomfortableness, shyness, and embarrassment as reasons for the cloak of darkness (Ben-Ze'ev, 2019). These statistics are suggestive to the degree couples genuinely wish to be exposed both physically and psychologically to their partner.[39]

Self-disclosure, in turn, self-exposure, is also a primary building block for fostering intimacy in relationships. Ira Reiss (1988), using the example of a turning wheel to demonstrate this concept, suggests in the first stage, we develop a rapport with another by cultivating a sense of comfortableness with each other, and a mutual desire to deepen the relationship. This leads to the second stage of self-revelation. Partners start to share their more intimate thoughts, feelings, and worries with each other.[40] This, in turn, results in deepening their relationship with each other, as sharing such intimacies only occurs with special people

---

[39] There is also a point that must be made here as it relates to the topic of sex, especially sex within marriage. Each sexual encounter is not always motivated for the same reason. As the acclaimed author, psychologist, and sex therapist David Schnarch (2009) bluntly put it, sometimes we want to make love to our partner, while other times we just want to F#@&! In other words, it would be a mistake to assume couples seek and consent to sex with their partner just for one purpose only; regardless, intimacy should at times serve as one of these purposes.

[40] This idea has been confirmed time and again. Most recently, Sarkisian and Gerstel's (2016) research showed how single adults are more likely than married adults to stay in touch with, provide help to, and receive help from their parents, siblings, neighbors, and friends, suggesting we are more likely to turn to our spouse to meet our needs than other persons who make up our social networks.

in our lives. This now takes us to the third stage, where we describe our emotional connection to the other person as love or being *in love* with him or her. Ego boundaries collapse, and all the world becomes possible. Consistent with M. Scott Peck's insights, this is a necessary stage if the relationship continues to cultivate to the fourth and final stage where real intimacy now begins to take root. This intimacy reflects "needs which, as they are fulfilled, express the closeness and privacy of the relationship shared. For example, the need for emotional support and sympathy are expressions of the underlying need for intimacy. We have other needs, but they are not related to intimacy and are thus less relevant for explaining love relationships" (Reiss, 1988, p. 102).

Essential to self-disclosure is trust. Our partner needs to keep it secret, referring primarily to intimate secrets. The human psyche is a complex phenomenon and may extend to deep places which—if you believe the tale Sigmund Freud was suggesting—there are even parts of the psyche that are too deep for one ever wholly to come to terms knowing about himself or herself. Not all self-disclosure is intimate. I might have no qualms letting anybody and everybody know I would love for my next automobile purchase to be a Jeep Gladiator but would be very hesitant to share my lifelong dream of buying a cowboy hat, moving out west and joining the Wyoming Water Ballerina Troop (of which only one of these disclosures is true). Intimate disclosures must be honored, and its secrecy kept by our partner. Such a violation of trust serves as a poignant reminder of just how alone we are in the world; by exposing our vulnerable flank, we risk degrading future opportunities to build intimacy in our relationship. For instance, the concept of the *work-spouse* has, in recent years, become part of our modern lexicon, referring to a growing trend where a collegial office relationship becomes an emotionally intimate relationship but not a physically intimate relationship. We begin to share those deeper self-disclosures to the work-spouse that ought to be reserved for the actual spouse.

Intimate relations build through acts of commitment which extend far beyond sexual fidelity. Inherent in such commitment is the belief in the other's trust, faithfulness, loyalty, and unwavering support. I will laugh at my wife's joke when sitting around a table with friends, even if it is not at all funny. She will agree with my analysis of the event around the same table, even if it makes absolutely no sense to her. Commitment always means publically taking your partner's side. At those awful times when despair inflicts our partner, we go to them, and we know our partner will come to us in like moments. Much for the same reasons, our partner can depend on us to lie to them about how lovely their new haircut looks.

Getting right to the point, intimate relationships matter. Even more to the point, marriage matters! Not all intimate relationships are the same, meaning not all intimate relationships can offer the same degree of rewards and benefits. To be clear, this is not a moral statement suggesting that some types of intimate relationships are bad or wrong and, therefore, should be avoided. Such stones are most certainly left unturned in this discussion. Instead, the suggestion here is one where the benefits in which intimacy can enrich our lives are most likely to be found in a marriage. Marriage is different from other ways in which couples may choose to pair themselves. Therefore, the costs, as well as the benefits to marriage, differ accordingly, too. There is no better way to arrange two people that yields more value from such an arrangement than from marriage. Married people, for instance, report higher levels of happiness, lower rates of mental illness, are better off financially, have children more likely to complete high school and less likely to be convicted of a juvenile crime, less likely to be the victim of domestic violence (especially women), and have a longer life expectancy (especially men) than those who are single, dating, or cohabitating (Waite & Gallagher, 2000).

Nonetheless, this is a book on social problems, not a book on making a case for marriage. Instead, the topic of marriage is being addressed here as it relates to an emerging social problem, and this point, our society has experienced a significant shift in the proportion of adults who are not married. During the 1960s, 31% of the adult US population was unmarried, and today about 45% of the adult population is unmarried (Jackson, 2018). To the extent marriage offers greater opportunity to cultivate benefits of intimacy, the adult population is now more estranged from these marital benefits.

Declining Marriage Signifies Declining Intimacy

It was sometime in the early 1980s the US divorce rate hit its height with about 5.5 per 1,000 in the population experiencing a divorce. After that, the statistic appeared to fall at a steady pace, and by 2009 it was now at 3.4 per 1,000 in the population (Cox & Demmitt, 2014). This might seem to suggest we were learning from the mistakes made in our past. Finally, a statistic to celebrate. Not so fast! At the same time, social scientists saw some other trends co-occurring, which might muddy the waters. For instance, couples are now waiting much longer to get married. It was once considered the norm to graduate from high school and get married; otherwise, graduate from high school, go to college, and then get married. The average age of first marriage for men was once 23-years back in 1950 and increased to 29-years of age in 2015; for women, it was 20-years of age in 1950, and 2015 increased to 27-years of age (Jackson, 2018). Therefore, if couples are waiting longer to get married, it suggests couples experience fewer years overall of married life, and—obviously—if there are fewer people in the population who are married, there are going to be fewer of them who are divorced. The logic is as simple as knowing that your chances of ever being bitten by a rattlesnake go down as you spend less time in the woods and more time on the New York City sidewalks.

Moreover, today, we are seeing purposefully more people deciding to stay single permanently; they never want to be married (DePaulo,

2014).[41] Several factors may be influencing this trend. We are now witnessing more women than men who are completing a bachelor's degree, suggesting women are not as interested in marrying men who have obtained less education or have less income than they do. In other words, women today have a *marriage market*[42] with fewer eligible men to choose from than they once had in the past. Still, even if there may be a growing population of never-married adults who are not interested in establishing such relationships now or even sometime in the future, most adults want to be married at some point in their life (Pepping, MacDonald & Davis, 2018). Based on the psychological literature, the desire to be married suggests a healthy goal to have. Recent research indicates it is unhealthy to be single in the long term. Single people experience higher rates of insomnia, anxiety, and depression (Adamczyk, 2017). Single people are more likely to postpone making major decisions in their life due to anticipating the possible effect it might have on a future (but yet to be identified) spouse (Jackson, 2018).

---

[41] Approximately 27% of all households consisted of adults living alone in 2010 compared to 17.1% in 1970, with the majority of those being women, according to the US Census Bureau (2011).

[42] It is just a mistake to say that we find our mate out of an *ocean* of opportunity. Instead, the opportunity to find a mate is directed towards designated shelves in the *marriage market*. For example, when women are looking for husbands, they are less likely to marry down in age; whereas, men who are looking for wives are more likely to be open to the prospect of marrying a woman who is significantly younger than he is. Again, women looking for husbands do not tend to be as attracted to men who are less educated and earn less money than she does. None of us are that interested in finding a spouse who devoutly believes in a faith that differs from our devout beliefs. You see, we shop for potential spouses in markets, not oceans.

Figure 8.1, Age of first marriage for men and women (US Census Bureau, 2018)

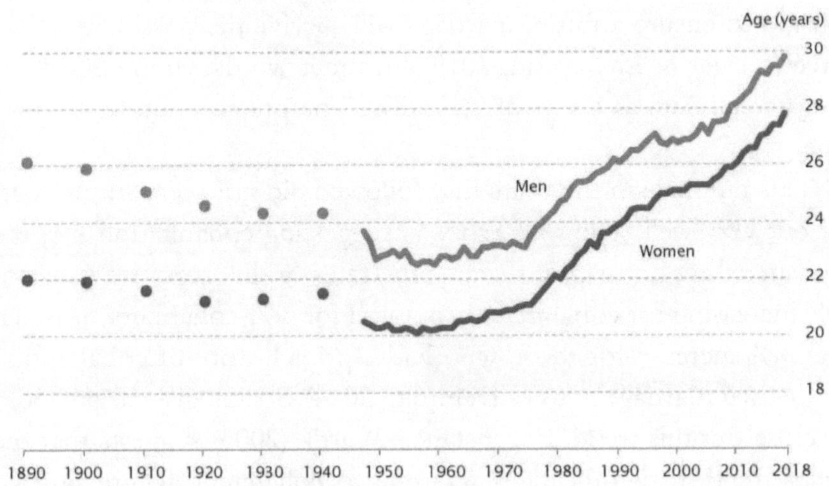

Also, divorce rates have probably been trending downward, in part, due to the exponential increase we have witnessed in *cohabitation* rates going up. The progressive trend has been for couples who would otherwise be able to consent to legally marrying each other, instead opting to move in together and reside with their partner.[43] We have seen a 29% increase in cohabitation rates in the decade following 2007, with roughly half of all cohabiters falling under the age of 35 (Stepler, 2017). Again, the height of the US divorce rate took place during the early 1980s and about 20 years later we then saw a spike in cohabitation rates go way up, and these rates have continued to rise in the years that have followed, suggesting the trend started with a goal in mind: to protect a future marriage from divorce. These folks experienced first-hand their parents' divorce and never wanted to experience divorce for themselves in their marriages. Most never-before-

---

[43] Most of the research on cohabitation is based on heterosexual relationships. Do not assume there is bias taking place. Only recently has legal marriage for homosexual couples had been established in many states. The option of marriage over cohabitation was not legally available as it has been for heterosexual couples. It is for this reason the available data is based primarily on heterosexual cohabitation.

married cohabiters enter into the relationship with the idea it will allow each of them to more effectively assess the overall quality of the relationship to ensure a future marriage will survive the possibility of divorce (Geiger & Livingston, 2019). In other words, young-20-somethings cohabitate as a sort of "test drive" before committing to marriage.

This rationale in the years that followed did not seem to prove itself out very well. The research was suggesting cohabitation had the opposite effect on marital success; the rates of divorce were substantially increasing for cohabiters than it was for non-cohabiters, as much as a 50% increase for those who had a prior history of cohabitation before their marriage (Cox & Demmitt, 2014). Sociologists began looking closely at this trend. For instance, Wartik (2005) suggests that the higher trend in divorce rates was due to cohabiters' failure on two fronts. First, these couples began cohabitating with partners who were "good enough to live with" but "not yet good enough to marry." For instance, take out a lined sheet of blank paper. Now start writing down the minimal qualities of a person whom you would ever consider marrying (i.e., age, intellect, attractiveness, income, humor, and so forth). Now go ahead and flip that sheet of paper over and write down the minimum qualities of a person whom you would ever consider cohabitating with as a partner. Wartick is suggesting the list is longer for marriage. In other words, we are more likely to settle on a possible cohabiter than we would for a prospective spouse. This is how the process begins. In time, as increasing levels of age, education, and income continue to decrease the possible pool of eligible marrying partners, and as we get subtle (and perhaps even direct) pressure from friends and family that it is time to marry, we do so with that person who may not have made the list to start with.

Second, these high divorce rates may be the result of failing to engage in real marital commitment. Cohabitation is, after all, based on a compromise, while marriage is based on a promise. Cohabitation starts with the idea if the "going gets tough, I can just leave at any time," but in marriage, "I have to see this problem through. What other option do I have?" The term *commitment* is too often used too lightly. It is not based on signing a 12-month lease with someone or sharing the expense of a new couch together; it refers to a pledge, allegiance, and faithful loyalty which binds the two together thoroughly. I am not attempting to be overly optimistic with the use of the term, appreciating the topic of marriage began here by looking at divorce rates and understanding that not all marriages that survive are happy-marriages.[44] I am a pragmatist and understand some marriages stay together just to see the game through to determine the winner after someone dies first. Nevertheless, marriage is a commitment, and we do see married folks more likely to be engaging in committing behavior over those who cohabitate. Go ahead and ask 100 people who are married (not 50 couples) and who are the same age, let us say 30-years-old if they share with their spouse a 30-year commitment on a mortgage, invest in a retirement account together, or named their spouse as the beneficiary on a life insurance policy. Now ask these same questions to 100 people (not 50 couples), who are also 30-years-old but who are cohabitating these same questions. You will see a different number of responses when directly asked about committing behaviors. Married people are more like to engage in such practices.

Again, the intention of this discussion on declining marriage rates is not to advocate for the importance of marriage and persuade folks from abstaining from cohabitation, but rather point out a possible adverse effect declining marriage rates may have on society. With less marriage, this discussion has suggested there is less opportunity to experience deep intimate connections with another and allowing feelings of isolation to fester. To this end, marriage matters.

---

[44] An old man walks into court with his attorney. The judge asks what's the matter he wishes to bring to the Court's attention. The old man says, "I want a divorce!" The judge sees just how old and infirmed the man looks as his walker supports him as he stands. "How many years have you been married?" the judge asks. To which the old man replies, "Fifty-eight years as of last month." Now more confused than ever, the judge asks, "Why do you want a divorce after being married for so many years?" The old man starts to shake in his walker, face red, he screams, "I JUST CAN'T TAKE IT ANY MORE!"

Isolation in Higher Education

"They'll show up if you offer them free pizza." Over twenty years of sitting in on college meetings trying to come up with innovative ideas for getting students to show up for an informational session on the upcoming study abroad trip, discussion on the ongoing internship we offer at the local veterans' homeless shelter, and so forth, it comes down to food. College students love pizza, especially when it is free! Some things never change; then again, some things have changed so very much on the college campus. Social change—in and of itself—certainly does not constitute a social problem, but systemic change that fundamentally affects the way education is constructed, engaged, delivered, and assessed may nudge towards experiencing a social problem, especially if these changes are estranging us ever further from each other and increasing our sense of isolation. To this point, two trends have been slowly fermenting over the last decade and a half in higher education which is decreasing our opportunity for meaningful social interaction, thereby contributing to an increase in social isolation.

First, today's college students are concerned about their grades. They are overly concerned about their grades. True, students who attended Aristotle's Lyceum in Ancient Greece were concerned about their grades, too, but I am suggesting this is probably all students are concerned with in their classes today. Everything is driven extrinsically towards the next upcoming exam. Should an event occur in the news that happens to be related to an idea discussed in class, and the professor attempts to explore this connection with students, this almost always results in the inevitable professor-cringing question: "Will we need to know about this on next week's exam?"

Also, forget controversy in the classroom. About the only debate left these days is when the final grade is 89.5%. This latter point may be related to developmental changes with this current generation of students, where they bring to the discussion less self-confidence and fear over being declared on the wrong side of the issue (Twenge, 2017). Second, the steady trend has been to move away from the traditional brick-and-mortar classroom in favor of the virtual classroom, typically referred to as *distance education*. Babson Survey Research Group (2016), reveals distance student enrollments had increased every year since 2012 when they first began keeping track of the data, with the most recent gain showing over 30% of all higher education students are now taking at least one class online. Growth, however, was uneven; public institutions grew by 7.3%, private non-profit institutions by 7.1%, while private for-profit institutions had their distance enrollments decline by 4.5%. "The growth of distance enrollments has been relentless," explains the study's co-author, Julia E. Seaman; the rate of online enrollment has "gone up when the economy was expanding, when the economy was shrinking, when overall enrollments were growing, and now when overall enrollments are shrinking." The report shows that the number of students studying on a physical campus has dropped by over one million (1,173,805, or 6.4%) between 2012 and 2016. Some of the data from this report are rather sobering. For instance, public institutions command the most considerable portion of distance education students (67.8 %); these enrollments are highly concentrated, as 5% of institutions account for almost half of all distance education students; 52.8% of all students who took at least one distance course also took a course on-campus; online enrollments remain local: 56.1% of those who took only distance courses reside in the same state as the institution at which they enrolled. Additionally, international online education is not an actual phenomenon, as international distance enrollments only represent 0.7% of all distance students located outside of the United States.

Likewise, the academy has been responding to this trend too. As the economy has continued to improve in the years following the Great Recession, college enrollment has declined somewhat, leaving colleges and universities scrapping amongst each other for their fair share of the pie, referring to student enrollment. Schools are promising their customers an effective, streamlined curriculum that will not clutter up the path towards graduation and degrees. To this end, today, more emphasis is being placed on measuring the course's *Major Learning Outcomes* (MLOs) than on those other qualitative aspects of the course, which once played somewhat greater importance. For example, a new stamp of approval is having online courses credentialed through *Quality Matters* (QM), which is a non-profit organization that has established a rubric for reviewing MLOs for online courses ensuring the course measures and assesses the student on all MLOs. QM adopts…

> core principles to create a culture of continuous improvement, …[appreciating] keeping learners engaged is different in online courses. Getting them past the 'packaging'—the mechanics of the course—so they can focus on content and learning objectives can be a challenge. That is where our research-based Rubrics and Standards really shine: they provide objective, evidence-based ways to evaluate the components of online learning. The commitment? It is significant. The impact? Substantial! (QM, 2016, n.p.)

Students are, in turn, responding positively to this reorientation to isolating the MLOs as the essential purpose for taking the course. A recent study by Hanover Research (2017) reports 60% of students feel that online learning has improved their grades, and 61% of students feel the online modality is either "extremely" or "very" helpful in preparing for exams. The same report is also suggesting that students find online instruction is improving their studying efficacy by reducing the amount of time required for studying.

The Hanover Research study also reports a revealing and striking trend: online courses are "not strongly associated with student-to-student interaction" (2017, n.p.). Moreover, the report did not speak of student-to-faculty interaction other than to point out "students are overwhelmingly likely to use email to contact professors" (n.p.). From the faculty perspective, online instruction from start to finish is grading, grading, and more grading. For faculty, assessing MLOs is the norm. From the students' perspective, however, online courses do have the familiar feel of the *independent study* courses from back in my generation, where over the summer, our professor might give us a reading list and assign writing topics that were then returned at the end of the term. Even when online courses require making a *reply* following the student's *post* to another student's post, the replies are formulaic where all the correct rhetoric is used, demonstrating online civility over actual critical thinking, debate, and discussion. For example, a fellow student replies and comments to another student's post:

> I respect not everyone views this issue as I do. We all bring our unique life experiences to a topic such as the one we've been exploring in this week's module. I appreciate reading your thoughts, as I find them to be eye-opening and so valuable to me as I come to terms with what my true position ought to be on this very important topic our professor has guided us through this week.

At all costs, avoid using ALL CAPS in any reply! Reading the class transcript from this week's post assignment, where post follows by reply, is as if we are replacing "real and actual" relationships with "as if" relationships.

I once took a group of students to The Hague for a Model United Nations (UN) competition serving not as faculty but more as a chaperone. One of my students, whom I will refer to as Billy, became overwhelmed with anxiety when he learned most of the students competing from the other schools were either graduate students or law students. "I do not even have a bachelor's degree; how am I expected to compete against all these other people?" We spent many hours in the hotel's lobby going over his presentation. Although I found the fact the UN competition was taking place in one of the actual courtrooms used by the International Court of Criminal Justice to be more intimidating, Billy overlooked this fact and continued to be anxious about his presentation; even once he completed it, he continued to go on second-guessing himself. His group, however, took second place in the event, and Billy was one of only three students awarded the opportunity to come back to serve as one of the program's facilitators for next year's Model UN competition. I got to know Billy over the week.

He grew up poor and worked a night shift at a liquor store to help support his disabled mother and younger brother. Billy never believed he would achieve more in life than, perhaps, becoming a manager of a liquor store. I received a short email from Billy about a year ago. Such notes always begin with, "I am sure you do not remember me…" but go on to say, "I'll be graduating from law school next week… Thank you." Of course, I remember Billy, but I honestly cannot remember even three names of students who are currently taking my online class that I just finished grading work from just three hours ago.

To be clear, at no time in this discussion am I suggesting learning does not occur through online pedagogy, or the quality of learning acquired using online instruction is inferior to that of face-to-face classroom instruction. Students most certainly learn through online instruction. Our discussion, instead, is addressing the latent concern of human interaction and socialization.

Jim Dean, Sharon Masters, Douglas Harper, and Carl Davis were some of my previous faculty who made a difference in my life, not just my professional direction, but in my life. Jim Dean, who was also the minister of the church I attended, taught my first college class and the first A I ever earned in college. Trust me, earning that first A means everything; otherwise, it is no more than an anxious idea. I stopped by Dr. Master's office to ask if she might write a letter of recommendation for graduate school. I rambled and said something to the effect I was not sure if I would be able to handle graduate school. She smirked (pointing out some smirks are good). Dr. Harper routinely had us meet at his house for our sociological theories class and would cook each of us omelets (along with cold beer) as we discussed Weber and Durkheim. These relationships mattered. To this day, I believe it is the relationship that "teaches," not the book, rubric, or online platform. Not to the same degree as marital relationships, but the relationships we form with some of our teachers along the way are deeply personal. We come to the college campus bringing with us our hopes and dreams for the future. For many of us, this is the place where we start to carve out from these hopes and dreams an actual reality. The process exposes our vulnerability, and the connections we make with others are essential. In my teaching, I try to let students know when I pass them in the hallway, "Excellent job on that paper; I am so proud of you!" or "Much better job on that second quiz. I can tell you are studying more." I want students to know their teacher thinks of them, not just the MLOs for the course. College today is stressful, expensive, and the vending machines always seem to be sold out of Pop-Tarts and Red Bull, but it is nice for students to know they are not alone.[45]

---

[45] When the end of our career looms out there closer than the start of it does in the rearview mirror, thoughts on what the future will bring may oftentimes start to sour. My own fear concerning the future of higher education centers around *Massive Open Online Courses* (MOOCs), which are essentially a "Skinner box-like" classroom with sometimes thousands of students swarming around in it. The course is primarily self-paced, as well as self-taught without a professor leading students or even an available resource for students, as faculty are not part of the MOOC. Once the objectives for the module are achieved, the next module opens for the student to move onto. MOOCs are cheap, and their efficacy is based entirely on how "outcome" is operationalized. If success is limited to achieving a minimum of 70% of the MLOs, then MOOCs are effective. But, ignore my earlier comments that learning does take place through means of online instruction. Here, the nature of MOOC instruction differs substantially, as the focus for online instruction as it exists in the higher education's curriculum today is on building tools for critical thinking and enriching the student's knowledge base, especially the capacity to think "freely." For MOOCs this is not the case; within this educational world, the focus is on "training." Consider for moment, how companies (not schools) offer their employees "training," not "education."

As the current debate on free universal college deepens, and questions begin to center around costs, our nation could actually offer an associate's degree (2-year degree) at an overall minimal cost through MOOCs. But, would such a degree have any actual value, and if so, where would such market value be found? To this question, perhaps, universally free MOOC degrees would basically establish a two-tiered educational system. The elite, private colleges and universities, with their dorms and faculty-based instruction, would provide bourgeoisie degrees offering this tier of the society access to upper-class careers and lifestyles, while MOOC-based degrees would limit graduates to the rungs of the working-class in both income and lifestyle. Effectively MOOC degrees become the new certificate for the "proletariat" class. Correct, I am suggesting a move towards MOOC education only works in a two-class social system where, in this case, there is effectively no longer a middle-class.

Summary

This chapter has pointed out our innate psychosocial need to connect to others. Socialization is required if we want to avoid loneliness, depression, anxiety, and the like. Socialization is the only effective means available to us for addressing our existential isolation in this world. When we connect intimately with our spouse, personally engage in our education, and exchange screen-time for face-time, we are committing ourselves to others and cutting through the angst of our isolation and able to experience our inalienable right for happiness.

This chapter has also shown how this innate need is being challenged and compromised to such an extent as to identify this as an emerging social problem. We are exchanging face-time with screen-time and removing actual human contact in the process. We are replacing the commitment and intimacy of marriage with other, less intimate relationships predicated on less commitment between partners. We are replacing our physical presence and interaction in social institutions like the college classroom and in doing so, manipulating the focus to experience measurable outcomes over socially intrinsic needs.

The chapter which follows takes what has been discussed here to the next level of analysis. The human connection may cut through feelings of loneliness and isolation, but so what! It matters not unless there is a reason for it all. Going out for a picnic in the park to forget about your problems is merely ignoring the facts: there is no money in the account, and the landlord is evicting you tomorrow. Human connection and intimacy only matter if there is some actual meaning in life to be had from it.

9   **Social Meaning**

Several years ago, the Florida Legislature placed a cap limiting the number of credit hours a resident could accumulate while pursuing a bachelor's degree utilizing the in-state tuition rate. Once exceeding this limit, set only a modest amount required above what is necessary for a bachelor's degree, students then must pay the out-of-state tuition rate. Clearly, the state's intent was to reign in escalating education expenses. After all, why should the state bare the cost for an 18-year old student entering college to become a criminal forensic anthropologist who then changes his academic major the following year, now intent to become an art therapist, but again changes his major before the midterm to astrologic physics with an emphasis in deep space proton reactions? It can quickly become expensive for a state to underwrite some of the tuition expenses associated with changing one's major. Nevertheless, changing one's mind and pursuing different academic interests is rather typical for young college students as they attempt to find their life's meaning. Neither criticism nor praise on this new legislation, merely an observation pointing out that the state is now placing greater emphasis for first-year college students to quickly identify their academic *purpose* over the potentially more expensive alternative of finding their life's *meaning*.

Our purpose typically is operationalized on our job description. *Purpose* refers to what we have been tasked to accomplish, which might be to sell cars, study and pass exams, grade exams, clean the house, and so forth. Purpose refers to the roles we each perform. *Meaning*, on the other hand, implies a more profound existential connotation; it gets to the reason *why* we function this way, versus that way, or any other way our aim should so choose. Once identified, meaning as it applies to one's life holds great significance and importance, which may be cherished even more than one's own life. However, here lies the existential philosopher's plight: acknowledging we have *free will* means, in turn, also acknowledges there is an inherent plan embedded into the human fabric directing us towards our life's meaning. *Meaning* then is only what we each make of it. Albert Camus referred to this plight—having to exist in a world where we seek so desperately to find meaning in life for our self, yet there is no true meaning to be had—as *absurd*, and maybe best explored in his *Myth of Sisyphus* (1955) who was cursed by the gods to roll a rock up a mountain only to be faced with the same task at the start of each and every day for all eternity.

> I leave Sisyphus at the foot of the mountain! One always finds one's burden again. But Sisyphus teaches the higher fidelity that negates the gods and raises rocks. He too concludes that all is well. This universe henceforth without a master seems to him neither sterile nor futile. Each atom of that stone, each mineral flake of that night-filled mountain, in itself forms a world. The struggle itself toward the heights is enough to fill a man's heart. One must imagine Sisyphus happy. (Camus, 1955, p. 112)

The horror of knowing we are responsible for making our own life's meaning certainly helps to explain the wanderlust of the college freshmen desperately changing majors akin the bride's equal hope when she asks to try on the next dress. Moreover, for the unlikely few who seem to have found their life's meaning, which also serves as a passion, this may come with its misfortune as well. Few who find meaning in life also seem to manage any reasonable assemblage of balance with it. Such passions can quickly turn on us as compulsive addictions. One only needs to look no further than the artist touched with achieving perfection.

It is the absence of meaning which captures the focus for this chapter. Psychiatrist and Holocaust survivor Viktor Frankl refers to this existential absence in the patient as *Sunday neurosis*, describing it as "that kind of depression which afflicts people who become aware of the lack of content in their lives when the rush of the busy week is over and the void within themselves becomes manifest" (1959, p. 123). When the day is finished, we find all that is left inside of us is boredom, langur, and lassitude. Again, Frankl refers to this as "that kind of depression," suggesting there is something more to it than just a pathological awareness of being sad. It is less of a physical state of being *depressed*, and more like a constant gnawing ennui. The day is over, and we are left with only our empty, hollow self.

To fill this void, we grab onto anything, just as long as it does not remind us of our empty husk of existence, even if it is momentary. Obviously, the answer is not found inside the bottle, but distraction and diversion just might be found inside there, and that is enough. So, we fill out the hours stupefied in pornographic flesh on the computer, even more, alcohol, emotionless relationships, binging through the next Netflix series, earning even more money, eating more food, and perhaps one day we say to our self: *what the hell, it is only heroin!* As a psychiatrist, this is the place Frankl repeatedly started his work with patients, helping them identify some meaning in their lives. Sadly, what lies on the surface may seem so far out of reach is the nearest and most natural thing to grab on to. I remember early in my wife's legal career, an old partner retiring from the firm. He was a widow with few hobbies or interests and retirement was not a good fit for him. He met up with a few of the younger lawyers for lunch, sharing a few stories about the firm from back in the 1970s. My wife suggested he write a history about the law firm, and instantly a reason to get up the next morning was right there in front of him.

Frankl saw Sunday neurosis saturating his midcentury time period. It was everywhere. As we analyze the demographics on rates of depression, addiction, and suicide, there is even more cause for alarm today. It is through this existential lens of meaning our focus will address two trends: the current opioid epidemic, but after the legalization of marijuana has first been explored. Meaning is not just something each of us needs in our personal lives, but meaning—not just purpose—is something a nation needs as well, and an absence of it is clearly a social problem.

Distracted (Marijuana)

"Marijuana does not kill anyone. The worst thing that can happen is for someone to fall asleep if they were to smoke too much." Right? After all, that is the message saturating our society in recent years.[46] There is nothing dangerous about marijuana; in fact, it is a miracle substance with properties to cure everything from diabetes to Alzheimer's disease. Anyone who would suggest otherwise is either a prude who probably never tasted a beer before or is somehow connected to the pharmaceutical industry, concerned THC will be the end to their financial dynasty. Yet, here we are with the topic of marijuana now being explored as a social problem, and not just your run-of-the-mill social problem but an emerging social problem which holds the potential to cause a significant ill effect on our society. The intent here—to be precise—is to identify marijuana in the context of a social problem, not to engage in public service messaging to promote abstinence of its use.[47] Nevertheless, the drug's efficacy and safety need to

---

[46] The perceived harmfulness of marijuana has decreased significantly since 1991, from an estimated 84.0% in 1991 to 53.8% in 2014 (Keys, Wall, Cerdá, et al., 2016).

[47] Again, I never confound my role as an academic with my personal moral footing. Any discussion on drugs is just that, academic. Personally, I have never tried an illegal drug, not even marijuana. Bruce Alexander's theory on drug use, which follows shortly in this chapter, best explains—perhaps—the reason for my abstinence.

be addressed first, as this message is not coming from underneath the high school bleachers today; the message today is based on an organized campaign from Big Business funding tens of millions of dollars to lobbyists to court politicians' votes. The campaign is logical and organized, starting first with decriminalization,[48] followed by legal medicalization, and eventually legalized recreational use.

Marijuana is not safe. Sure, maybe it is safer to smoke marijuana than it is to drink liquid bleach, but that is like suggesting placing a filter on a cigarette makes smoking tobacco as medicinal as eating salmon for dinner tonight. True, it is highly unlikely someone will smoke enough marijuana at one point in time and die from it, but the same can be said for tobacco's safety as well. What is the likelihood of dropping dead from smoking five packs of Marlboro cigarettes in a single day? The risk in tobacco use is not what happens at the moment the product is consumed; it is from what happens later on down the road after ongoing continued use. To the point: marijuana is not safe.

Some of the myths out there today advocating marijuana's efficacy center around various mental health benefits resulting from it, which is also suggested to be less expensive than other more dangerous pharmaceuticals. For instance, there are plenty of websites out there suggesting marijuana is a cure for *Posttraumatic stress disorder* (PTSD),[49] but

---

Nonetheless, I challenge the reader to identify anywhere in this chapter where my personal moral compass reveals itself while engaging the topic of drug use, recreational or otherwise.

[48] A common mistake is to assume decriminalization puts an end to any further need for other restrictions on marijuana use for those seeking to ensure its availability for either medical or recreational purposes. Not true. "Oftentimes, when a person hears the phrase 'decriminalization,' whether it is a drug or a different crime, it is assumed that there are no penalties associated with it. However, that is generally not how marijuana decriminalization laws work. When states enact laws that decriminalize marijuana possession, it means that there will be no resulting jail time for first-time offenses" (Scheft, 2015, p. 122).

[49] PTSD is a psychiatric condition resulting from exposure to a traumatic (meaning horrific) event. Symptoms may include: intrusive memories, nightmares, persistent avoidance of stimuli related to the event, flashbacks, disruption of memory about the event hypervigilance, and exaggerated startle responses (APiA, 2013).

this is not based on actual academic, scholarly research, meaning to suggest it is helpful in the treatment of PTSD is placing the cart well ahead of the horse. As O'Neil, Nugent, Morasco, et al. (2017) report, the academic literature is insufficient to draw such conclusions at this time. More research is needed to reach such a conclusion based on accepted academic standards. However, their exhaustive review of the current body of scholarly research and studies that are still ongoing contraindicates marijuana use for treating PTSD. Those who had no prior history using marijuana until suggested for their PTSD were more likely to show violent behavior and have their PTSD symptoms worsen. Additionally, O'Neil et al.'s (2017) analysis suggest those who use marijuana as a treatment were more likely to be unemployed, less financially stable, and express higher levels of suicide ideation than those non-users also having PTSD. Finally, those medicinal benefits which there is supporting evidence come from the cannabidiol (CBD) element of cannabis, which is not related to the plant's psychoactive properties (Berenson, 2019).

There is—in fact—a growing body of literature to support a causal link between marijuana use and *psychosis*.[50] Today's marijuana is not the same drug as what was being smoked at the *Jethro Tull* concerts back in the 1960s and 1970s, as the concentration of tetrahydrocannabinol (THC)[51] is exponentially stronger today. Back then, THC concentrations were about 2%, and today it is about 25% for the marijuana sold

---

[50] *Psychosis* refers to a break with reality. A person who is psychotic is not able to process information from their surroundings against the ideas taking place in their mind. They often hallucinate, experiencing noises, or voices that are not there. These hallucinations may also be visual, olfactory, or tactile. Delusions are also typical with psychosis were firmly held false beliefs are present. Even when confronted with clear and convincing evidence, the delusion persists. These delusions may be related to persecution (i.e., "The government is plotting to kill me.") or grandeur (i.e., "I have magical powers and can teleport to different planets."). Psychosis is typically a symptom related to schizophrenia, a disease that affects less than 1% of the population (APiA, 2013).

[51] Tetrahydrocannabinol (THC) is the principal psychoactive agent responsible for marijuana's psychological effect (i.e., getting high).

in a legal dispensary (Berenson, 2019). The *Lancet* recently reported scholarly research showing the risk of being psychiatrically treated for a psychotic event increases when both the THC potency and duration of use increases. The stronger the THC concentration, the more likely one is to experience a psychotic event. The longer one continues to use the drug, it becomes more likely one is to experience a psychotic event (DiForti, Quattrone, Freeman et al., 2019). What this study seems to be suggesting: those who already have a genetic predisposition for schizophrenia are elevating their actual risk for developing the disease by exposing themselves to THC. Those who continue to advocate on the safety of marijuana smirk at this unfolding research, suggesting it is just the sequel to *Reefer Madness*,[52] and academia's way to scare people away from using the drug. There is no estimate at this time on the effect marijuana is contributing on incidence rates for a psychotic-related disease like schizophrenia, but it is unlikely these numbers would ever approximate those suggested in *Reefer Madness*, especially when considering lifetime prevalence rates for schizophrenia are less than 1% (APiA, 2013). Nonetheless, suspected risk of homicidal or suicidal reactions from using antidepressant medication—which is far less than 1%—has caused the FDA to now require warnings to be placed on prescription bottles for children and adolescents prescribed this class of medication. If these risks are even at these lower required levels when prescribing antidepressants, the risks associated with marijuana ought to somehow be honestly shared with the consumer as well.

---

[52] Directed by Louis Gasnier, *Reefer Madness* was a 1936 propaganda film intended for teenage audiences with just one purpose: to terrify them into abstinence. The movie suggested that murder, rape, and complete madness (i.e., psychosis) might result from the tail-spinning effects of trying marijuana. The melodramatic acting ensured the movie was seen more like a comedy film, with 80-year old grandmothers—perhaps—the only age group who would have been scared straight from ever trying the drug for the first time if offered to her by some shady-looking guy named Jeff Spicoli at Wednesday's BINGO tournament in the nursing home.

A review of the empirical literature also calls into question popular opinions suggesting that prescribing marijuana as an effective pain-killer without attaching to it the same concerns for abuse and addiction, which is apparent with the use of opioids. Advocates have suggested legalization of marijuana for the treatment of chronic pain can also be an effective way to address the nation's current opioid epidemic. To these points, there is—in fact—scholarly research suggesting marijuana can reduce neuropathic pain, but its benefits tend to last for about four hours with the long term efficacy diminishing in about 15-weeks, while exposing the user to possible elevated risk for adverse cardiovascular effects, testicular cancer, transitional cell cancer, and suicidal behaviors (Nugent, Morasco & O'Neil, 2017). Additionally, the argument that marijuana legalization will naturally benefit the current opioid epidemic is baseless, spurious speculation. As Berenson (2019) explains, some pro-legalization groups started to point out that those states legalizing the medical use of marijuana were reporting fewer deaths from opioid overdoses. The problem with this argument: those states first to legalize medical marijuana were out west, while the opioid epidemic first took root in the east, particularly in the Appalachians. This spurious data corrected itself as the opioid crisis marched westward, and as the legalization of marijuana moved eastward.

The environmental and adverse life-effects from marijuana use are also evident from a review of the empirical literature. The typical user is male, between the ages of 18 and 29-years of age, Hispanic (male)/African-American (female), and residing on the West Pacific Coast of the United States (Kerr, Lui & Ye, 2017). The national trend shows a steady increase in the use of marijuana (see Table 9.1; Kerr et al., 2017), with an overall increase of 79.12% from the years 2000 to 2015, with men representing most of the statistic (67.05% increase). For those between the ages of 18 and 29-years, there has been a 49% increase in use for men and 62.33% increase for women. "The passage of medical marijuana legislation, in particular allowing medical marijuana dispensaries or home growing, under varying policy regimes since 1996, is potentially relevant to marijuana use trends" (Kerr et al., 2017,

p. 473). Studies have shown, with both adolescents and adults, those states with medical marijuana laws in place have higher rates of marijuana use than in those states where the use of the drug is still illegal (Keyes et al., 2016). It is not just more convenient access to the drug that seems to be getting at the root of these numbers. Instead, it is the user's perception of marijuana's safety. As perceived harmlessness from using the drug decreases, the rate of its use increases. The data suggests legalizing medical marijuana use, in turn, supports the belief that marijuana is a safe drug to use. Keyes et al. found a 35.95% change in difference[53] in those who first perceived marijuana as being *unsafe* to now believing the drug to be *safe* following the passage of legalized medical marijuana use.

Table 9.1, Percentage of population reporting any marijuana use in the past year, National Alcohol Survey (Kerr, Lui & Ye, 2017)

YEAR	**2000**	**2004-05**	**2009-10**	**20014-15**
All	7.20%	6.70%	10.20%	12.90%
All male	8.80%	9.10%	13.30%	14.70%
All female	5.70%	4.40%	7.30%	10.60%
By age (yrs)	**Males**			
18–29	19.60%	17.70%	23.20%	29.20%
30–39	8.80%	11.90%	16.20%	14.80%
40–49	7.70%	7.60%	12.90%	11.70%
50–59	3.60%	6.30%	11.20%	11.60%
60+	0.50%	1.50%	1.80%	7.00%
	Females			
18–29	14.60%	12.30%	16.90%	23.70%
30–39	6.90%	3.90%	10.10%	15.00%

---

[53] This value determines the change from one amount to a lesser amount in terms of percent decrease by providing the original quantity followed by the new quantity. The difference is computed by dividing the two quantities and multiplying the result by 100 (% decrease = original value – new value/original value x 100). In this instance, Keyes et al. determined 84.0% of their sample perceived marijuana as harmless in 1991, and then in 2014, 53.8% of the sample now perceived marijuana as safe.

40–49	4.70%	4.50%	6.30%	8.70%
50–59	2.10%	1.80%	4.00%	7.30%
60+	0.00%	0.50%	1.00%	1.90%
By race	**Males**			
White	7.60%	8.80%	13.40%	13.40%
Black	11.20%	16.80%	18.10%	16.40%
Hispanic	12.90%	4.70%	10.10%	19.10%
Others	12.70%	9.90%	11.90%	15.80%
	Females			
White	5.70%	4.50%	8.20%	10.10%
Black	4.70%	4.20%	7.60%	13.40%
Hispanic	5.90%	2.10%	2.80%	9.30%
Others	6.50%	8.80%	5.80%	12.80%
By region	**Males**			
Mid-Atlantic	9.10%	9.20%	10.50%	11.80%
N. Central	7.90%	8.70%	17.60%	13.70%
NEngland	16.60%	11.60%	17.40%	10.50%
Pacific	11.30%	10.90%	17.00%	21.40%
S. Coast	7.50%	7.80%	12.10%	18.30%
South	7.00%	9.00%	8.10%	10.20%
	Females			
Mid-Atlantic	4.70%	4.00%	6.60%	13.10%
N. Central	5.10%	4.40%	8.50%	7.90%
NEngland	8.80%	4.20%	4.70%	13.10%
Pacific	8.10%	7.60%	9.20%	16.40%
S. Coast	5.10%	1.40%	6.70%	8.90%
South	5.00%	5.00%	6.20%	8.60%

These trends showing higher use of the drug along with diminishing societal attitudes that marijuana is harmful appears to be part of a logical and intentional plan being played out by the new marijuana industry which is quickly morphing into the next new Big Business industry similar to that of Big Tobacco and Big Alcohol corporations. Big Marijuana is predicted to reach $44 billion by the year 2020 (Begley, 2016). "Even as commercial marijuana [business] interests try to distance themselves from these other industries, they have admitted to copying approaches…" used by their business predecessors (*Alcoholism Drug Abuse Weekly*, 2016, p. 1). Even beyond employing similar lobbying strategies, Big Marijuana's marketing campaigns are now suggesting other drugs (i.e., cigarettes and alcohol) are more dangerous than theirs is while marketing to younger age populations, "as 19-year-olds buy a lot more stuff than 29-year-olds" (p. 6). They are increasing the potency and decreasing the pricing at the same time. They are downplaying any of the research suggesting their product might be harmful. They are also now dispatching their lobbyists back to the same politicians who they once argued in front of for the need to allow home-growing for personal medical use but to now press for legislation to criminalize for home cultivation of marijuana within a 25-mile radius of any retailer.

Although health risks are present and medicinal benefits weak, marijuana as an emerging social problem centers on the drug's ability to asphyxiate a person's will for finding any meaning in life. Quickly, life's meaning fogs out as the smoker settles on their life's purpose to just being high. The new status takes shape: *pothead*. This title is not being used derogatorily, as it is not an insult; instead, it is a *status* defining anticipated roles. A pothead refers to one who has low social status, little is expected by way of vocation or economic contribution, and minimal trust is given—as there is more of an eye of suspicion directed towards him or her—since the *Reefer Madness* stereotype persists to some degree. Their status requires a level of aloofness, as is always the case with marginalized people, for this is what *stigma*[54] looks like. The

---

[54] *Stigma* does not result from a behavior itself; rather, it refers to the ways a society devalues one as a human being. A person may steal a car, be arrested for the crime, and holds the official title of the thief. Stigma now follows as a community treats this person as something less than a fully intact person, having upon him or her a

pothead exists, at one level or another, on the fringes of society. Maybe he or she works off the books because legitimate employment is not possible. Even if marijuana use is legal, it will still prohibit employment when drug testing is a prerequisite, and no employer entrusts to someone stoned at various points in time throughout the week any real responsibility (i.e., teach a child, oversee the money, or care for the sick). They may refer to themselves as artists or musicians, but they are not gainfully employed, living either with gaggles of like friends or in their parents' basements.

As an emerging social problem, this status of pothead is not so much a concern for adults. Of course, there are always those who wish to transition from one status to another following a divorce or unemployment. Instead, this new status of pothead is of particular concern for our adolescents and young adults who appear to be the primary targets for this new Big Marijuana Business. The real danger for this population is the drug's ability to snip way their inherent wanderlust and existential thirst to find themselves and cultivate a unique contribution that may be of some benefit to the world, rather left to pursue a lifestyle of avolition. Life's meaning and pipe dreams originate from altogether different places and are seldom, if ever, congruent with each other. For the last couple of decades, we have witnessed an extension of adolescence. As noted in the previous chapter, young adults are waiting longer to get married, as they are living at home longer. They are taking longer to finish college, and once finished, confronted with entry-level salaries insufficient to manage their new student loans. In short, it is tough to break out of adolescence and move forward into the adult world these days, and to do so while pursuing actual meaning in one's life only adds to this challenge. It has always been challenging to make it in this world. Sisyphus can undoubtedly attest to the fact: rolling rocks is no easy business. Who would deny Sisyphus a little

---

permanent veneer of suspicion, undeserving of even securing legitimate employment, or being ineligible to vote. Although their debt to society is paid for the act, he or she will never be seen as being equal within society.

weed to ease his aching back and to alleviate the horror of his day-to-day reality, but in this alternate reality, I no longer believe Camus would "…imagine Sisyphus happy." This gets to the quick with identifying marijuana as an emerging social problem. Now, the use of this drug is supported by politicians and adult populations who drive by legal dispensaries on their daily commute with absolute indifference. Perhaps, they had heeded their accountant's advice and invested in this growing business opportunity. The cost may be a *lost generation*, but not in the sense of what Hemmingway and Fitzgerald wrote of in *The Sun Also Rises* and *The Great Gatsby*.

The sociologist attempts to understand how a society idly stands by on the sidelines watching a young generation disengage from middle-class goals, instead choosing to pursue getting high over actual meaning in their lives. To this end, our analysis takes us in two directions. This is where we will pause to leave the discussion for now. First, in the chapter that follows, we will again look at this problem from a different angle: the disappearing middle-class. Rapidly, we are becoming a society of *haves* and *have not's*. The conflict theorist might conclude that giving young people marijuana may keep them from noticing and screaming over the unraveling of their middle-class hopes. Second, these concerns over marijuana may have gone unnoticed, occurring in the shadows and overlooked by a different sort of drug epidemic that first made its appearance in the poor, coal mining communities of the Appalachians, but now is a national concern. Marijuana abuse does not require *narcan*[55] kept nearby and at the ready, but opioid abuse does. A concern with marijuana is its ability to numb the user, but the concern with opioids is its ability to kill.

---

[55] *Naloxone*, better known as *narcan* is an opioid antagonist, often used for a complete or partial reversal of an opioid overdose. It is now routine for police, not just EMS to carry this drug with them, as encountering acute opioid overdoses is becoming much more customary. There has been some debate about needing a prescription for the medication, and if knowing the medication is close by might encourage ongoing opioid abuse.

Defeated (Opioids)

As a young man, Bruce Alexander wanted to study love, and there was no higher authority in psychology to study under than Harry Harlow (see Chapter 8). By the time Alexander showed up to the rhesus monkey lab at the University of Wisconsin—Madison, his professor, had become a hardened "chain-smoking, poetry-writing, alcoholic..." (Blum, Introduction), and Alexander took notice of this later quality. A bit of a radical himself, Alexander left the United States for Canada to avoid the draft for the Vietnam War and embarked on a long academic career studying addiction, not love. Morphine became his drug of choice, and rats were his preferred subjects. The nervous systems of rats are very similar to humans, making them a practical choice to work with.

By the late 1970s (Hadaway, Alexander, Coambs & Beyerstein, 1979) and early 1980s (Alexander, Beyerstein, Hadaway & Coambs, 1981), Alexander's research began to change its focus and started looking at the environment as a contributing force in the addiction process. In a series of experiments, typically referred to as the *Rat Park Studies*, Alexander tested the forces of chemical tolerance and withdrawal against the boundaries of the environment. His rodent participants were divided up and assigned to one of two housing situations: cage or rat park. The former referred to a standard cramped, metal cage designed to house research animals. Rat park, however, was different in almost every regard. The rats were not isolated from each other; they lived in this nearly 200-square-foot space together with fresh cider chips, wheels to run on, and murals painted on the walls.

These rats were offered endless opportunities to get high through two fluid options: plain old, flat tap-water or morphine[56] water laced

---

[56] Starting around the beginning of the Nineteen Century, the field of chemistry began to focus on isolating the active agents from natural products, like opium. German pharmacist Wilhelm Serturner was responsible for first extracting a crystalized substance from the plant that proved to have a narcotic effect when he first

with some sugar. In the caged environments, the rats went immediately to the morphine option and stuck with it. However, the rats assigned to live in the park turned their snouts up to the morphine, preferring the tap water. Alexander's explanation for this observation was pretty straight forward: it is the environment that addicts, not as much the chemicals. Alexander even took those rats who had been sustained on the morphine water and relocated them to rat park, and these rats proceeded to self-withdraw. In other words, Alexander was not making a bizarre claim that physiological experiences of tolerance and withdraw are fictitious. He observed his morphine-addicted rats withdrawing from the drug. Instead, Alexander's argument focused on environmental elements as having more considerable influence over what kept the rats going back once again to the morphine.

Alexander's thesis is still considered somewhat controversial, especially within a medical-model culture which prefers to explain addiction as a disease. This *disease model* argues that some people have a genetic predisposition to a particular drug, and once significantly enough exposed to the drug, the disease now establishes itself—*tolerance* sets in, which now requires more of the drug to experience a similar high-like experience. In the absence of the drug, *withdrawal* rages the body with symptoms which may include a racing-heart, sweating, chills, nausea, and headaches, which are so overwhelming to the addicted, they must obtain more of the drug. All free will, at this point, is lost. Once again, Alexander is suggesting these physical aspects to addiction take a backseat to environmental forces. It is an over-simplistic explanation to suggest those who are addicted need a long weekend respite at a nearby Ritz-Carlton Resort or relocation from substandard housing to homes equipped with two-car garages, plush wall-to-wall carpets, and digitized dishwashers. Alexander is not taking a position that socioeconomics is the chief culprit, as even the wealthy and elite in our society

---

administered it to dogs; in fact, Serturner's had extracted from opium all of its narcotic attributes. He named this new substance *morpheus* after the god of sleep, but the name was modified later to morphine (Miller, 2014).

face drug addiction, too. Instead, Alexander suggests that environments in which we feel—and perhaps actually are—trapped, unable to find any slack or release from are what confines us are the actual root of the problem.

Let us take Bill and Erma as an example. They are a middle-aged couple who have been married for 20-years and share three children. The oldest child is 20-years-old and is now out of the home. The other two children still live in the home. Bill was in college when he met Erma, who was then 18-years-old and had dropped out of high school when she turned 16-years-old. Within only two months after they first met, Erma was pregnant, and their daughter was born two weeks after they got married. Bill went on to complete college, works in insurance, and provides a decent standard of living for his family. Erma has never held a job. Both like to drink—a lot! Bill, however, can put down the bottle anytime. Erma, however, is an alcoholic. She cannot go so much as a day without having a few drinks. She can become very ugly when she drinks, saying the vilest and nasty comments to her children, that is if she has not first passed out before they get home from school. The disease model for addiction takes the position Erma, unlike Bill does not share the same genetic propensity for alcoholism. Using Alexander's theory, however, the analysis would center on Erma's horrible marriage. She suspects Bill has cheated on her throughout the marriage (which he has many, many times), but she cannot leave. She has no education or job opportunity. Moreover, Bill has convinced her she is no longer physically attractive or intelligent enough to ever attract the attention of another man. If she were ever to leave him, she would be alone. Like her children, she is utterly dependent on Bill. She is trapped in a "cage" with alcohol offering the only respite for her misery. In other words, when Alexander refers to the environment, he is suggesting a rather complicated and confounded phenomenon. Moreover, this complexity is equally matched by the complexity of the substance used.

The Making of an Epidemic

The opioid epidemic may turn out in the end to be the most lethal ever to strike the United States. The number of deaths resulting from overdoses has already exceeded those from the height of the AIDS epidemic, the total number of US lives lost in the Vietnam War, and the number of lives lost annually in car accidents. The Centers for Disease Control and Prevention estimates 70,200 people died from opioid-related overdoses in 2017, with the highest gains resulting from fentanyl; Figure 9.1 clearly expresses the dramatic increase in deaths associated with this epidemic (National Institute on Drug Abuse, 2019).

Figure 9.1, National drug overdose deaths including all ages from 1999 to 2017

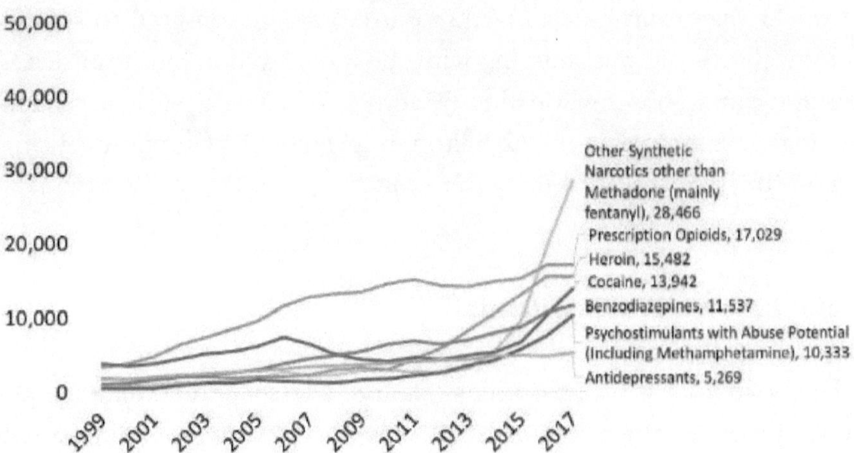

This rise in opioid overdoses can be traced back to the initial introduction of OxyContin onto the market by the Big Pharma company, Purdue. Their sales representatives aggressively marketed the drug to physicians emphasizing its slow-release mechanism, which was promised to work better than any of the other opioids already on the market, while also claiming it was addiction proof. Because of the slow-release, patients would not need to be hitting the bottle every four hours; the benefits would last a full twelve hours (McGeal, 2018).

"Soon, for-profit pill mills, staffed by unscrupulous providers who signed scores of blank prescriptions for others to dispense, could be identified by long lines of people awaiting refills to avert the agonies of withdrawal or to sell as a source of income" (Volck, 2019, p. 36).

Particularly hard hit was the coal-mining regions of the Appalachians, which had already been economically devastated through government regulations that nearly put a halt to the coal-mining industry. As Macy (2018) explains, by 2004 OxyContin was the most prevalent prescription abused in the US, and in the wake which followed the medical industry's response was the second wave of the epidemic as the addicted sought illegal means to secure their drugs which were either now being restricted access to or were just cheaper than the prescriptions filled legally at the local pharmacy. The illicit drugs of choice were either heroin or fentanyl (which is a synthetic opioid exponentially stronger than morphine). In 2007 Purdue finally admitted to a single felony charge of "misbranding with the intent to defraud or mislead," resulting in a $634 million fine (Macy, 2018). Not a particularly substantial penalty against the $2 billion in revenue OxyContin was bringing in for Purdue during its better years.

Pain: Physical and Existential

The above discussion on opioids—and to a lesser extent, marijuana—has approached the problem as an *epidemic*, suggesting it is widespread, unwelcomed, and harmful to those who have been touched by it. Inherent in this term—as well—is the idea of *disease*. An epidemic is used when referring to the quick and rapid spread of a disease, like the flu, for example, suggesting the adversity is resulting from an event beyond one's willful control. The debate centering around addiction as a disease is far from resolved. Many in the addictions field contend the problem does have a possible connection to our genes, thereby removing voluntary control over the behavior, which is no different from other diseases such as diabetes or cancer.

> The fundamental assumption is that individuals make choices that
> are in their best interests. Since addiction is self-destructive, the log-
> ical implication is that addicts cannot be voluntarily choosing to use
> drugs. Since the symptoms of diseases are involuntary, then addic-
> tion must be a disease. (Heyman, 2009, p. 99)

The challenge to this particular disease model is the absence of organic evidence. There is genetic evidence, even genetic testing, linking one's biology to the risk of cancer, but there is no genetic test (or another objective test) to identify such a link between one's biology and risk for addiction. Instead, the basis for this disease model explaining addiction rests primarily on the argument we do not voluntarily engage in self-destructive behavior, but this assumption is flawed, which explains why there is no universal agreement on the disease model for addiction. First, the argument is flawed because there are instances that point to the fact that human beings do engage in potentially self-destructive behaviors. College students routinely procrastinate all weekend right up to Sunday night before starting the essay due first thing on Monday morning. At some point in the mating ritual, a spouse makes a conscious decision to have an extramarital affair. People knowingly make bad choices from time-to-time aware of the consequences that are likely to follow.

Second, by looking at the biological connections to explain addiction, the existential connections are overlooked. Addiction makes logical sense when explained as a means for treating existential pain, especially the type of pain that comes from despair. The difference between *despair* and *suffering* for Viktor Frankl is, with the latter, there is *meaning*. People who are in a state of despair are without meaning attached to their suffering. Many of Frankl's patients were paraplegics or quadriplegics who came to see him following their spinal cord injuries. More than one of these patients went on to train to become psychotherapists themselves to work also with those who, too, were victims of spinal cord injuries. Their psychotherapeutic work did not ameliorate their ongoing suffering from their injuries; instead, it offered a reason to exist with it. Frankl's wisdom comes straight to the point: without meaning, we are left with the pain that is already there.

The etiology of pain often alluded to throughout this chapter, is considered both physical or psychologically rooted, but it is a mistake to dichotomize pain into the categories of physical or psychological, where one is purely biological in its experience, while the other bites at the psyche absent any direct neurological basis. Pain does not dichotomize this way. The nature of what it feels to experience pain, to hurt, and agonize is not altogether different when explained by the psychologist versus the physician. When explored, the similarities become evident.

One commonality between pain associated with both physical disease and injury and mental illness is its range of both presence and absence. Not all disease hurts. A physician assessing a patient for possible diabetes may ask questions about frequent urination, excessive thirst, and dizziness, but the physician does not usually ask the patient about his or her experience of physical pain. The same holds when evaluating for the presence of schizophrenia; here too, the patient is not asked to report their level of pain. Besides, there are instances where it seems illogical to report feeling pain. For example, many people who experience the loss of a limb report pain, sometimes agonizing pain over the part of the body that is now gone; this is called *phantom limb pain*. There are also those instances that not to feel pain makes no sense, as is the case when walking over hot coals while in a meditative state.

The second point of commonality between pain associated with physical disease, injury, and mental illness is that both forms share similar makeups. An analysis of the various characteristics making up the phenomenon of pain speaks towards both the physical and organic as well as the psychological and inorganic. To this end, attempts to define the nature of pain tend to involve the interaction of three confounding attributes. First, pain involves our senses. The transduction of pain is—in part—based on what we touch, see, smell, and hear. The odor of decaying, rotting food may swiftly result in gaging and vomiting just as a piercing noise has us cupping our ears to deafen the sound. Our sensory systems (i.e., eyes and ears) are responsible for *transduction*, meaning the sensory organs (i.e., eyes) convert a raw stimulus (i.e., lightwave) into a format interpretable to the nervous system. Second, pain involves emotion. Accompanied by pain is an internal, affective state.

It is possible to experience psychological states of fear, anger, rage, alarm, disgust, and dread during moments of pain. The emotional expression witnessed for one who has just had a car door slam on their hand is indistinguishable from the anguish witnessed by another just learning the tragic news a loved one has died. Consider the pain disorder *asymbolia* where one is, in fact, physically sensitive to painful stimuli, but there is no emotional distress over the pain; one is capable of feeling pain without pain hurting the person. There is a sort of dissociation taking place, much like when one experiences the benefits of morphine. Emotions are essential to the full experience of pain (Grahek, 2007). Finally, pain involves cognition. There must be an internal perceptual awareness of the experience, referring to the active meaning-making process occurring while interpreting the sensations and emotions. Perception is a cognitive process and significantly influences our personal experience of pain. Perception's role in the experience of pain helps to explain why pain awareness can change; although, there has been no change in the intensity of the pain stimulus. For instance, we have all had the experience of being distracted, perhaps in a conversation, losing immediate awareness of a headache or toothache that may have seemed intolerable just a moment prior. Additionally, numerous research studies have shown how catastrophizing anticipated pain does heighten actual pain outcomes (Nermo, Willumsen & Jonhsen, 2019; Hodges, Tsao & Sims, 2015). Walking into the dentist's office, anticipating pain will result in the experience of more considerable pain during the procedure.

The role perception plays in making emotional meaning may also help to explain why interpreting some sensations painful for some may also be interpreted as pleasurable to others. Consider, for example, *sexual masochism disorder* (SMD) which refers to a type of *paraphilia*, meaning one has an "intense and persistent sexual interest other than sexual interests in genital stimulation or preparatory fondling with phenotypically normal, physically mature, consenting human partners" (APiA, 2013, p. 685). In other words, a paraphilia refers to sexual arousal or sexual gratification by unusual means. With SMD, sexual arousal, pleasure, and gratification for the person are associated with experiencing humiliation, being beaten, and exposed to suffering. An essential component in making a diagnosis of SMD is "personal distress." Should one express no alarm, concern, or distress over this sexual interest, the diagnosis is not made, suggesting the sexual expression of masochism is normal? Thus, some people (which the APiA skeptically estimates to be less than 2% of the population) experience such pleasurable emotional states as euphoria, excitement, joy, and love by being struck by the hand or other objects, having hot wax poured on the body, or pinched with clamps.

Many experts in the field of pain study have attempted to classify and logically organize the phenomenon of pain. Some have done so based on pain's duration as either chronic, acute, or transitory. Other attempts have organized pain around body locations (i.e., abdominal or cranial) or etiological factors like inflammation versus nerves. In the field of psychology, however, classification tends to organize pain as being either *psychogenic* or *algopsychalia* in nature. *Psychogenic pain* refers to an experience of pain resulting from psychological distress (Alexander, 2012). A student's anxious fear over tomorrow's classroom presentation results in a migraine, or he experiences gastrointestinal pain the week after his girlfriend left him for another man. The pain is not fictitious nor expressed as a ploy for attention. Suggesting an aspirin or antacid is as helpful as a remedy in such circumstances as if the headache resulted from excessive reading or heartburn following a spicy meal.

Algopsychalia pain, on the other hand, is experienced at the emotional level. It refers to a cognitive awareness of personal suffering, a mental pain with no expectation of linking it to a biological source (Blom, 2010). It is what suicidologist Edwin Shneidman has referred to as "psychache" (2002). There is a crisp recognition this pain comes, not from the nervous system, but from being human. The recognition may only exist at the emotional level absent the ability to articulate in language the feelings of loneliness, despair, and estrangement that tend to accompany it often. Perhaps, one of the most poignant descriptions of algopsychalia comes from journalist William Styron's memoir reflecting on his battle with depression:

> What I had begun to discover is that, mysteriously and in ways that are totally remote from normal experience, the gray drizzle of horror induced by depression takes on the quality of physical pain. But, it is not an immediately identifiable pain, like that of a broken limb. It may be more accurate to say that despair owing to some evil trick played upon the sick brain by the inhabiting psyche, comes to resemble the diabolical discomfort of being imprisoned in a fiercely overheated room. And because no breeze stirs this caldron, because there is no escape from this smothering confinement, it is entirely natural that the victim begins to think ceaselessly of oblivion. (1990, p. 50)

Algopsychalia pain is intrapsychological, meaning the stimulus experienced is inorganic, occurring only within the mind because there is not an evident and apparent sensory system involved in transduction. This assumption may be accurate, or it may be mistaken. The idea humans have five senses (i.e., hearing, vision, taste, smell, and touch) is wrong. Our senses also include thermoception (temperature), mechanoreception (vibration), equilibrioception (balance), proprioception (kinesthetic), and chemoreception (internal chemical levels such as sodium). There is still debate on the actual number of senses human beings are capable of possessing. Perhaps, algopsychalic pain results from the transduction of a stimulus accompanied by an intense emotional perception resulting in pain response.

A final commonality between physical/organic pain and psychological/inorganic pain pertains to the mutual benefits of psychotherapy. It would seem talking to a psychotherapist about one's pain helps curb the experience of pain. Pertaining specifically to physical/organic forms of pain, cognitive-behavioral therapy (CBT) is helpful across a wide range of pain syndromes. Targeting a patient's beliefs and expectations about his or her pain help the patient adjust to their experience with pain, report lower frequencies of painful episodes, and report a reduction in their experience with pain intensity (Thomas, Wilson-Barnett & Goodhart, 1998). Thus, the experience of pain may also serve as a bridge for understanding the connections between organic and inorganic forms of the disease. As H. G. Well reminds us, "For it is just this question of pain that part us" (1986, p. 100).

Final Remarks

Drug use, abuse, and addiction have been discussed from an existential point of view by looking at it as steaming from loss of meaning in life. Such meaning implies a more profound existential connotation; it gets to the reason *why* we pursue any goal in life. *Meaning* then is what we each make of it. When we have no meaning in life, drugs like OxyContin, heroin, fentanyl, and marijuana may be used as a means for treating this pain. The existential pain these drugs are attempting to mask over may exceed any pain associated with the drug's withdrawal.

This chapter has associated a state of meaninglessness as an emerging social problem. To this point, drug use has been looked at as a remedy—or at least a psychological escape—from this state of meaninglessness. Perhaps, the concerns with marijuana have not garnished sufficient public attention as our nation's attention has finally been captivated by the deadly opioid epidemic.

Nowhere in this chapter, however, is it suggested "meaning in life" is the silver bullet to drug addiction. The mere suggestion that such problems can be univocally resolved goes beyond hubris to now sounding more like a typical cable news pundit's commentary on any one of our nation's problems. Drug addiction is painfully complicated. This attribute of "meaning in life," nevertheless, needs to be part of this multifocal debate. In an earlier footnote from this chapter, I made a personal disclosure; I have never used drugs. I have never even tried marijuana. I contributed this to having a clear sense of meaning in my life. Yet, in the act of complete and honest disclosure, I can imagine a life that is different from the one I currently live where I would use them.

It is imperative—both personally and nationally—to have and to pursue meaning in life. There must be a reason beyond the shallow excuse to punch a clock by 9:00 AM to get out of bed every day. Maybe the reason to punch that clock is to ensure one's children never have to; meaning is found in such a sacrifice. Nations need to pursue meaning in the life of their society, too. Policies that benefit some—especially at the sacrifice of others—ought to strive for cultivating a national sense of meaning, not simply to ensure the "have's" continue to have more at further cost to the "have not's." It is to this debate our discussion now turns towards in the last chapter.

10   Conclusion: Making it Better for the Middle-Class

Karl Marx and Friedrich Engels' *The Communist Manifesto*, first written in 1848, was just that: a manifesto. The document was a political outcry. "It is high time that Communists should openly, in the face of the whole world, publish their views, their aims, their tendencies, and meet this nursery tale of the *specter of communism* with a manifesto of the party itself" (1964, p. 55). They write with a purpose in mind; their manifesto is a call to action, complete with goals supported by the authors' self-declared wisdom. Their manifesto ends with: "Let the ruling classes tremble at the Communistic revolution. The proletarians have nothing to lose but their chains. They have a world to win," they say, ending with their final word, "UNITE!" (p. 116). Marx and Engels viewed the plight of the downtrodden, whom they called the *proletariat*, resulting from the ruling *bourgeoisie*, those who were members of the power elite and used their authority to control and to exploit the proletariat. The only legitimate means to rectify this social problem, as Marx and Engels saw things, was through a political revolution.

William Golding (1982) referred to this political theory of communism, for which so much fuss has been made, as "simplistic" and a "bore." Golding suggests, in turn, "The simplistic popularization of their ideas has thrust our world into a mental straightjacket from which we can only escape by the most anarchic violence" (p. 187). "So it goes,"[57] as political manifestos are met with absolutism in return.

This book began pointing out that politics is a flawed solution to most social problems. It is most certainly a *tool*, but it is most certainly not the *key*. In addressing the challenges bought on by social problems, politics ought to be used for sure, but not as the single answer in and of itself. We learned long ago in this nation the decree of the king is hollow in these matters; it is the will of the people that matters, not the rhetoric of yet another leader promising to unshackle and free the masses of their "chains." We are endowed with inalienable rights and the existential freedom to both engage and pursue these rights. As a collection of people forged together in a shared society, we are correct in believing the common problems we face are resolvable. Politics is an excellent solution to get a new traffic light installed at the busy intersection, but as a grand solution in resolving a social problem, political solutions are unlikely to ameliorate the concern to a degree over that which political rivals gin up their base in opposition. Social problems are involved, with confounding issues at play. Nevertheless, as has been said on several occasions throughout this book, a defining attribute of a social problem is the belief that something can be done to turn the tide and ameliorate its condition. If this were not the case, the problem would then be identified as an *existential threat*, as defeat is inevitable should sociologists be so foolish to seize command.[58]

This final chapter is not a manifesto and does not advocate any recipe or course of action necessary to resolve these emerging social problems identified and discussed in the previous chapters. Advocacy

---

[57] I can't help myself sometimes. "So it goes," is a phrase used throughout Kurt Vonnegut's novel, *Slaughterhouse-Five or The Children's Crusade: A Duty-Dance with Death* (1969), which may be said to be the best anti-war novel written.

[58] Refer back to Chapter 1. An existential threat was defined as a problem without a sociological solution. Hitler's attempt to dominate the world was used as an example. The only solution to avoid societal annihilation was political. Had sociologists taken the lead and attempted to defeat the problem of Nazism rather than the federal government, the outcome of World War II would have been distinctly different.

requires following the directions to achieve a promised outcome, but debate begins with an idea which then follows with a moment of silence before the mutual exchange of volley of debate resumes. This is how the *public square* ought to work. The intent is to assemble in this final chapter the many ideas, data, and speculations discussed in this book into some order and logic and begin a discussion on ameliorating these emerging social problems.

The reader is charged now with the responsibility to approach the following discussion critically, looking for flaws and biases. The reader is expected to argue back throughout the chapter. Be on guard for possible bias from the search engines used in identifying data upon which positons have relied on. Throughout this book, I have pulled old, yellowed-out books now brittle to the touch from my bookshelf to support positions taken; were these the right books? Be mindful that I have matured into my middle-aged years working all the while in a community college setting. To what degree is my own schema used to assess matters been distorted as a result? Where has my own moral bias seeped into the discussion, necessitating more professional distances be given? Choices are being made to identify some concerns as *manifest*, meaning primary while others as *latent*, meaning secondary in their level of concern; is rearrangement required? Remember what Jürgen Habermas (1989) told us about the public square. This is not the space for compromise and finding some patch of common ground to settle upon. The public square is that place carved out in a free society for confrontational debate; we are all equals in this space; no academic credential or professional title offers anyone of us a higher footing and greater authority while we are inside the public square; in this space, we are all equals.

Turning the Tide on Emerging Social Problems:
A Remedy for the Melting Middle-Class

The reach and effect of social problems extend beyond just the personal experiences of people. Social problems refer to a social phenomenon which, either places at risk or compromises the sustainability of societal functioning or the inalienable rights of those impacted directly or indirectly by these social problems. It is to this latter point of the individual's inalienable rights this book has taken a less traditional approach to an analysis of social problems. The traditional approach is more likely to emphasize societal contributions. In this book, however, it has been argued the existence and validation of an individual's inalienable rights occur through reflection on the "givens" of existence, which include: death, freedom, responsibility, and establishing meaning in life. The failure to do so results in the individual experiencing existential angst and despair. However, this is also potentially infectious to the societal as well. Social institutions can reciprocally absorb this despair, too, taking the form of a social problem.

Moreover, throughout this book, social problems have been identified as being dynamic. Social problems do not stagnantly rest on either extreme of the dynamic continuum; they are not to be found squarely within the individual nor just within the social institution. Rather social problems arduously exist somewhere within those points between the continuum's extreme ends. Social problems are active, as a sort of sociological friction which regularly occurs, always rubbing between these two points of the individual and societal.

Although all social problems are operationalized using the same criteria, social problems still differ from each other; they are not the same. Likewise, the level of threat social problems pose may also differ from each other. For example, three of your foes each pick up three separate rocks, hurling them at you, but the rock you need to be most concerned with is the one that is going to strike you first. To this end, four qualities have been identified, providing context to any social problem. First, social problems vary in their degree of ethical alignment between respective positions of morals and values, where *values,* refers to those things people genuinely care about, and *morals* refer to those ways motivation for our bonded behavior is shared through human emotions and experiences. As the degree of congruency between these two ethical attributes increase, social problems take on less severity. In turn, the more these two attributes become incongruous with each other, the more socially risky the problem becomes. Second, as attention is misdirected away from the societal interests to various positions about a social problem, possible risk, and harm to society increases, especially as the degree of involution increases; whereby, the social problem is entangled with multiple layers of complexity in the many different positions taken. Instead, sociological attention is best when redirected away from a particular position and focuses on social interests instead. Third, when the free, open, and reciprocal exchange of communication is present, the severity of risk decreases but will otherwise remain high when debate falls upon deaf ears indignant to acknowledging any other possible alternative position. Finally, as aegis authority increases, so too does the inherent risk associated with social problems. In other words, when a few sources of social authority maintain influence and control over a specific social problem, the level of social risk rises.

This book has limited its focus only on those *emerging social problems* which pose the most immediate and significant threat to societal functioning. In Chapter 5, the effects technology is now imposing on our most succinct inalienable rights for freedom of thought and freedom of speech were presented by identifying two emerging social problems: thinking[E] and the virtual public square. Chapter 6 identified the reduction in the ranks of the middle-class, decreasing birth rates, and restrictive college costs all as emerging social problems. Finally, this robust list ends with iDepression, declining marriage rates, legalization of marijuana, and opioid addiction, all explored in Chapters 7 and 8.

In the face of a list of social problems, sociological triage is essential. All are problems, but which one is most alarming, soonest to jeopardize ongoing social stability and perhaps the simplest and swiftest to address to quickly free up resources to once again rally the troops and move on to and apply to the next social problem. To this end, the *melting away of the middle-class* is identified now as that emerging social problem that is of paramount concern juxtaposed in the lineup of all the other emerging social problems identified in this book.

Why this emerging social problem and not one of the others? Based on the severity and risk of overall societal harm, the melting middle-class leads over those other emerging social problems discussed in this book. First, the middle-class represents that point on the socioeconomic ladder, bridging the difference in the range of inequality between those who have the most with those who have the least in our society. In other words, the middle-class is closer to the poverty line than are the wealthy, and they are also closer to experiencing complete economic independence than are the poor. This, in turn, offers the middle-class cognitive insight and perspective that is much more difficult for those positioned on the higher and lower rungs of the socioeconomic ladder to grasp. Therefore, the collapse of the middle-class will fundamentally alter a substantial cognitive schema which this particular class has traditionally provided our society in a manner potentially more devastating than any Google algorithm might otherwise have on our independent thinking.

For example, in more recent political cycles, socialism has been gaining popularity. Rhetoric favoring government established systems of free higher education for all, universal government health care, and a guaranteed income whereby the government issues monthly checks to all its citizens ensuring everyone's bank accounts are always just north of the poverty line, appears to be part of the mainstream for the National Democrat Committee's (DNC) platform today. The idea here is not that debate favoring more socialistic styles of government ought to be snuffed out in the public square; instead, it is that middle-class argument is ever-increasingly now absent in the public square. Karl Marx only spoke of two classes: proletariat and bourgeois. His argument favoring political revolution losses its bravado in the face of middle-class values. Without the presence of a middle-class, the risk of a radical shift in traditional governing political ideology is inevitable.

Second, identifying concern over a melting middle-class does not lead to nearly as polarizing debate as many other social problems appear to do. Quickly, sides are taken on topics the likes of abortion, systemic racisms within law enforcement, or climate change. Isolating focus on the middle-class would not appear to divide a population, at least not initially, but perhaps unite a population. Consider that most Americans, about 70%, self-report as being middle-class (Martin, 2017), but only 32% of Americans have a footing on this particular rung of the socioeconomic ladder (refer back to Chart 7.1). It might appear logical those Americans who are working-class may try to identify more with the middle-class, but the same logic still holds for many in the upper-class too; middle-class values are preferred over all others, leaving some outside of the middle-class to self-identify as being middle-class. Because the debate over the middle-class does not appear to be seeping in controversy, this emerging social problem is less likely to be censored, especially in the virtual public square.

Finally, there is another challenge when attempting to offer a remedy to social problems, and it is the same reason why we can only eat one cheeseburger at a time. There are limits to human capacities. Complex problems require *reductionist approaches*. Consider Eric Kandel's research on memory, winning him the Nobel Prize in Medicine and Physiology earlier in this century. He was the first to see and map out the process of memory shifting from short-term to long-term forms. However, this was only possible because he was first able to identify the simplest of subjects that might infer enormous implications on to humans. He settled on Aplysia, the giant sea slug. Their "large synaptic potentials made it possible to map neural connections cell by cell and eventually enabled me to work out for the first time the precise writing diagram of a behavior" (Kandel, 2006, p. 148). Social problems are no less complex and require reductionist approaches too. However, society—unlike the brain—is not tethered together by a neural web. In this environment, reductionism first requires identifying a principal concern, which is then followed by realigning both the *manifest* and *latent functions* of the phenomenon by using social will. By identifying the melting middle-class as the chief social problem to remedy, more of those other emerging social problems also discussed in this book will benefit latently. Herein, choices are suggested that will have secondary benefits to other facets connected to different emerging social problems. Thus, many of these other social problems are not being ignored; their remedies, too, are proposed soon.

Figure 10.1, Manifest and latency influences

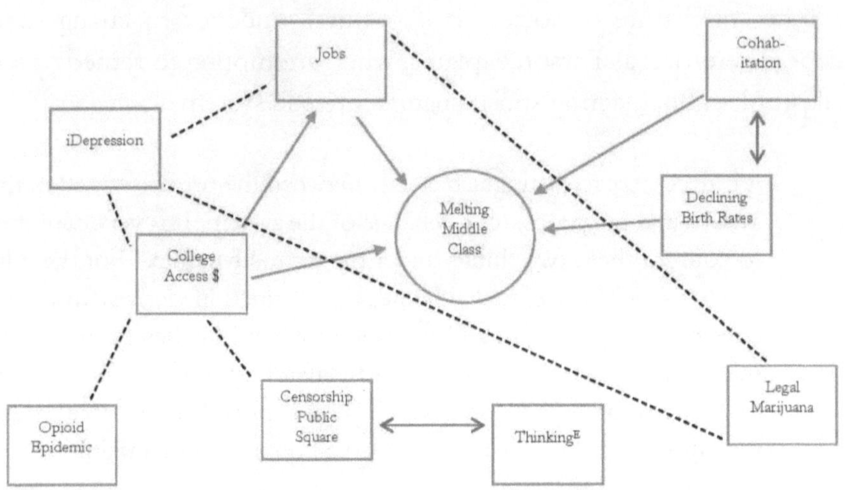

Latent influence, -----
Manifest influence, →

Change from within rather than from without. One undisputed fact about any social problem: both the concern and possible solution to ameliorate it is perplexing; there is no clear path illuminating an obvious and simple solution to remedy it. Approaching a social problem is much the same as approaching a mirage while wandering in the desert. The remedy to the problem appears to be so evident at times, but still always just out of reach. In part, this is because the very nature of social problems is a complicated and confounding phenomenon.

The first step to seizing the reigns of control is to effect change *into* the system rather than *onto* the system. According to sociologist Talcott Parsons (1951), social systems strive to achieve a state of social *equilibrium*, which refers to a societal state of balance. This social balance is achieved when all of the internal social systems and subsystems work cooperatively, dynamically, and mutually with each other by counter-balancing a change in one subsystem throughout some or all of the others. *Social chaos* results when a change imposed rapidly and profoundly onto society inhibits the systems and subsystems to counter-balance to correct for itself. In other words, Parson is suggesting an inherent feature of society is its natural tendency to change and adapt. Therefore, as Parson explains, when attempting to remedy a social problem by injecting social change into the system...

> it is necessary to distinguish clearly between the processes within the system and the processes of change of the system. It is very common to confuse these two things under the term "dynamic." For the purposes of our conceptual scheme, the distinction derives from the concept of equilibrium and the way in which this has been used in the present work. Beyond the most general meaning of the concept of equilibrium, the meaning which is most directly applicable here is that applying to what we have called a "boundary-maintaining" system. (1951, p. 323)

The goal to effectively remedy a social problem is to strategically inject a series of small changes into the system that, in turn, require the system to accommodate these changes through its inherent counter-balancing mechanisms. Attempts to effect change of the system at a macro level need to be avoided to protect against social chaos from resulting. Thus, the remedy suggested to correct this emerging social problem targets the systems (or social institutions) within society. Some of which may already appear to be functioning without any recognized problems. There are no "grand" strategies, like increasing the minimum wage to \$30/hour or forgiving all student loans, which exceed \$5,000 or more, as this is more likely to ensure a state of social chaos.

Figure 10.2, Reestablishing equilibrium

Phase 1: stable society experiencing equilibrium just before a social change

Phase 2: a social change has occurred within one of the social system affecting a change from a state of equilibrium to a state of disequilibrium

Phase 3: all other social systems have made small counter-balancing adjustments in order to reestablish a new state of social equilibrium

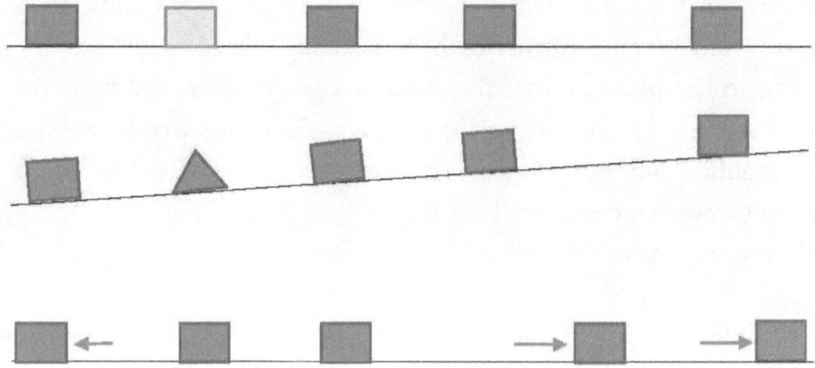

Reestablishing the Middle-Class

Without purposeful intervention, the middle-class will continue to diminish, and their benefits to our society will continue to recede until there is nothing left. Middle-class values are essential to the continued success and prosperity of our society. This is not to suggest the values and contributions made to our society by those classes perched on the socioeconomic rungs above and below pale in significance; they are just different from those of the middle-class. Therefore, the solution is not pulling down nor up those who lie outside the middle-class range.

A new middle-class cannot be drafted, nor can its values be reassigned to those who stand on these other rungs of the socioeconomic ladder; it must be forged and constructed from our society's creative ingenuity. It is possible to replenish the ranks of the middle-class. However, the steps suggested here in this chapter are neither apparent nor may be popular, but accomplishing this is possible.

Access to the middle-class is first—and foremost—established through jobs. Not all jobs are the same when it comes to the requisite skills, demands, and sacrifices necessary to succeed at them. Occupational success with these jobs requires the value system which the middle-class brings with them to the job site daily. In turn, these are the jobs that continue to build and cultivate middle-class values from the job site. For the reader who believes a child receives the same feelings of pride and accomplishment when receiving a little league trophy for coming in last-place as does the child on the first-place team, he or she will disagree with this suggestion already. In other words, economic redistribution where money flows down from the wealthier rungs of the socioeconomic ladder does not pull up the lower rungs into the middle-class. A middle-class status cannot be bought; it must be earned.

Middle-class jobs typically demand skills first requiring dedicated preparation and study. At the higher end of the middle-class range, these jobs may include physician, attorney, accountant, or business executive. At the lower end of the range, these jobs may include teacher, police officer, nurse, paralegal, or dental hygienist. As previously discussed, the current obstacle for those who have just recently trained through college programs for entry into these professions is student loan debt. A young middle school math teacher does not earn the economic benefits of his or her position because student loan payments keep one firmly anchored on the working-class rung of the ladder. Rebuilding the middle-class requires attention to the lower ranges for this group over the higher ranges, which starts with identifying affordable career training. College needs to be affordable once again. Young graduates cannot be handed student loan payments that out weight the value of their degrees and continue to expect young adults will flock to these pricy educational tracks.

Several politicians in the national spotlight, like Senator Bernie Sanders, have argued in favor of free college. Sander's platform is actually for *free college for all!* The oppositional party's response has suggested such an idea is unrealistic because it is unaffordable. After all, who is going to pay for it? There is a reasonable reply to the question: much of the money is already available; we are currently prepared to pay for it without having to dig yet deeper into taxpayers' pockets. The response to this challenge is for the financial responsibilities to be funded by the states through the use of *community college vouchers*. High school students who achieve a college-ready status at the start of their junior year would receive the option for completing their last two years at their local community college. State funding, otherwise used to pay for the high school, would be now diverted to the community college. With any possible luck, the difference in cost might require students to spend ten weeks in the summer to pay any difference in expenses for books or transportation expenses. Even federal student loans—at rates far lower than what the student would be applying for two years later— should be made available.

This suggestion also saves the state on current educational expenses. The state only needs to pay once for the student to take the same class. Instead of the state funding the cost of algebra as a junior in high school only to subsidize the cost of college algebra two years later, the state is now funding only one algebra class which is completed at the community college.

When K-12 state-based school vouchers have been proposed in the past, the outcry from school unions was fierce. Arguments proliferated on how such policies would unfairly place poor and marginalized families at risk; they could not afford to leave their poor and failing school, now experiencing even more draining resources. Nevertheless, outcome studies show that policies like school vouchers and charter schools do work. Moreover, the naysayers may point out all the reasons how high school juniors are not ready for college. Perhaps they are academically ready, but the critics argue not emotionally or psychologically prepared. Again, there have been decades and decades of data gathered on similar dual-enrollment programs on a smaller scale demonstrating its effectiveness.

Additionally, the statistics show that graduation rates decrease as students get older. Starting a student in community college at a younger age will increase the likelihood he or she will graduate and graduate in fewer years than it takes older students today to complete an associate's or bachelor's degree (National Student Clearinghouse Research Center [NSCRC], 2016). In turn, this will also increase the tax base with these, now graduates, assigned to middle-class tax brackets.

Figure 10.3, Time to a degree for associate and bachelor's degree earners by age and type of institution where a degree was received (NSCRC, 2016)

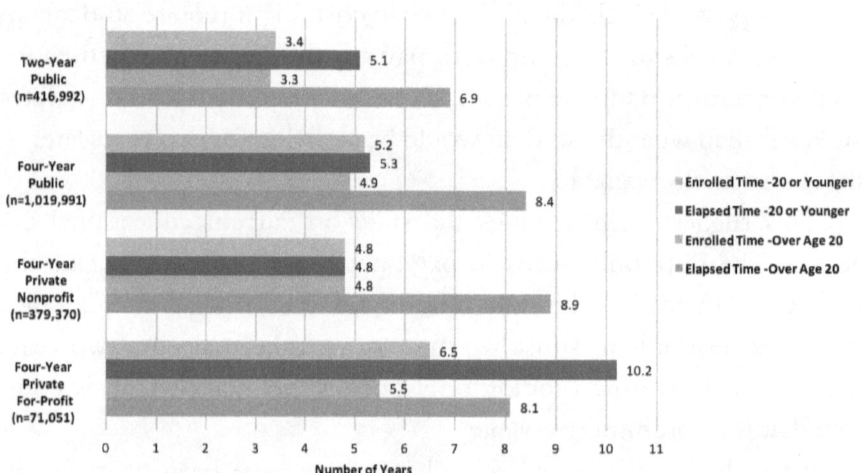

Recent graduates of Harvard University do not take jobs patrolling their neighborhoods, teaching third graders their multiplication tables, or administering insulin to patients in the local nursing home. Harvard graduates typically enter the bourgeoisie-track job market, while community college graduates pursue a humbler middle-class job market. However, Harvard graduates—unlike community college graduates—

typically receive a bachelor's degree. Many of today's entry-level positions now require the bachelor's degree that once an associate's degree, referring to the two-year degree typically granted at community colleges, would suffice (i.e., law enforcement and nursing). While some continue to require the bachelor's degree, which traditionally meant the community college graduate would then transfer on to a state university to finish the final two years (i.e., teachers). Moreover, there are many careers that a bachelor's degree would provide an advantage in the job market but are too vocational to capture the state university's interest to develop four-year programs around such career training (i.e., veterinarian-technician, human services, dental hygienist, or physical therapy assistant). States, therefore, should permit community colleges to develop and offer vocationally related bachelor degrees.

Again a public outcry should be anticipated from those who continue to associate stigma with the community college as being nothing more than the thirteenth-grade or believe these institutions are not equipped to teach at this level effectively. Unlike state universities, the community college classes are rarely—if ever—taught by teaching-assistants or have class sizes hurling upward into the hundreds resembling stadium seating at a sporting event, not a lecture on Hobbesian philosophy. True, the faculty at community colleges place importance on teaching over the value of research, which is not the case at most research-based universities. Moreover, this is not an original idea being proposed here; some community colleges do offer four-year programs leading to the bachelor's degree and have been doing so for decades now. There is data to support this approach does work. Students graduate and enter into professions, like public school teaching, excelling in their chosen field, and holding far less student loan debt. Moreover, the debt these students do have is more manageable in relation to their salaries. Additionally, these community colleges build their programs around the needs of their respective community; keeping their students local, benefits these students who are more likely to have additional social support available to them (i.e., family) to address those many other needs that go hand-in-hand with college degree completion and overall success in the classroom.

A preemptive caveat is suggested: if the state is going to underwrite the cost of the student's education, students are expected to attend face-to-face classes, or at least a majority of classes need to be taken in a face-to-face modality, not online. Decreased socialization—which is the net result for online instruction—is associated with higher rates of depression. Adolescents in this age range need more opportunities to socialize, not less. Again, there is nothing inherently wrong with online instruction as it relates to learning outcomes. Students can learn through online instruction; nonetheless, courses using this modality are better reserved for older-working adults or limited summer course-work.

Let us pause to access once again the costs as well as the social impact for what has just been proposed so far. The state already provides for the cost of public education as well as a substantial amount of tuition costs for in-state residents attending local community colleges or state universities. Economically, both the state and federal government benefit with higher tax revenue once the student graduates and is now in the workforce two years sooner. True, some teachers/professors may find it necessary to shift from one institution to another based on the flow of students. For example, some high schools may need fewer teachers, but the community college will be in demand of new faculty. The economic looser in this proposal will more likely be the state university who will have to find other means for paying for their new edifies, multi-million dollar gyms, and bloated administrative staff than saddling down undergraduates with debt equaling the size of mortgages for three-bedroom homes.

This proposal does not limit free choice. Students are still permitted to apply to those out of state universities ranked as being the top party schools or the ivy league. Students graduating from community colleges are not prohibited either from transferring on to private colleges or the ivy league, as this is already routine. Finally, community colleges are not being asked to compromise on their mission to offer open-access to college. Once those high school students who were deemed not to be a college-ready graduate from high school or others who have earned a GED may still be offered access to the community college. These institutions have always addressed the needs of diverse student populations (i.e., Early College students, returning adults, GED graduates, or senior citizen enrichment) and are primed to continue to do so moving into the future.

Again, one of the causes for these skyrocketing college costs has been the result of the federal government getting into the student loan business, pushing private banks aside. Once again, private banks need to be brought back into this process. Just as is the case when loaning out for a mortgage, banks also need to be required to evaluate their level of risk. For instance, a bank will not approve a mortgage for $500,000 on a one-bedroom, 850 square-foot home located deep in the weeds of rural America that last sold six months ago for $75,000. The bank first needs evidence to support the fair market value of the product for which the loan is being given to purchase. Banks need to have standards in place to assess the value of the product they are offering to loan. This proposal is not unlike the same expectations banks now have following the real estate market crash back around 2010.

A middle-class cannot be imported. *Immigration*, especially *illegal immigration*[59] is not a reasonable remedy to our nation's population decline, especially as it concerns the middle-class. The argument coming from both the political right and political left over illegal immigration

---

[59] The meaning of language has the ability for its significance to be refashioned, scrubbed, and even eradiated from the academic lexicon. When the debate is set in the public square, language is of absolute importance. Words are the instrument for honest debate, and in the midst of debate, the debater has a responsibility to use words univocally, avoiding hollophrasis where what was once a word gets crumbled back to infantile banter and innuendo. Although some Google searches may suggest in the list of returned links where the term *illegal immigrant* is being used in a derogatory context, this does not render the term offensive. I use the term here for no other purpose than to differentiate behaviorally from a person who has secured the necessary legal status to be residing in the country versus a person who has not secured the necessary legal status to be residing in the country.

is deafening, the rhetoric is vile, and reasonable solutions to the argument are becoming pushed away further from view. The only point to this debate both Democrats and Republicans seem to agree on over this topic is that it is worth entrenching themselves over and to concede no point to their opponent. Here is where we also see the value when the sociologist appropriately extricates him or herself from the moral entanglements of the debate. Other topics take shape when the fog from dichotomous debate evaporates. A latent consequence from recent immigration trends has been an influx of new persons, which nearly accounts for the depreciation of people no longer being born due to plummeting birth rates, especially among the middle-class. A reasonable argument is made here; both sides of the political aisle are deliberately agreeing to disagree on this political issue because the latent benefit of building a replaceable new tax cohort is in place, and doing so ensures the immediate survival of other societal concerns (i.e., funding Social Security).

The problem of illegal immigration has not been addressed in this book up until this point. The purpose of doing so now is only to address one aspect of it; only that part of illegal immigration pertaining to the middle-class and population decline is relevant for the moment. This approach is not unusual; actually, it is typical to isolate and tease out only those aspects of a social phenomenon appearing to bleed into other areas of concern. Social problems cannot be resolved if they first are not proportionately managed.

We are a nation where people of other nations desire to come to and to be a part of. We are a good people and have a Dream to offer those who still hold out hope their life—the lives of their children—can be something much better than what it has been in their native country. This does not diminish the fact that our nation has also used immigration as a strategy to address those times when we have needed a growing citizenry. The valve on the immigration spigot has been adjusted over points in time and even closed completely at other points. The aperture for this immigration spigot, in part, has also been determined by the speed by which *assimilation* occurs, whereby immigrants adapt to one degree or another the norms and values of the dominant culture. Much like the term *illegal immigrant*, the term *assimilation* can also permit negative ideas to swell up quickly, but assimilation is no more than a tool applied by a dominant culture; like any tool, it can be misused. The concept is fundamental, "social institutions can be sustained over time only if the individuals who take part in them are affectively invested in the social role relationships of which they are constituted" (Fox, Lidz & Bershady, 2005, p. 5-6). The central point, the assumption has always been for those who willingly immigrate to our nation for their behavior and values to soon fall somewhere inside our society's wide range of norms and values.[60]

Illegal immigrants do not typically find themselves perched on the middle rungs of the socioeconomic ladder. Instead, they more likely to see the soles from middle-class shoes somewhere on the rungs above them. Illegal immigrants, by definition, do not have legal status to work, often casting them off into the vocational shadowlands. They must work under the table and off the books. Opportunity to exploit their labor, paying below minimum wage, to ignore child labor laws, extending the workweek without overtime compensation, and providing no benefits like healthcare or sick leave is too often the norm for this population. But, adding more rungs to the lower portions of the socioeconomic ladder does not—in turn—establish a middle-class by juxtaposition. Moreover, two possible confounding problems start to

---

[60] This topic is—and always has been—ripe for debate. My intent here is not to lob out yet another controversial topic. My use of cultural assimilation is narrowly applied to the center lane, not those more peripheral concerns. The bonds forging together our society cannot survive when its core values and fundamental laws do not find some degree of commonality in its belief and practice. An 8-year-old child cannot ever under any circumstance consent to having sex with a 30-year-old adult. Someone who is homosexual should never endure physical assault or be murdered because of his or her sexual identity, as no justification exists for such acts. A woman should not be told who she must marry; no jurisdiction should ever validate a marriage license where clear and obvious coercion is being imposed on the nuptials. Assimilation ensures a common set of values and behaviors (not morals) are assumed by all. Morality cannot be legislated through the creation of laws, but behaviors can be legislated. The laws currently in place that protect children, sexual orientation, and women are not up for negotiation or compromise, as these are infused within our inalienable rights.

come into focus by providing free community college tuition to college-ready high school juniors who are either illegal immigrants or the children of illegal immigrants. First, the college degree with its vocational emphasis may now have higher market value back in their native country, and the state's investment is lost. Second, those without the ability to speak a second language may be placed at a disadvantage. Surges in immigration—legal and illegal alike—result in forming culturally specific neighborhoods. This has historically been the case (i.e., China Town or Little Italy both in New York City and Germantown in Philadelphia) and continues to occur today. The need to learn English as a new language becomes less essential, while the need for police officers, teachers, and EMTs to be bilingual more essential.

Incentivizing Marriage and Family. The most obvious way to increase the ranks of the middle-class is for middle-class couples to have more children. Historically, *intergenerational social mobility* has been for children to grow up and to become a little better off than their parents, but not substantially better off than their parents. In other words, children from middle-class families tend to secure a little stronger footing on the middle-class rung of the socioeconomic ladder than that achieved by their parents. The clear and obvious challenge to this common-sense approach, however, is that couples today are waiting longer to get married, as discussed in Chapter 8 (see Figure 8.1), which means they are waiting longer to start having a family. Moreover, the costs associated with raising a family (e.g., childcare) and the burden of maintaining student loans are pressing many young couples to make a deliberate choice to either restrict family size—often meaning one child—or forgoing children altogether.

Strategies do exist that can help to promote stronger birth rates for the middle-class. The strategies suggested above, promoting college graduation and entry into the middle-class job market sooner, would also latently promote a shift in the age of first marriage back towards younger ages. Obviously, if couples are married sooner and working sooner, they will have children sooner, too. They will also be extending the range of years of fertility within their relationship, thereby increasing the likelihood of having larger families. Similar strategies can result from direct incentives offering greater tax incentives to couples by increasing the economic value associated with dependents. Other changes in the tax code would have similar effects too (i.e., authorize parents to add a son-in-law or daughter-in-law as a dependent who is under a designated age (i.e., 25-years) and is now residing in the parents' home, which has the latent effect of encouraging college graduation and possible in-home childcare. Such policies never have the net effect of benefiting every eligible person or drastically influencing the indented goal (in this case, increasing birth rates), but they do often have marginal effects and advance slowly towards the end goal.

Intent. The above discussion serves a single purpose, which is to offer a model for applying the various skills which have been interwoven throughout this book to critically interpret and debate on a plan to address and correct an emerging social problem. Although many social problems have been identified in this book, here, our concern and focus have been on our nation's decreasing citizenry within the ranks of the middle-class. The goal has been to provide a model that serves as the basis to engage the necessary and free debate on the matters that concern us most.

My goal for concluding this book is not with offering an answer that resolves the problem, but with an idea upon which to engage debate. Most works of non-fiction do not deviate much from the Aristotle model of fiction; the story rises with conflict to an inevitable climax, follows with a resolution, and ends with the six tritest words ever written: "… and they lived happily ever after." We like resolution! Our minds are cognitively wired to fill in the gaps, polishing down all the ambiguity until the world once again makes sense to us. Falling into this too familiar theme would be hubris. Social problems are not math equations, as there is no eloquent resolution to be had. Rather, we end on the point of ambiguity. Social problems are not solved in the ivy towers of academia or the chamber of the Capitol.

The answers to our social problems are fist articulated inside the public square.

Final Thoughts

This book began by pointing out, towards the end of his life, Sigmund Freud suggested civilization was inherently flawed. We enter into a social contract, to protect ourselves from the carnal lusts and violence by the hands of others, but by doing so, we are prohibited from perpetrating our similar desires upon others. As Freud explains, "…civilization is largely responsible for our misery, and that we should be much happier if we gave it up and returned to primitive conditions" (1961, p. 33). We are left with a social state where social problems are inevitable and without resolution.

This book has looked at the subject of social problems from a perspective somewhat contrary to that of Freud; although, this is not so unusual when analyzing social problems from a sociological point of view. It is, however, rather unconventional to place as much significance on existential influences when addressing the etiology of social problems. Sociologists today prefer the harder quantitative analysis expressed in elaborate statistical models over softer qualitative approaches. Moreover, sociology never embraced existential philosophy to the same degree as psychology, even though existential psychology never rose to prominent status as other schools of thought (i.e., neuropsychology or behaviorism).

By taking this existential perspective, a social problem is no longer seen as a phenomenon infiltrating itself into the social system, infecting it as a bacterial agent might do to its human host; rather, a social problem is now expressed as a systemic phenomenon resulting from the act of individuals connecting to their society. Dynamic friction takes place between the societal and the individual, and it is at this is this point of connection between the two, which identifies the etiology for social problems. To this end, social problems are considered as *emerging social problems*, centering around an existential framework.

Even though an existential perspective is far from the traditional way the topic of social problems is analyzed, this book has held to the sociological argument that social problems can be corrected, and our world is always capable of becoming something better than it once had been. The challenge—nevertheless—may be near the same as the process of unscrambling an egg and returning it—yoke and all—back into its shell. But, sociologists tend to be rather united in the belief that social problems, even emerging social problems, can be ameliorated.

The central theme has been the need to ensure that the necessary debate occurs in the public square. This space cannot be compromised. It is an essential space. Here in this space of the public square, we are stripped of all titles, rank, and status. We are equals who share in a common social community, universal alienable rights, and all working towards a common goal, which is to ensure when we speak of "… a bad moon a-rising," we are in the act of car-karaoke to Creedence Clearwater Revival… so much better than that Katy Perry!

References

Admczyk, K. (2017). Voluntary and involuntary singlehood and young adults' mental health: An investigation of mediating role of romantic loneliness. *Current Psychology, 36,* 888-904.

Alcohol Drug Abuse Weekly: News for Policy and Program Decision-Makers. (2016). Marijuana business interests following tobacco and alcohol playbook. *Author, (9),* 1-6.

Alexander, J. (2012). *The hidden psychology of pain: The use of understanding to heal chronic pain.* Balboa Press.

Alexander, B. K., Beyerstein, B. L., Hadaway, P. F. & Coambs, R. B. (1981). Effect of early and later colony housing on oral ingestion of morphine in rats. *Pharmacology Biochemistry and Behavior*, 15 (4), 571–576.

Altschul, J. (2018). It is time for Congress to treat Twitter as a publisher. *The Federalist*. https://thefederalist.com/2018/11/29/time-congress-teat-twitter-publisher

American Psychiatric Association. (2013). *The diagnostic and statistical manual of mental disorders, 5th edition*. Arlington, VA: author.

American Sociological Association. (2018). *American sociological code of ethics*. https://www.asanet.org/sites/default/files/asa_code_of_ethics-june2018.pdf

Asencio-Rhine, M. (February 20, 2019). Vandals paint #metoo message on Sarasota's kissing statue, police say. *Tampa Bay Times*. https://www.tampabay.com/news/publicsafety/vandals-paint-metoo-message-on-sarasotas-kissing-statue-police-say-20190219/

Babson Survey Research Group. (2016). Grade Increase: Tracking distance education in the United States. https://bason.quatrics.com/jfe/form/SV djbTFMIjZGYDNVb

Becker, H. S. (1963). *Outsiders: Studies in the sociology of deviance*. Free Press.

Begley, S. (2016). Marijuana's economic impact could hit $44 billion by 2020. *Time, March 14*, 67.

Bellafiore, R. (2018). Summary of the latest federal income tax data, 2018 update. Tax Foundation. https://taxfoundation.org/summary-latest-federal-income-tax-data-2018-update/

Ben-Ze'ev, A. (2019). Why people have sex with their eyes closed: The look of love and the look of sex. *Psychology Today*. https://www.psychologyday.com/us/blog/in-the-name-love/201901/why-people-have-sex-their-eyes-closed

Berenso, A. (2019). *Tell your children the truth about marijuana, mental illness, and violence*. Free Press.

Berkman, L. F. & Syme, S. L. (1979). Social networks, host resistance, and mortality: A nine-year follow-up of Alameda County residents. *American Journal of Epidemiology, 109 (2)*, 186-204.

Berlin, I. (1978). *Karl Marx, 4th ed*. Oxford University Press.

Bliss, W. D. (1897). *The encyclopedia of social reforms*. Funk & Wagnalls.

Blom, J. D. (2010). *A dictionary of hallucinations*. Springer.

Bloomberg. (2018). Top 3% of U.S. Taxpayers Paid Majority of Income Tax in 2016. https://fortune.com/2018/10/16/federal-income-tax-2016-2018/

Blum, D. (2002). *Love at goon park: Harry Harlow and the science of affection*. New York: Perseus Publishing.

Boeree, C. G. (2018). *Personality theories from Freud to Frankl*. Open Knowledge Books.

Bouchard, T., Lyken, D., McGue, M., Segal, N., & Tellegen, A. (1990). Sources of human psychological differences: The Minnesota study of twins reared apart. *Science, 250*, 223-229.

Bowlby, J. (1969). *Attachment and loss. Volume 1: Attachment*. Basic Books.

Bradbury, R. (2013). *Fahrenheit 451*. Simon & Shuster.

Bush, G. W. (2010). *Decision points*. Crown Publishers.

Camus, A. (1955). *The myth of Sisyphus and other essays*. Vintage.

Centers for Disease Control and Prevention. (1994). International notes certification of poliomyelitis eradication—the Americans, *Morbidity and Mortality Weekly Report, 43 (93)*, 720-722.

Cervantes, M. D. (2003). *Don Quixote*. HarperCollins.

Chang, K. (2007). Adult bipolar disorder is continuous with pediatric bipolar disorder. *The Canadian Journal of Psychiatry, 52 (7)*, 418-424.

Child Care Aware of America. (2015). Parents and the high cost of child care: 2015 report. Author. http://usa.childcareaware.org/wp-content/uploads/2016/05/Parents-and-the-High-Cost-of-Child-Care-2015-FINAL.pdf

Chitika. (2013). *The value of Google result positioning*. Perma.cc/7AGC HTDH.

Coan, J. A. & Sbarra, D. A. (2014). Social baseline theory: The social regulation of risk and effort. *Current Opinion in Psychology, 1*, 87-91.

Camus, A. (2013). Death in the soul. In, *Algerian Chronicles*. Belknap Press.

Coleman, J. W. & Cressey, D. R. (1993). *Social problems, 5ᵗʰ ed.* Harper Collins.

Cooper, D. (1967). *Psychiatry and anti-psychiatry*. Paladin.

Cox, F. D. & Demmitt, K. (2014). *Human intimacy: Marriage, family, and its meaning*. Wadsworth Cengage learning.

Damasio, A. (1999). *The feeling of what happens: Body and emotion in the making of consciousness*. Hardcort Brace.

Darley, J. M. & Latané, B. (1968). Bystander intervention in emergencies: Diffusion of responsibility. *Journal of Personality and Social Psychology, 8 (4)*, 377-383.

DePaulo, B. (2014). A singles studies perspective on mount marriage. *Psychological Inquiry, 25*, 64-68.

de Jouvenel, B. (1957).   Huntington, J. F. (trans.) *Sovereignty: An inquiry into the political good*. Cambridge University Press.

Di Forti, M., Quattrone, D., Freeman, T. P., Tripoli, G., Gayer-Anderson, C., Quigley, H., Rodriguez, V., Jongsma, H. E., Ferraro, L., La Cascia, C., La Barbera, D., Tarricone, I., Berardi, D., Szöke, A., Arango, C., Tortelli, A., Velthorst, E., Bernardo, M., Del-Ben, C. M., Menezes, P. R., Selten, J.-P., Jones, P. B., Kirkbride, J. B., Rutten, B. P. F., de Haan, L. Sham, P. C., van Os, J., Lewis, C. M., Lynskey, M.,

Morgan, C., Murray, R. M. & the EU-GEI WP2 Group. (2019). The contribution of cannabis use to variation in the incidence case-control study. *Lancet Psychiatry, 6 (5),* 427-436.

Doran, J. M., Marks, L. R., Kraha, A., Ameen, E. J., & El-Ghoroury N. H. (2016). Graduate debt in psychology: A qualitative analysis. *Training and Education in Professional Psychology, 10,* 3-13.

dos Reis, S., Zito, J. M. Safter, D. J., & Soeken, K. L. (2001). Mental health services for youth in foster care and disabled youths. *American Journal of Public Health, 91,* 1094-1099.

Duckworth, A. (2019). Research. https://angeladuckworth.com/research/

Duckworth, A. (2018): *GRIT: The power of passion and perseverance.* Scribner.

Duckworth, A. L., Peterson, C., Matthews, M. D., & Kelly, D. R. (2007). Grit: Perseverance and passion for long-term goals. *Journal of Personality & Social Psychology, 92, (6),* 1087–1101.

Durkheim, E. (1951). *Suicide: A study in sociology.* Free Press.

Easterbrook, G. (2003). *The progress paradox: How life gets better while people feel worse.* Random House.

Ebbinghaus, H. (1913). Memory: A contribution to experimental psychology (No. 3), Teachers College, Columbia University, New York.

Epstein, R. (2019). Why Google poses a serious threat to democracy, and how to end that threat? *American Institute for Behavioral Research and Technology.* https://www. judiciary .senate.gov/imo/media/doc/Epstein%20Testimony.pdf

Epstein, R. (2016). Can search engine rankings swing elections? *New Internationalist.* https://newint.org/features/2016/07 01/can-search-engine-rankings-swing-elections

Epstein, R. & Robertson, R. E. (2019). The search engine manipulation effect (SEME) and its possible impact on the outcomes of elections. American Institute for Behavioral Research and Technology. https://www.pnas. .org/content/pnas/ 112/33/E4512.full.pdf?with-ds=yes

Erikson, E. H. (1949). *Childhood and society.* W. W. Norton.

Eysenck, J. H. & Wilson, G. D. (Eds.). (1973). *The experimental study of Freudian theories.* Methuen & Company.

Fontanella, C. A., Hiance, D. L., Philips, G. S., et al. (2014). Trends in psychotropic mediation used for Medicaid-enrolled preschool children. *Journal of Child and Family Studies, 23,* 617-631.

Fox, R. C., Lidz, V. M. & Bershady, H. J. (Eds.) (2005). Introduction. In authors, *After Parsons: A theory of social action for the Twenty-First Century.* Russell Sage Foundation.

Frances, A. J. (2018). We have too many specialists & too few general practitioners. *Psychology Today, 1.* https://www.psychologytoday.com/us/blog/saving-normal/201601/we-have-too-many-specialists-too-few-general-practitioners

Frey, W. H. (2018). Us population growth hits 80-year low, capping off a year of demographic stagnation. Brookings, December. https://www.brookings.edu/blog/the-avenue/2018/12/21/us-population-growth-hits-80-year-low-capping-off-a-year-of-demographic-stagnation/

Freud, S. (1961). *Civilization and its discontent.* Norton.

Freud, S, (1912). Selected papers on hysteria and other psychoneuroses. *The Journal of Nervous and Mental Disease, Chapter II.*

Freud, S. (1961). *Five lectures on psycho-analysis.* W.W. Norton.

Frankl, V. E. (1959). *Man's search for meaning.* Beacon Press.

Frankl, V. E. (2000). *Recollections: An autobiography.* Basic Books.

Fromm, E. (1956). *The art of loving.* Bantam Books.

Frosh, S. (2011). *Feelings.* Routledge.

Gardner, H. (1983). *Frames of mind: The theory of multiple intelligences.* Basic Books.

Geiger, A. W. & Livingston, G. (2019). Eight facts about love and marriage in America. Fact Tank: News in the Numbers, Pew Research Center. https://www.pewresearch.org/fact-tank/2019/02/13/8-facts-about-love-and-marriage/

Gelles, S. (2018). Censorship on the web is winning. *EConent.* http://www. econtentmag.com/Articles/Column/Creative-Data/Censorship-on-the-Web-is-Winning-127734.htm

Gladwell, M. (2005). *Blink: The power of thinking without thinking.* Little Brown.

Goffman, E. (1961). *Asylums: Essays on the social situation of mental patients and other inmates.* Anchor Books.

Golding, W. (1954). *Lord of the flies*. Faber & Faber.

Golding, W. (1982). Belief and creativity. In author *A moving target*. Farr, Straus & Giroux.

Gore, A. (1992). *Earth in the balance: Ecology and the human spirit*. Houghton Mifflin.

Google. (n. d.). Building a stronger future for journalism. https://news initiative. withgoogle.com/

Guest, J. (1976). *Ordinary people*. Penguin Books.

Grahek, N. (2007). *Feeling pain and being in pain (2ⁿᵈ ed.)*. The MIT Press.

Habermas, J. (1989). *The structural transformation of the public sphere: An inquire into a category of bourgeois society*. MIT Press.

Hadaway, P. F., Alexander, B. K., Coambs, R. B. & Beyerstein, B. (1979). The effect of housing and gender on preference for morphine-sucrose solutions in rats. *Psychopharmacology, 66* (1), 87-91.

Hains, T. (January 22, 2019). Ocasio-Cortez: The world is going to end in 2 years if we do not address climate change. RealClear Politics. https://www. realclearpoltics.com/video/ 2019/01/ 02/ Ocasiotez_the _world_is_going_to_ end_in_ 12_years_if_we_dont_ Address_climate_change.html

Hall, W. & Weier, M. (2016). Lee Robin's studies of heroin use among US Vietnam veterans. *Addiction, 112*, 176-180.

Hanover Research. (2107). 2017 digital study trends survey: Results prepared for McGraw-Hill by Hanover Research. https://s3.amazonaws.com/ecommerce-prod.mheducation.com/unitas/highered/explore/sites/study-trends/2017-digital-trends-survey-results.pdf

Hari, R., Henriksson, L., Malinen, S. & Parkkonen, L. (2015). Centrality of social interaction in human brain function. *Neuron, 88,* 181.

Harrington, A. (2019). *Mind fixers: Psychiatry's troubled search for the biology of mental illness*. Norton.

Hazan, C. & Shaver, P. (1987). Romantic love conceptualized as an attachment process. *Journal of Personality and Social Psychology, 52,* 511-524.

Hedegaard, H. (2018). Suicide mortality in the United States, 1999—2017. Centers for Disease Control & Prevention, NCHS Data Brief, 30.

Heidegger, M. (1991). *Nietzche, volume one and two*. Harper.

Heyman, G. M. (2009). *Addiction: A disorder of choice*. Harvard University Press.

Hodges, P., Tsao, H. & Sims, K. (2015). Gain of postural responses increases in response to real and anticipated pain. *Experimental Brain Research, 233 (9)*, 2745-2752.

Holt-Lunstad, J., Smith, T. B. & Layton, J. B. (2010). Social relationships and mortality risk: A meta-analytic review. *Public Library of Science, 7 (7)*.

Horton, P. B., Leslie, G. R. & Larson, R. F. (1991). *The sociology of social problems, 10th ed.* Prentice Hall.

Ishiguro, K. (2005). *Never let me go: A novel*. Vintage.

Jackson, J. B. (2018). The ambiguous loss of singlehood: Conceptualization and treating singlehood ambiguous loss among never-married adults. *Contemporary Family Therapy, 40*, 210-222.

Jacoby, R. (1975). *Social amnesia: A critique of conformist psychology from Adler to Laing*. Beacon.

James, N. (2018). Recent violent crime trends in the United States. Congressional Research Service. https://fas.org/sgp/crs/misc/R45236.pdf

Janis, I. L. (1971). Groupthink. *Psychology Today, 5 (6)*, 43-46 & 74-76.

Kandel, E. R. (2006). *In search of memory: The emergence of a new science of mind*. W. W. Norton.

Kerr, W. C., Lui, C. & Ye, Y. (2017). Trend and age, period and cohort effects for marijuana use prevalence in the 1984-2015 US National Alcohol Surveys. *Addiction, 113*, 473-481.

Keyes, K. M., Wall, M., Cerdá, M. Schulenberg, J., O'Malley, P. M., Galea, S., Feng, T. & Hasin, D. S. (2017). How does state marijuana policy affect US youth? Medical marijuana laws, marijuana use and perceived harmfulness: 1991-2014. *Addiction, 111*, 2187-2195.

Kutchins, H. & Kirk, S. A. (2003). *Making us crazy, DSM: The psychiatric bible and the creation of mental disorders*. Free Press.

Lenzer, G. (2009). *The essential writings of Auguste Comte and positivism*. Transaction Publishers.

Leon-Guerrero, A. (2019). *Social problems: Community, policy, and social action, 6th ed.* Sage.

Liazos, A. (1972). The poverty of the sociology of deviance: Nuts, sluts, and perverts. *Social Problems, 20,* 10-120.

Lieberman, M. D. (2003). *Social: Why our brains are wired to connect.* Crown Publisher.

Liebert, D. (1998). The married widow: A correlational study of grief and social support networks amongst non-residential spouses of long-term care nursing home residents (Doctoral dissertation). University of Sarasota, Department of Psychology & Behavioral Science: Sarasota, Florida.

Liebert, D. (2013). Psycholiterature in the classroom: The pedagogical benefits of using literature with psychology students. Presented at the British Psychological Society Conference, November 8-10. York, England.

Liebert, D. (2017). *It is not about Freud but it is all about Freud: Development of a contemporary psychology.* Open Knowledge Books.

Liebert, D. (2017). *Points on madness: Essays on abnormal psychology.* Open Knowledge Books.

Loftus E. F., Coan, J. & Pickrell, J. E. (1996). Manufacturing false memories using bit of reality. In L. M. Reder (ed.), *Implicit memory and metacognition* (pp. 195-220). Psychological press.

Loftus, E. & Ketcham, K. (1991). *Witness for the defense: The accused, the eyewitness, and the expert who puts memory on trial.* Martin's Press.

Loftus, E. & Ketcham, K. (1994). *The myth of repressed memory: False memories and allegations of sexual abuse.* St. Martin's Press.

Lu, W. (2019). Adolescent depression: National trends, risk factors and healthcare disparities. *American Journal of Health* Behavior, *43,* 181-194.

Lukianoff, G. & Haidt, J. (2018). *The coddling of the American Mind: How good intentions and bad ideas are setting up a generation for failure.* Penguin Press.

Luther, M. (1523). Secular authority: To what extent should it be obeyed.

Macy, B. (2018). *Dopesick: Dealers, doctors, and the drug company that addicted America.* Little Brown.

Maier, P. (1933). *American scripture: Making the Declaration of Independence.* Alfred A. Knoph.

Make Our Schools Safe. (n.d.). *About.* https://makeourschoolsssafe.org/

Maldonado, C. (2018). Price of college increasing almost 8 times faster than wages. *Forbes*. https://www.forbes.com/sites/camilomaldonado/2018/07/24/ price-of-college-increasing-almost-8-times-faster-than-wages/#1a26e32866c1

Maldonado, S. (2019). San Francisco high school to paint over historic George Washington mural. NBC Bay Area. https://www.nbcbayarea. com /news/local/San-Francisco-to-Paint-Over-Historic-George-Washington-Mural-512249811.html

Malraux, A. (1934). Chevalier, H. M. (trans.) *Man's fate*. The Modern Library.

Maslow, A. H. (1968). *Towards a psychology of being (2nd ed.)*. Van Nostrand Reinhold Company.

March for Our Lives. (2019). How we save lives. https://march foroutlives.com/

Marshall, G. (1994). *The concise Oxford dictionary of sociology*. Oxford University Press.

Martin, E. (2017). 70% of Americans consider themselves middle-class—but only 50% are. *CNBC*. https://www.cnbc.com/2017/06/30/70-percent-of-americans-consider-themselves-middle-class-but-only-50-percent-are.html

Marx, K. & Engels, F. (1964). *The communist manifesto*. Pocket Books.

Mazzie, P. (2019). Racist comments cost conservative Parkland student a place at Harvard. *New York Times*. https://www.nytimes.com/2019/06/17/us/ parkland-kyle-kashuv-harvard.html

McClelland, J. & Werling, J. (2018). How the 2017 Tax Act affects CBO's projections. Congressional Budget Office. https://www. cbo.gov/publication/53787

McGreal, C. (2018). *American overdose: The opioid tragedy in three acts*. Public Affairs.

Miller, R. J. (2014). *Drugged: The science and culture behind psychotropic drugs*. Oxford University Press.

Mills, C. W. (1956): *White collar: America's middle-classes*. Oxford University Press.

Mills, C. W. (1959). *The sociological imagination*. Oxford University Press.

Mojtabai, R., Olfson, M. & Han, B. (2016). National trends in the prevalence and treatment of depression in adolescents and young adults. *Pediatrics*, 138 (6).

Moreno, C., Laje, G., Blanco, C. et al. (2007). National trends in outpatient diagnosis and treatment of bipolar disorders in youth. *Archives of General Psychiatry, 64 (9)*, 1032-1039.

National Institute of Drug Abuse. (2019). Overdose death rates: Revised January 2019. Author. https://www.drugabuse.gov/related-topics/trends-statistics/overdose-death-rates

National Science Foundation, National Center for Science and Engineering Statistics. (2013). National survey of college graduates public use microdata file and codebook. https://setat.nsf.gov/dpwnload/

National Student Clearinghouse Research Center. (2016). Time to degree—2016. https://nscresearchcenter.org/signaturereport11/

Neisser, U., Boodoo, G., Bouchard, T. J. J., Boykin, A. W., Brody, N., & Ceci, S. J., et al. (1996). Intelligence: Knowns and unknowns. *American Psychologist, 51,* 77–101.

Nermo, H., Willumsen, T., Johnsen, J. A. K. (2019). Prevalence of dental anxiety and associations with oral health, psychological distress, avoidance and anticipated pain in adolescence: A cross-sectional study based on the Tromso study, fit futures. *Acta Odontological Scandinavica,* 77 (2), 126-134.

Nicas, J. (2017). Google has picked an answer for you—Too bad it is often wrong. *The Wall Street Journal.* https://www.wsj.com /articles/googles-featured-answers-aim-to-distill-truthbut-often- get-it-wrong-1510847867

Nugent S. M., Morasco, B. J. & O'Neil, M. E. et al. (2017). The effects of cannabis among adults with chronic pain and an overview of general harms: A systematic review. *Annuals of Intern Medicine, 167 (1),* 319-331.

O'Niel, M., E., Nugent, S. M., Morasco, B. J., Freeman, M., Low, A., Kondo, K., Zakher, B., Elven, C., Motuapuaks, M., Paynter, R. & Kansagara, D. (2017). Benefits and harms of plant-based cannabis for posttraumatic stress disorder: A systematic review. *Annual of Internal Medicine, 167 (5),* 332-341.

Orwell, G. (1987). *Nineteen eight-four.* Everyman's Library, Alfred A. Knopf.

Palahniuk, C. (2008). Catching up with… Chuck Palahniuk. *Paste.* https://www.pastemagazine.com/articles/2008/09/catching-up-with-chuck-palahniuk.html

Parson, T. (1951). *The social system.* Routledge.

Parsons, T. (1977). *Social systems and the evolution of action theory.* The Free Press.

Peck, M. S. (1978). *The road less traveled: A new psychology of love, traditional values, and spiritual growth.* Simon and Shuster.

Pepping, C. A., MacDonald, G. & Davis, P. J. (2018). Toward a psychology of singlehood: An attachment-theory perspective on long-term singlehood. *Current Directions in Psychological Science, 27 (5),* 324-331.

Peters, X. (2019). Florida Sheriffs Bob Gualtieri and Grady Judd promoted arming teachers on NRA TV. *Orlando Weekly*. https://www.orlandoweekly.com /Blogs/archives/ 2019/ 01/07/ florida-sheriffs-bob-gualtiari-and-grady-judd-promoted-arming-teachers-on-nra-tv

Pethokoukis, J. (2018). The great American melt up. *Commentary, July/August*, 37-40.

Pinker, S. (2018). *Enlightenment now: The case for reason, science, humanism, and progress.* Penguin.

Pressley, A. (2018). I believe survivors. I believe Christine Blasey Ford. And I still believe Anita Hill. *Boston Globe*. https://www.bostonglobe.com/ opinion/2018/ 10/06/believe-survivors-believe-christine-blasey-ford-and-still-believe-anita-hill/tlJebzeHjKyhsLqDwRqoWI/story.html

Proffitt, D. R., Stefanucci, J., Banton, T. & Epstein, W. (2003). The role of effort in perceiving distance. *Psychological Science, 14 (2),* 106-112.

Pulphus, D. (2016). *Untitled # 1*, painting. Quality Matters. (2016). Grounded in research. Driven by best practices. A community that puts learners first. https:// www. qualitymatters.org/why-quality-matters

Quart, A. *Squeezed: Why our families can't afford America.* CCCO.

Reiss, I. L. (1988). *Family systems in America (5th ed.).* Holt.

Ritzer, G. (2009). *Enchanting a disenchanted world: Continuity and change in the cathedrals of consumption.* Sage.

Rogers, C. R. (1986). *Freedom to learn: A review of what education might become (2nd ed.).* Merrill Publishing Company.

Rosenhan, D. (1973). On being sane in insane places, *Science, 179,* 250-258.

Rosenthal, R. & Jacobson, L. (1966). Teachers' expectancies: Determinants of pupils' IQ gains. *Psychological Reports, 19,* 115-118.

Rubin, L. (1976). *Worlds of pain: Life in the working-class family.* Basic Books.

Sapolsky, R. M. (2004). *Why zebras do not get ulcers: The acclaimed guide to stress, stress-related diseases, and coping (3rd ed.).* Holt.

Sarkisian, N. & Gerstel, N. (2016). Does singlehood isolate or integrate? Examining the link between marital status and ties to kin, friends, and neighbors. *Journal of Social and Personal Relationships, 33 (3),* 361-384.

Sartre, J.-P. (2007). *Existentialism is a humanism*. Yale University Press.

Scharch, D. (2009). *Passionate marriage: Keeping love and intimacy alive in committed relationships*. W. W. Norton.

Scheer, H. (2019). Pinterest and Twitter are trying to censor Live Action, a pro-life group. *The Federalist*. https://thefederalist.com/2019/07/12/pinterest-twitter-trying-censor-live-action-pro-life-group/

Scherf, A. L. (2015). The societal and economic impacts of recent dramatic shifts in state marijuana law: How should Minnesota proceed in the future? *Journal of Public Law & Policy, 36 (1)*, 119-160.

Scherr, S., Haim, M. & Arendt, F. (2019). Equal access to online information? Google's suicide-prevention disparities may amplify a global digital divide. *News, Media and Society, 21 (3)*, 562-582.

See it now. (1995). CBS television interview of Jonas Salk, MD. Aired on 4/12/1955.

Sendak, M. (1963). *Where the wild things are*. Harper Collins.

Shakespeare, W. (1998). *The tempest*. Oxford Press.

Shneidman, E. L. (2002). *Autopsy of a suicidal mind*. Oxford University Press.

Singer, D. G. & Revenson, T. A. (1997). *How a child thinks: A Piaget primer*. International Universities Press, Inc.

Sit, R. (2018). More than 2 million in 90 percent of voting districts joined march for our lives protest. *Newsweek*. https://www.newsweek.com/ march-our-lives-how-many-2-million-90-voting-district-860841

Slater, L. (2004). *Opening Skinner's box: Great psychological experiments of the Twentieth Century*. Norton.

Smail, D. (2005). *Power, interest, and psychology: Elements of a social materialist understanding of distress*. PCCS Books.

Sperber, J. (2013). *Karl Marx: A Nineteenth Century life*. Liveright Publishing Corporation.

Spitler, K. (2007). Bipolar disorder diagnosis increases in children and adolescents. *Neuropsychiatry, 8 (10)*, 1-23.

Steinbuch, Y. (2019). Parkland shooting reports backs arming teachers, slams police response. *New York Post*. https://nypost.com/2019/01/03/parkland-shooting-report-backs-arming-teachers-slams-police-response/

Steplier, R. (2017). Number of US adults cohabitating with a partner continues to rise, especially among the 50 and older. *Fact Tank: News in the Numbers, Per Research Center*. https://www.pewresearch.org/fact-tank/2017/04/06/number-of-u-s-adults-cohabiting-with-a-partner-continues-to-rise-especially-among-those-50-and-older/

Stringer, H. (2016). Got debt? *Monitor on Psychology, 47 (4)*, 52-56.

Styron, W. (1990). *Darkness visible: A memoir of madness*. Oxford Press.

Sykes, C. J. (2016). *Fail u.: The false promise of higher education*. St. Martin's Press.

Szasz, T. S. (1974). *The myth of mental illness: Foundations of a theory of personal conduct*. Harper and Roe.

Tatum, S. & Klein, B. (2017). Controversial painting removed from capital. CNN. https://www.cnn.com/2017/01/13/ politics/controversial-painting-to-be-re-moved-from-capitol/index.html

The Brown University Child & Psychopharmacology Update. (2014). Moving forward on treating DMDD: Stimulants, parent training, and CBT. author.

Thomas, V. N., Wilson-Barnett, J. & Goodhart, F. (1998). The role of cognitive-behavioral therapy in the management of pain in patients with sickle cell disease. *Journal of Advanced Nursing, 27 (5)*, 1002-1009.

Tolstoy, L. (1960). *The death of Ivan Ilych and other stories*. Signet Classics.

Turman, M. (1965). The functionalist approach to social problems. *Social Problems, 12 (4)*, 379-388.

Twenge, J. M. (2017). *iGen: Why today's super-connected kids are growing up less rebellious, more tolerant, less happy and completely underprepared for adulthood*. Atria Books.

Umberson, D. & Montez, J. K. (2010). Social relationships and health: A flashpoint for health policy. *Journal of Health and Social Behavior, 51 (suppl)*, S54-S66.

U.S. Census Bureau. (2018). Decennial censuses, 1890 to 1940, and current population survey, annual social and economic supplements, 1947 to 2018. https://www.census.gov/data/tables/time-series/demo/families/marital.html

United States Census Bereau. (2018). Nevada and Idaho Are the Nation's Fastest Growing States. https://www.census.gov/newsroom/press-releases/2018/esti-mates-national-state.html

United States Department of Education. (2011). The condition of education. National Center for Educational Statistics. Washington, D.C.

U.S. Department of Education. (2018). Prepared remarks by U.S. Secretary of Education Betsy DeVos to federal student aid's training conference. https://www.ed.gov/news/speeches/prepared-remarks-us-secretary-education-betsy-devos-federal-student-aids-training-conference

U.S. Department of Education, National Center for Education Statistics. (2019). Tuition costs of colleges and universities. *Digest of Education Statistics*. https://nces.ed.gov/fastfacts/display.asp?id=76

Verria, L. & Galdorisi, G. (2012). *The kissing sailor: The mystery behind the photo that ended World War II*. Naval Institute Press.

Volck, B. (2019). Roots of the opioid crisis. *Christian Century*, March, 36-37.

Waite, L. J. & Gallagher, M. (2000). *The case for marriage: Why married people are happier, healthier, and better off financially*. Random House.

Wartik, N. (2005). The perils of playing house. *Psychology Today, July/August*, 42-52.

Weber, M. (1949). *The methodology of social science*, (trans. & ed., Edward H. Shils & Henry A. Finch). Free Press.

Well, H. G. (1896). *The island of Dr. Moreau*. Heinemann, Stone & Kimball.

Winerman, L. (2016). The debt trap. *The Monitor on Psychology*, 47 (4), 44-46.

Wright, R. (1994). *The moral animal: Why we are the way we are/The new science of evolutionary psychology*. Pantheon Books.

Yalom, I. (1980). *Existential psychotherapy*. Basic Books.

Index

www.ingramcontent.com/pod-product-compliance
Lightning Source LLC
Chambersburg PA
CBHW051437250726
48655CB00001B/98